£13.50

Debussy in proportion

A musical analysis

Debussy in proportion

A musical analysis

ROY HOWAT

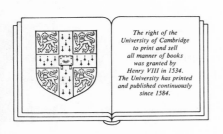

The right of the
University of Cambridge
to print and sell
all manner of books
was granted by
Henry VIII in 1534.
The University has printed
and published continuously
since 1584.

CAMBRIDGE UNIVERSITY PRESS

Cambridge
London   New York   New Rochelle
Melbourne   Sydney

Published by the Press Syndicate of the University of Cambridge
The Pitt Building, Trumpington Street, Cambridge, CB2 1RP
32 East 57th Street, New York, NY 10022, USA
10 Stamford Road, Oakleigh, Melbourne 3166, Australia

First published 1983
First paperback edition 1986

Printed in Great Britain
at the University Press, Cambridge

Library of Congress catalogue card number: 81-21580

British Library Cataloguing in Publication Data

Howat, Roy
Debussy in proportion
1. Debussy, Claude
I. Title
780'.92'4   ML410.D28

ISBN 0 521 23282 1 hard covers
ISBN 0 521 31145 4 paperback

To Ian Kemp

Contents

Preface

Debussy's writings are too well sprinkled with pungent remarks about analysis to be of comfort to anyone contemplating analysis of his music. 'Grownups ... still try to explain things, dismantle them and quite heartlessly kill all their mystery', he complained in 1901, in his very first piece of published musical criticism. But his attitude was not so simple. 'The need to understand – so rare among artists – was innate in Rameau. Was it not to satisfy that need that he wrote his *Traité de l'harmonie* ...?', we find him writing some years later. The contrast suggests he had strong feelings about what was useful and what was futile in musical analysis, as well as a constant sensitivity towards whatever in music defies words. If this book takes the analytic plunge, then, it is with the belief that an understanding of some of the mechanisms Debussy used for organizing and conveying his inspirations – consciously or not – should only enhance our awareness of the real mystery that lies inviolable behind the inner strength of his musical ideas.

Since the analyses here are intricate, and trace some strict logic, it is as well to say straight away that they constitute no attempt to contradict the well-documented view of Debussy as a thoroughly instinctive artist, a communicator of the elusive momentary intuition. But if logic is visible in the score, it is there whether the composer was conscious of it or not; if he was conscious of it, the fact does no injury to the potency of his instinct. The more original and mysterious the intuition, the more precise new techniques have to be found to communicate it successfully. Jules Laforgue, one of Debussy's literary idols and another thoroughly intuitive artist, took up the cudgels for this argument in his *Notes d'esthétiques*, countering Ernest Renan's contention that knowledge and science weaken instinct. 'That is to misunderstand the word *instinct*', Laforgue argues back; 'In art there will always be, as there always was, instinct and reflection, inspirational or divining instinct and knowledge or science.' In fact the question of this duality was at the heart of the artistic circles in which Debussy moved in his formative years, and is discussed thoroughly in Chapter 11 below, as it gives added impetus to the preceding analyses.

To accompany the analyses, four of Debussy's works are reproduced here in their entirety as Appendix 3: the song 'Spleen' (from the *Ariettes oubliées*), and the piano pieces 'Clair de lune' (from the *Suite bergamasque*), *L'isle joyeuse*, and 'Reflets dans l'eau' (from the first series of *Images*). For the main analysis, though – of *La mer* – this is impracticable, and the reader will have to obtain a score to

ix

follow the analysis properly. The same applies to the other works studied more briefly in Chapters 3 and 11 and in Appendix 2; all of them are easily obtainable. The opportunity has been taken of presenting the four pieces in Appendix 3 in corrected editions.

All references to literary sources in the text are identified by author and title or date of publication, plus page number if apt; the sources can then be identified in full from the Bibliography. This method helps to avoid a jungle of notes.

Preparation of the book has been enormously helped by the use of computer to store and edit the text; for invaluable help in this, and for many perceptive comments, I am indebted to Andrew Uttley. In 1973 the Centre de Documentation Claude Debussy opened at Debussy's natal town of St Germain-en-Laye, and I was fortunate to be able to work there throughout 1976. To its former *animatrice* Mrs Margaret G. Cobb I am grateful for information and encouragement which have continued in large measure since her retirement from the Centre Debussy in 1976. Professor Ian Kemp supervised this work's initial preparation as a doctoral thesis (Howat 1979); for his encouragement and guidance I owe a large debt of gratitude, and to him the book is dedicated with affection.

This whole venture was made possible by a research grant from the Scottish Education Department, followed by a Research Fellowship from Jesus College, Cambridge; to them I express thanks. Many other friends and colleagues have contributed ideas, critical comments and useful information; I beg forgiveness for not filling pages with all their names. Special thanks are due, though, to Roger Nichols and Dr Robert Orledge, who gave of their time to read and discuss the work in progress, supplying much helpful advice and information. I am also grateful to Mme I. Goüin for the opportunity to work on Debussy material in the library of her late brother François Lang, at the Abbaye de Royaumont, France; and to Mrs Louise Varèse for allowing me to study Debussy's annotated printed copy of *La mer*. Debussy's stepdaughter Mme G. de Tinan (the former Dolly Bardac) kindly allowed me to examine Debussy manuscripts and proofs in her possession, and reminisced fascinatingly about her childhood years in the Debussy household. ('Il était très secret', though, was the only information she could furnish on how Debussy worked.) Rosemary Dooley and Eric Van Tassel, of Cambridge University Press, have my gratitude for their encouragement and patient help in bringing the book *au point*. In addition to those acknowledged specifically in the following chapters, others who have been of particular help include the firm of Durand et Cie; Dr John Gage; Dr Douglass Green; Richard Langham Smith; M. François Lesure; M. Jean-Michel Nectoux; Dr Marie Rolf; Professor Julian Rushton; Mrs Eileen Uttley; and the staffs of the Pendlebury, Rowe, History of Art and University Libraries, Cambridge, the Bibliothèque Nationale, Paris, The Pierpont Morgan Library, New York, the Humanities Research Center of the University of Texas at Austin, and the Sibley Music Library of the Eastman School of Music at the University of Rochester.

Chapter 3 and Appendix 2 below contain some material previously published in Howat (1977), included here by kind permission of the editors of *Music & Letters*. Music examples 1, 4, 6, 7, 27 and 28 are reproduced by kind permission of Durand S.A., Editions Musicales, and Société des Editions Jobert, Paris.

Roy Howat
Cambridge, 1981

Note: In this book, where pitches are named in a specific octave, the following code is used (c′ = middle C; each octave is deemed to begin on C and rise to B): C–B c–b c′–b′ c″–b″ c‴–b‴.

PART 1

Exposition

'You must take measurements. And you must square out your paper.'
– W. Somerset Maugham

Chapter 1

Proportional structure and the Golden Section

Proportional balance in any piece of music is something we tend to take instinctively for granted – provided it is instinctively satisfactory. If a painting or
building is clumsily proportioned, any sensitive observer can see the fact in an
instant; in music, though, we have to hear the piece through to make the
equivalent evaluation. Nevertheless, this aspect is equally vital in music, whether
the composer applied it merely by instinct or by careful design. Most experienced
listeners know the instinctive feeling of either sluggishness or breathlessness that
results from a musical framework, or a part of one, too large or too small to
contain its musical argument or to balance its surrounding formal sections. This
reminds us that it is not just the mathematical proportions themselves that
matter, but also whether they are well matched to what they contain.

When this twofold balance sounds well managed, how did the composer
achieve it? – purely by instinct, by design, or by a mixture of the two? Whatever
the answer, can the resulting sense of coherence be matched with any demonstrable system of architecture in the music? – a question of special interest with
music which, like much of Debussy's, diverges radically from conventional
musical forms.

Some answers to those questions have prompted the writing of this book. The
primary one is the discovery that much of Debussy's music contains intricate
proportional systems which can account both for the precise nature of the
music's unorthodox forms and for the difficulty in defining them in more
familiar terms. Most important of all, they show ways in which the forms are
used to project the music's dramatic and expressive qualities with maximum
precision. These systems are based principally on two ratios traditionally associated with formal balance in many fields of art and science: exact symmetry or
bisection, as achieved by dividing into halves; and the ratio known as the Golden
Section.

As the concept of Golden Section is central to this book, some explanation of it
is apt here. Recognized since ancient times as important in architecture, painting
and natural organic growth, the Golden Section (Golden Mean, Golden Ratio –

henceforth 'GS') is the way of dividing a fixed length in two so that the ratio of the shorter portion to the longer portion equals the ratio of the longer portion to the entire length. In mathematical terms, $\frac{b}{a} = \frac{a}{a+b}$. Fig. 1.1 shows this. The ratio's exact value is irrational, its decimal places continuing indefinitely; it approximates to 0·618034... (a little under two-thirds) of the length measured.

Fig. 1.1: Golden Section

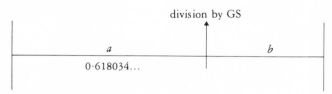

division by GS

a b

0·618034...

Its special characteristic is shown in Fig. 1.2. C divides the line AB by GS; D is then added to divide AC by GS. But in doing so, D also divides the whole length AB by GS in the other direction, the shorter portion lying to the left. No other ratio has this property. The system of Fig. 1.2 can be extended inwards and outwards by GS with similar results, producing a network of interlocking GS divisions in both directions, and this is the main reason not only for the special place of GS in Classical mathematics (particularly as Euclid's 'extreme and mean ratio') but also for its importance in organic structuring.[1]

Fig. 1.2

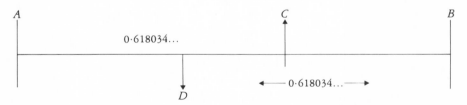

A C B

0·618034...

D

←— 0·618034... —→

The irrational value of GS can be expressed in a more manageable way. It is *approached* more and more closely by the ascending numbers of the 'Fibonacci' summation series 0, 1, 1, 2, 3, 5, 8, 13, 21, 34, 55, 89, 144... Each number in this series, as well as being the sum of the previous two terms, gives the nearest whole number to the GS of its two neighbouring terms in the series. For example, 34 × 0·618034 = 21·013...; 34 ÷ 0·618034 = 55·013... Indeed, any summation

1. F. Lasserre (1964, 76–106) traces the importance of GS in Classical mathematics. Its role in nature is documented by A. H. Church (1904), S. Colman and C. A. Coan (1912; 1920), T. A. Cook (1903; 1914) and D'A. W. Thompson (1917), who list examples ranging from snail shells to sunflowers, pine cones and catkins.

The exact value of GS, also traditionally represented by the Greek letter ϕ, is $\frac{\sqrt{5} \pm 1}{2}$; the plus value gives 1·618034... (GS by extension) and the minus value gives 0·618034... (GS by division). The two numbers are reciprocals: $\frac{1}{1·618034} = 0·618034$ and vice versa.

series in which each term is the sum of the previous two terms approaches nearer and nearer to a geometric series with its successive terms linked by GS. Thus we can start, for example, by adding 1 and 3, producing the series 1, 3, 4, 7, 11, 18, 29, 47, 76... The ratio 1:3 is far (0·3333...) from 0·618034; 3:4 is less so (0·75), 4:7 better (0·5714...), 7:11 better yet (0·63636...), 11:18 already accurate in its first two decimal places (0·6111...) and so on. From 4, 7 upwards that series gives nearest whole numbers to GS.[2]

Fibonacci's series also provides a simple way of calculating the GS of any number (demonstrated on page 7 below), so that no great mathematical skill is needed to manipulate numbers in this way. This prompts the question of whether the proportional patterns in Debussy's music were designed consciously or intuited subconsciously, a question discussed more in the following pages. Whatever the case, one's attention is attracted by how often well-defined sections in Debussy's music follow Fibonacci's numbers at strategic places – the 55 bars of introduction to the last movement of *La mer*, the 21 bars of introduction to 'Rondes de Printemps' from the orchestral *Images*; the 34 bars comprising the first 3/8 section of *Jeux*; the 34 bars of build-up to the climactic coda of *L'isle joyeuse* (bars 186–219 –pages 219–20 below), and likewise to the recapitulation of *Masques* (bars 236–69); the first reprise in 'Reflets dans l'eau' after 34 bars and the beginning of its climax after 55 (pages 196–8 below). The following chapters trace many more examples, relating them musically and proportionally to what surrounds them.

Lucid and objective general surveys of GS, its history and use in the visual arts, and the varying attitudes taken towards it at different times, are provided by P. H. Scholfield (1958) and R. Wittkower (1949; 1960). One of the best-known modern applications of GS is the Swiss-French architect le Corbusier's 'modulor', first announced in 1948, a GS-based architectural grid produced by extending the GS system of Fig. 1.2 above to follow the vertical proportions of the human body. Le Corbusier was anticipated earlier this century by two writers in particular, Matila Ghyka and Jay Hambidge, who produced numerous volumes on the Golden Section (listed in the Bibliography below), basing their theories on artistic and archaeological evidence, and in some cases on esoteric traditions. Hambidge's arguments were not all watertight, and the enthusiasm his theories roused in some circles was equalled by the disparagement they suffered in others, the arguments for and against sometimes showing more passion than reason. GS had earlier taken a place in the theories of the German scientist, psychologist and parapsychologist extraordinary Gustav Fechner,

2. The Fibonacci series takes its nickname from that of the medieval mathematician Leonardo da Pisa (1170 – 1250), known to his contemporaries as 'Figlio Bonaccio' (son of Bonaccio), and instrumental in establishing the use of Arabic numbers in Europe. The 3, 4, 7. . . series is known as the Lucas sequence, after the nineteenth-century French mathematician Edouard Lucas; it has a simple relationship to the Fibonacci series in that $11 = 3 + 5 + 3$, $18 = 5 + 8 + 5$, $29 = 8 + 13 + 8$ and so on, allowing the two sequences to coincide and interact. The importance of this will be seen in the following chapters.

whose work, as we shall see later, was known to the French Symbolists with whom Debussy associated in early years. Fechner's attempts (1876) to prove an instinctive visual preference for GS were discredited after his death, when it was found he had suppressed some possibly contradictory evidence; but recently I. C. McManus (1980) has, to his own surprise, partly vindicated Fechner.[3]

There is no doubt, though, about how significant a role GS plays in organic nature. Indeed one of Hambidge's severest critics was the same Theodore Cook (1922) whose treatises on GS in organic nature (1903; 1914) are still standard reference works. Whatever the whole truth is about GS in art and psychology (and the field has not been one monopolized by the most objective of investigations), if GS is seen to be consistently present, and above all influential, in the musical forms analysed here, it calls for study, whether it came about through instinct, design or both.

Golden Section in musical forms

One of the clearest applications of GS in Debussy's music occurs in the two sets of piano *Images* of 1905 and 1907. In 'Reflets dans l'eau' (reproduced on pages 194–200 below), the first of the 1905 set, the principal climax, at bars 56–61, lies symmetrically over the piece's overall point of GS (after 58 bars out of a total of 94 – it makes only about 1% overall difference to the calculation whether or not one allows for the digressions from the predominating 4/8 metre in bars 11 and 23). If this example lacks immediately obvious precision, 'Mouvement', the third of the 1905 *Images*, is less ambiguous, with a sharply focused principal climax in bars 109–10, again placed precisely over the overall point of GS in the middle of the bar 110 (Ex. 1). 'Cloches à travers les feuilles', the first of the 1907 *Images*, is even more precise, with only half a bar of *fortissimo* at its climax, again exactly at the point of overall GS (in the second half of bar 31, also shown in Ex. 1 – remembering that bars 9, 11, and 15, in 2/4, count as half the value of the surrounding 4/4 bars). All three pieces begin and end quietly, giving maximum force to their dynamic shapes.

Three out of six *Images* make a sufficiently high tally to prompt closer attention, both to the music and to the questions that naturally follow. Does it signify anything worthwhile in musical terms? If so, what about the other *Images* whose climaxes are not thus placed? In the pieces mentioned, are the GS climaxes proportionally isolated, or might they involve more complex proportional networks?

The three questions are most easily answered in reverse order. As already suggested, these musical climaxes are also the structural climaxes of intricate

---

3. Dr McManus's conclusions, based on much more sophisticated experimental equipment and thorough analysis than were available to Fechner, are the more remarkable in view of his initial expectation (communicated to me in conversation) of disproving Fechner.

Ex. 1

(a) 'Mouvement', bars 109–10

(b) 'Cloches à travers les feuilles', bar 31

proportional systems which, when analysed, account for the sequence and positioning of all the important musical events in the pieces involved. The system of logic revealed by these analyses can then account in equal detail for the forms of the remaining *Images* and other works by Debussy. The musical significance of all this is discussed throughout the present book: Chapter 2 discusses the analytical techniques involved, and detailed proportional analyses follow from Chapter 3 onwards.

Two other fundamental questions follow. Of these the first – whether the proportional schemes were the result of conscious design or purely of a highly refined subconscious instinct – is discussed at various stages of this book. To the second question – whether or not this technique was unique to Debussy – a more immediate answer presents itself in the form of a number of proportional studies of the music of various composers. Among the many such studies that seek or find only approximate proportions,[4] there are a few significantly accurate or comprehensive discoveries: for example, Marcus van Crevel's astonishingly complex numerological analyses (1959; 1964) of two masses by Obrecht, some of which findings are paralleled by Brian Trowell's recent work on Dunstable

4. J. H. Douglas Webster (1950) and C. Pascoe (1973) cover the widest ranges of composers from this aspect, though their methods of analysis severely limit what they can positively conclude. They are discussed in more detail, together with a number of other proportional investigations, in Howat (1979), Chapters 1 and 2.

(1979); various types of proportion found by John Rutter (1975) in music by Haydn, Mozart and Beethoven; and, though not always quite accurate, Ernő Lendvai's proportional analyses (1971) of Bartók's music. Lendvai's findings are the more striking here in view of Bartók's admiration for Debussy's music.[5] Some precise proportional structures in music by other composers are shown briefly in Appendix 2 below, which also lists some more existing proportional analyses in music. In the main, though, this book restricts itself to Debussy, not only for reasons of space but also because the techniques involved will be seen to be crucial to Debussy's style – whether he was consciously aware of them or not.

This brings us back to the first question, still unanswered, of Debussy's awareness or otherwise in proportional matters. Full discussion of this is reserved until Chapter 11, since much of the most important musical evidence will emerge only in the intervening analytical chapters. Suffice it here to mention two basic pieces of evidence, one general and one specific.

First, none of Debussy's surviving manuscripts contains any signs of numerical calculations concerning structure.[6] This however is inconclusive, and also not surprising. Most of these manuscripts are the final copies given to the engraver; an artist as meticulous as Debussy was over the visual presentation of his scores – both manuscript and printed – would hardly have been so unprofessional as to deliver his finished product with scaffolding still attached. In any case these final copies are mostly third or fourth drafts of the works concerned, by which stage their forms would be well established.[7] Apart from these final copies, only a very small number of sketches have survived. Debussy is known to have destroyed the large majority of his sketches, and, while that proves neither side of the question, it could be conjectured that the few sketches which remain are those that divulge no secrets – a person as secretive as Debussy being especially unlikely to allow himself to be seen in such a compositional state of undress. No firm conclusion can therefore be drawn from the above.

The second, more positive piece of evidence is a letter of August 1903 from Debussy to his publisher Jacques Durand. Returning the corrected proofs of the *Estampes*, Debussy writes:

You'll see, on page 8 of 'Jardins sous la pluie', that there's a bar missing – my mistake, besides, as it's not in the manuscript. However, it's necessary, as regards number; the

---

5. Similarities in procedure between the two composers are documented in Howat (1977; 1983).

6. The numbers found on some of the drafts in short score for his orchestral works (for example, that of *La mer*, a manuscript discussed in Chapters 6–9 below) refer to the proposed (and actual) pagination of the full scores he prepared from the short scores. In this sense at least, he took his measurements and literally squared out his paper (cf. page 1 above).

7. See Debussy (1927) pages 18, 20, 140, 155 and 156 for some of Debussy's own allusions to the extent to which he recopied his works. For example, at his death were left four complete autograph manuscripts of *Jeux* (one of them now untraced since being auctioned by Emma Debussy in 1933).

divine number [*elle est nécessaire, quant au nombre; le divin nombre*], as Plato and Mlle Liane de Pougy would say, each admittedly for different reasons.[8]

This leaves no doubt that at least on that occasion Debussy was consciously constructing with numbers. Tantalizingly, the exact terms are left unspecified; *divin nombre*, however, is more likely to signify *nombre d'or*, the usual French term for GS, than any other known possibility – particularly since 'Jardins sous la pluie' is indeed built on a GS–symmetrical pattern, one whose maximum accuracy depends on the bar added to the proofs by Debussy. Moreover, the bar in question (bar 123, missing in the autograph)[9] is not essential to the music's grammatical sense, being merely a repetition of the previous bar. (Ex. 2 quotes both the manuscript and printed versions of the passage; the piece's proportions are investigated in Chapter 10 below.) Debussy's concluding banter, characteristic of his correspondence, does not demean the passage's significance; otherwise rather inexplicable in the context, it could be an attempt to mask his self-consciousness at raising the subject at all. Even if this piece of evidence is not absolutely conclusive, Debussy's statement certainly gives us good reason for investigating numerical possibilities in his musical forms.

Debussy would have had ample opportunity to learn about GS through his constant associations with painters and other artists; that interest in GS was endemic in the visual arts at that time is documented by the exhibition in Paris by the *Section d'or* (Golden Section) group of painters in 1912. This is all discussed more fully in Chapter 11, along with other possible ways in which Debussy's attention could have been drawn to proportional techniques in art. It is worth saying straight away, though, that number and proportion were ideas much in circulation among the French Symbolist artists with whom Debussy mixed in his formative years.

It need hardly be added that Debussy has never before enjoyed fame as a mathematician. But, as mentioned on page 3 above, there is an easy way of finding the GS of any number, by breaking the number down into Fibonacci components. Thus a number chosen at random, for example 347, can be broken down into 233 + 89 + 21 + 3 + 1. GS of this by Fibonacci procedure is 144 + 55 + 13 + 2 + 0·6 = 214·6. 347 × 0·618034 by long division yields 214·45... Other random examples are 66 which yields 41 and 40·79... respectively by the two methods, and 86 which yields respectively 53 and 53·15... Obviously the Fibonacci method is reliable easily to the nearest whole number, which is as near

8. Autograph letter in the archives of Durand et Cie; published in Debussy (1927, 10). Liane de Pougy (diplomatically rendered in the published version as 'X. de Z.') was a well-known Parisian *demi-mondaine*. *Le divin nombre* as applied to her suggests a pun on the expression connoting 'the divine few' or 'the elite' (synonymously *le nombre des élus*), which would be consistent with her *demi-mondaine* reputation. By an odd coincidence, in later life she married a relation of Matila Ghyka.

9. Music department of the Bibliothèque Nationale, Paris: Ms. 988. This, the only known autograph of the three *Estampes*, is the manuscript used by the engraver. The extract reproduced in Ex. 2 forms the last system on page 4 and the first on page 5 of 'Jardins sous la pluie'.

These are part of 0, 1, 1, 2, 3 5 8, 13, 21, 34, 55, 89, 144, 233

Ex. 2: 'Jardins sous la pluie',
(a) Bars 118ff reproduced from Debussy's autograph (by courtesy of the Bibliothèque Nationale, Paris)

(b) Bars 120–5 of the printed version after Debussy's proof alteration

as musical notation can approach anyway. Edward Lockspeiser's definitive work on Debussy (1962; 1965) has probably destroyed any lingering notions of the composer as an anti-intellectual who eschewed understanding of what he was about. Dreamer in a more special sense he was, but one knowledgeable about an enormous range of subjects, and with a mind of exceptional retentive power. It would be less than reasonable, then, to consider him incapable of the elementary addition and subtraction involved in the above method of calculating GS. Whether or not he consciously did so is of course another question, as yet undecided. But the point here is that the possibility cannot be ruled out on technical grounds.

Similarly, the idea of Debussy using such scientific means of formal regulation (consciously or not) is quite compatible with his known distaste for musical *formules*. Taken exactly (and especially in French usage), a formula is a prescribed method, convention or recipe – a definition applicable to such constructions as fugue, sonata form and so forth. Debussy's own use of the word – for example, 'la formule wagnérienne' in an article of 1902 (Debussy, 1971, 61) – confirms this. By contrast, GS is a natural principle, like the harmonic series, whose physical existence antedates mankind. As such it would hardly be disregarded by Debussy, were he aware of it. When he wrote, more than once, about his musical 'search for a world of sensations and forms in constant renewal', his aim was evidently to free music from rigidly stereotyped forms.[10] At the same time his concern for proportional balance within his formal freedom is well documented in his own writings – the most notable example being the second piece of *En blanc et noir*, in which he restored to the proofs a long passage previously cut from the manuscript, explaining to Jacques Durand (Debussy, 1927, 143) that 'concern for proportions absolutely demanded this change'.[11]

Two objections are sometimes raised to the idea itself of investigating proportional coherence in musical form. The first is the opinion that such coherence merely springs from a fairly ubiquitous proportional instinct, and is thus banal or unimportant. The second is the opinion that the human mind cannot instinctively evaluate precise temporal proportion on such a scale, and thus that such proportional plans are musically irrelevant. Clearly both objections cannot apply at once, as they are mutually exclusive. If, on the one hand, such precise and logical proportional schemes are indeed a result purely of instinct, then the existence of this instinct is proved (at least on the composer's part, even if it may be less developed in many listeners). If, on the other hand, such instinct does not exist, then the structures can only have been designed intentionally. (It will be seen that they are too comprehensive and accurate for there to be any possibility of their being merely fortuitous.) But for Debussy, of all composers, instinct and design would never have been so arbitrarily detached: it is a safe assumption that any conscious compositional techniques, proportional or otherwise, would have been used for ensuring maximum accuracy in the music's instinctive effect – and that they would be rejected unless the musical results felt instinctively correct to him. That is to say, if Debussy designed such schemes consciously, the implication must be that he also believed in a corresponding proportional instinct.

But scepticism from both the reader and the analyst is a healthy safeguard against jumping to conclusions; in the matter of proportional analysis it is the more understandable in view of rampant inaccuracy in many existing studies on the subject. It is essential therefore to define the methods by which the following

10. 'La recherche d'un monde de sensations et de formes incessamment renouvelé' (Debussy, 1971, 56 and 114).

11. The superseded shorter version can be found in the autograph copy (Music department of the Bibliothèque Nationale, Paris: Ms. 989). Other examples of Debussy's sensitivity to proportion are his Cello Sonata, of which he wrote in 1915: 'J'aime les proportions et la forme presque classique, dans le bon sens du mot' (Debussy, 1927, 142); and a review in which he praises Lucien Capet's *Poème* for Violin and Orchestra: 'La liberté de sa forme n'en contrarie jamais l'harmonieuse proportion' (Debussy, 1971, 220).

analyses and measurements are to be undertaken, what degree of accuracy is to be sought as acceptable, and precisely what the analyses can tell us about the music. To this the next chapter is devoted.

One other danger has to be guarded against. Proportions can too easily become the type of study where one finds whatever one wants by looking hard enough. The main safeguard against this is constant vigilance with regard to the musical logic of the systems discovered here, and the light they cast on other structural aspects. That many of Debussy's early works betray *no* sign of any proportional systems, even after exhaustive examination, is of additional reassurance here that the schemes found in the more mature works are not merely wishful analytic thinking. Those musical structures without any detectable proportional schemes are investigated and discussed in Chapter 4.

A more positive corroboration can be added. In the mature works whose proportional systems are analysed, it will be seen that the systems are comprehensive to the extent that not a single significant musical event in any of the pieces defies their logic or lies outside them. The proportional structures will also be seen to have maximum possible accuracy in musical terms: in the case of any small inaccuracy there is always a musical reason – and sometimes another proportional one – why the system could not be made more accurate. In this regard the following chapters discuss some last-minute changes Debussy made to scores – in one case after publication – all of which improve proportional accuracy. An example already seen is the bar he added to 'Jardins sous la pluie', specifying number as the reason. Therefore proportional structure in Debussy's music is not theory but demonstrable fact. The element of hypothesis concerns only how aware Debussy was of it, and, if aware, his reasons for using it.

Chapter 2

Analytical aims and methods

In dealing with Debussy and proportions, this book has two fundamental aims. The first, already outlined in Chapter 1, is simply to demonstrate these proportions in the music. The second follows from this: to trace ways in which these are influential in defining and conveying the music's dramatic and expressive qualities. The more detailed analysis necessary for this second purpose inevitably makes some of the book less easy reading than it might otherwise have been, but this should need no apology: apart from the subjective view that any musical analysis without this second aim appears to me futile, the second aim is at least partially necessary in this case to establish the book's primary argument. Proportional structures are *per se* abstract: in music they can have real existence only in terms of the music's other structural functions. Awareness of other structural aspects is therefore necessary not only to be able to detect the presence of proportional structures, but also to be able to determine their significance. It should hardly be necessary, then, to add that the following proportional analyses make no attempt to belittle the relevance of other analytical approaches.

The challenge of Debussy's unorthodox formal systems has stimulated a rich variety of such approaches. Jean Barraqué follows a practical composer's approach to many immediately audible aspects of Debussy's music, such as rhythmic and dynamic animation (1965; 1972; posth.). Felix Salzer's modified Schenkerian analyses (1952) risk – and incur – the wrath of fundamentalists who consider Debussy and Schenker incompatible.[1] Jean-Jacques Nattiez (1975, 330–56) finds linguistic models in *Syrinx*. Edward Lockspeiser (1962; 1963; 1965) and Vladimir Jankélévitch (1949; 1968; 1976) approach from a more subjective angle, observing and classifying both small- and large-scale expressive and emotional habits or tendencies in the music – in complete contrast to Robert Moevs's minute intervallic classifications (1969). Arnold Whittall (1975) considers the role of modal and tonal contrasts and juxtapositions in the dramatic gradation and impact of pieces as diverse as *L'isle joyeuse*, *Jeux* and the *Prélude* 'Voiles'. Nicolas Ruwet (1962), another linguist, investigates Debussy's habit of building structural blocks of symmetrically repeated motives or bars. These

---

1. Oswald Jonas, in his notes to the American edition of Schenker's *Harmony* (1954, viii), sweeps Salzer's analyses aside as being 'possible only through misinterpretation of Schenker's basic theories, first of all of his concept of tonality, and therefore ... doomed to fail'.

diverse approaches (the list is nothing like exhaustive) are mentioned here for two reasons: first, because they provide structural parameters necessary for defining proportional systems; second, because their number and variety have still not succeeded in accounting for any comprehensive system of logic and balance in Debussy's forms, or in consistently relating any such system to the expressive substance of each piece.

For example, it is not difficult to identify the first movement of *La mer* as a five-part sectional form; the problem is, why did Debussy choose a five-part sectional form to organize the sensations conveyed by that movement? Or, in the piano *Images* of 1905, why should 'Hommage à Rameau' and 'Mouvement' have clearly defined ternary-plus-coda outlines whereas 'Reflets dans l'eau' resists any such simple classification? If we recall Debussy's battle-cry, 'a world of sensations and forms in constant renewal', his juxtaposition of the words *sensations* and *forms* implies a degree of inseparability of these two aspects in his mind. In view of this the question is not merely 'What is the form?', but rather 'Why is the form as it is, and how does this relate to the music's expression?'

A main reason for the failure of existing analyses to account for Debussy's formal systems is that they tend to treat separate musical functions in isolation, finding few ways in which these are organically integrated. (This is no implied condemnation; it merely points out the nature of such specialized analysis.) Since proportional analysis, by contrast, has no option but to involve other structural aspects, its significance will be determined in this book by whether it can throw further light on the other structural aspects, and whether it can link those other aspects together and relate them to the music's expression in ways that explain something of the exact nature of Debussy's forms.

To do this, the proportional analyses consider the music's dynamic shape in an architectural sense, and as an integral formal function. Surprisingly few analyses of Debussy's music consider dynamic shape at all, and those that do tend to fasten only on isolated aspects – a principal climactic point, for example. Yet dynamics are one of the most immediately palpable aspects of Debussy's mature music, most of which is strongly characterized and focused by an undulating tidal flow of dynamic intensity – especially significant in a work like *La mer*, where the dynamic ebb and flow has a broadly programmatic as well as an abstractly dramatic function. This tidal effect is generated not only by dynamic peaks and troughs, with the intermediate crescendos and diminuendos, but also by all the types of formal definition – particularly changes of harmonic tension, or varying degrees of rhythmic animation – that articulate the approaches to and recessions from those peaks. In most of Debussy's music dynamic peaks tend to be precisely focused: 'Jeux de vagues' from *La mer* is one of the best examples, with a sequence of short dynamic peaks increasing in intensity until the final explosion at figure *38*. It is reasonable to infer that other aspects of the music might be organized so as to direct the listener's attention most forcibly towards these climactic points. This, we shall see, is the case, not only applying to isolated movements but also sometimes linking different movements of a work.

Obviously, to follow every detail of structure, every change of harmony, would be as impossible in a book this size as it would be tedious. What is aimed at here is a more qualitative approach to structural aspects: transitions of harmony, tonality, modality, texture, rhythm, phrase structure and melody that define audible turning points in the music. Harmonically and tonally, for example, the emphasis is on setting the individual harmonic steps within a larger framework, by grouping them together qualitatively in terms of tonal stability or instability, diatonicism or chromaticism, changes of mode, or static or dynamic qualities – tracing what Arnold Whittall calls 'the skilfully balanced relationship between chromaticism and diatonicism [that] brings tension and dynamism to [Debussy's] music' (1975, 271). Debussy's phrase structure reveals similarly skilful balancing, between blocks of symmetrical phrases on the one hand, with their effect of regularity, against the relative instability of asymmetrical phrases on the other.[2] As one might expect, the musical turning points defined by such contrasts and sections coincide with the nodal points of GS and symmetrical sequences in the music, again involving dynamics.

The vital property of all these functions is their audibility: any sensitive ear, even if untrained in harmonic theory, can detect changing dynamics, a new melody, or the increased turbulence or density when stable gives way to shifting harmony, symmetrical to asymmetrical phrases. (Any orchestral player will confirm how much easier it is to count bars when they follow groups of four, indicating the greater instinctive effect of stability – or, in some cases, momentum – from four-bar phrasing.) So the proportional systems on which these qualitative musical functions are built can be taken as having, at least primarily, the functional purpose of leading the listener, via the music's form, to its expression. One might say that the music is trying to tell us how to listen to it. (The numerological connoisseur will see that this is quite different from the cabbalistic number systems traced by Ulrich Siegele (1978) in music by J. S. Bach.)

Structural counterpoint and arithmetical accuracy

One of the problems in defining Debussy's formal systems results from his fondness for staggering the turning points associated with various musical functions, so that, say, the music's tonal and motivic events follow separate rates of change. The last two pages of 'Reflets dans l'eau' are a good example (pages 199–200 below), with the return to the opening tonality in the middle of a phrase (bar 69) and the final return of the piece's principal thematic motive in the

2. Debussy's interest, as early as 1889, in qualitative contrasts between symmetrical and asymmetrical phrase structure is documented in Maurice Emmanuel's transcriptions of Debussy's classroom conversations with his teacher Ernest Guiraud (in Lockspeiser, 1962, 204–8).

middle of another phrase (bar 78). This visible and audible structural counterpoint will be seen, in the following chapters, to correspond to counterpoints of two or more proportional sequences running simultaneously. Each one is normally associated with a different structural aspect – this is important, if the principle is to be musically viable – and the sequences usually converge on centres of structural or dramatic focus, or on the end of a movement. The principle is in effect a large-scale type of polyrhythm; it reaches its highest degree of sophistication and complexity (among the works studied here) in 'Jeux de vagues' from *La mer*. The idea is known in recent music: the composer Elliott Carter (Edwards, 1971, 111–15) has described his own use of similar large-scale polyrhythms, based on symmetrical sequences – as well as mentioning his reluctance to disclose this for many years after the music's composition.

In order to relate two or more such sequences within one movement, it has sometimes evidently been necessary for Debussy, whether consciously or not, to stretch or compress one or more of them very slightly. This is shown in the following analyses whenever it occurs. Such small deviations do not invalidate the proportional systems, though, since GS, having an irrational value, is in any case impossible to obtain with full accuracy in numerical terms. The question rather is how much deviation is permissible, or how closely one can approach the exact irrational value in terms of the music's natural flow, for example, without inappropriate disruption of the metre: whether to the nearest beat of pulse, to the nearest bar, or to some alternative nearest practicable point of measurement. Instances will be seen, too, when the metre *is* interrupted for this purpose, the interruption itself marking a musical nodal point in the same way that the interruption of a sequence of four-bar phrases would do. (Regular metre is, of course, itself a symmetrical proportional sequence.) There is also the question of whether to spread unavoidable inaccuracies, however small, as evenly as possible throughout the various proportional sequences in operation, or whether to concentrate the inaccuracies in the structures of lowest musical significance. All this applies whether as a result of instinct or design on Debussy's part.

It will be seen that rarely does any inaccuracy exceed one of the units by which the proportions of the piece in question are being measured (the methods of measurement are discussed on pages 15–21 below) unless a good reason for this can be demonstrated in terms of structural counterpoint or other structural exigencies. An example that sometimes arises is the need not to disrupt a sequence of four-bar periodicity which itself forms part of another proportional structure. In such cases the percentage amount of the inaccuracy is supplied, showing that normally such inaccuracy is spread as evenly as possible in percentage terms among the various sequences present. The exceptions to this are when some musically less important sequences carry a larger share of inaccuracy, in order to give maximum accuracy to the more dominant ones. The majority of these inaccuracies will also be shown to be less than 2% of the musical 'distance' being measured – an amount too small to impair the effectiveness of the

14

proportional systems. Indeed, for a composer so fond of the expression 'sans aucune rigueur', one who would never imprison music in formulae, the accuracy Debussy attained is astonishing.

One would not expect the advocate of 'sensations and forms in constant renewal' to be enslaved by proportional techniques. Much of the fascination of the proportional investigation here comes from the ingenuity with which Debussy wields his proportions, whether consciously or not. No system ever appears the same way twice; indeed, much of the later music seems to be using proportions to take decided structural risks, and many of the proportional structures are far from obvious to the initial search. The obvious, in keeping with other aspects of Debussy's technique, is avoided more and more; it is for this reason that any relevant proportional analysis has to remain alert to apparent inaccuracies or inconsistencies.

Methods of measurement

Are temporal proportions in music to be measured by clock time or by the music's notated pulse? For some recent music (for example, Karlheinz Stockhausen's *Fresco* and *Mikrophonie II*) the former method is specified in the score by strict timings. But music with a defined internal metrical pulse is more problematic. Any recording producer will vouch for the enormous variations in duration between different performances of any one work, or sections within it. Probably the most extreme known case was described by the conductor Albert Coates, who recalled performing times for Scriabin's *Divine poem* ranging from ninety minutes under Nikisch's baton, and an hour under Koussevitsky's, to Scriabin's own time (apparently with no cuts) of thirty-eight minutes! (Aronowsky, 1959, ix–x). The moral of the story is that, in practice, a composer cannot assure a piece's proportions in clock time if its notated dimensions are fixed and if an internal metrical pulse has to be followed. True, many of Bartók's scores contain precise timings; but Bartók took pains to explain (for example, in the preface to the violin-and-piano score of his Violin Concerto of 1938) that the timings were intended merely as a guide. For him, sensitivity to nuance evidently had priority. All the more, then, for such a refined exponent of nuance as Debussy, if proportions are to be accurately guaranteed by the composer, this can only be practicable in terms of the metrically notated dimensions.

'All very well,' the listener will say, 'but what about the way I hear the music?' It seems reasonable to suppose that for the involved listener the music's audible pulse provides a more vivid or emphatic articulation of time than his watch does, even if he is aware of the presence of fluctuations in that pulse such as accelerando, ritardando or rubato. Ernő Lendvai takes this view (1971, 26). But the problem is more complex. Do other events in the music, regardless of its tempo, affect the listener's awareness of time? Does this vary with the listener's mood or state of concentration? And what about Henri Bergson's theories about temporal perception? All this is too subtle and subjective to admit of academic proof, and to expatiate on it at the necessary length – and, inevitably, inconclusively – would be inappropriate here.[3] If this appears to be dodging the issue, the answer is that ultimately the issue is one not crucial to this book. The primary concern here is with what Debussy actually wrote; since the proportional structures to be described in the following chapters work with maximum accuracy and musical logic when measured by the notated pulse, there is no option but to conclude that Debussy either designed or intuited them in those terms. This applies even if such pulse is only one of various ways, some of them perhaps simultaneous, in which we experience time when listening to music.

It is worth adding that existing rhythmic theories and analyses, including Nicolas Ruwet's work on Debussy's symmetrical phrase structures (1962), tacitly take this as read: indeed, without dependence on the notated rhythms they would be helpless. A minim followed by a crotchet (provided there is no notational or tempo modulation between them) is always regarded there as a ratio of 2:1, even if an accelerando or ritardando in force at that point might make the ratio in clock time more like 2:0·93 or 2:1·24 (to take two of an infinite number of possibilities). If these analyses are relevant to one's instinctive reception of music, it is logical to infer that any larger-scale extension of the same temporal instinct (which must exist at a local level, otherwise rhythm, metre and rubato would be redundant) would continue to work on the same basis.

Some problems of pulse measurement

By what units is this musical pulse to be measured? A movement whose metre is constant, such as the finale of *La mer*, presents no problem, as it can logically be measured by bars. A piece like 'Pagodes' (from *Estampes*) is also quite simple: as it is predominantly in 4/4, its two bars of 2/4, at the same crotchet tempo, can each be counted as the equivalent of half a 4/4 bar, or alternatively the entire piece can be counted in minim beats or half bars. Either way the proportions yielded – which are what matter here – are identical. In 'Hommage à Rameau' from the piano *Images* of 1905 (analysed in Chapter 10), the irregularities of metre are frequent enough to make counting in fractions of bars unwieldy; the most convenient method there is to take the piece's constant minim beat as the standard unit of measurement.

3. The reader who wishes to explore this subject further is referred to the following books and articles: Robert Erickson (1967), Marie-Louise von Franz (1974), Michael R. Rogers (1977), Pierre Souvtchinsky (1939), Karlheinz Stockhausen (1959), and Igor Stravinsky (1947). Chapter 1 of Howat (1979) discusses some of these. Elliott Carter (1977) frequently takes up the topic, especially in the chapters 'The time dimension in music' and 'Music and the time span'. Henri Bergson (1910) is also basic reading here, although it is worth noting that Edward Lockspeiser (1965, 278), describing similarities between Debussy's and Gaston Bachelard's views of water and dream symbolism, contrasts them both with Bergson's outlook.

L'isle joyeuse brings a new problem (see the reproduction of the entire piece on pages 209–21). Since it is in a mixture of 4/4 and 3/8 bars, linked by the relationship ♪ = ♪ (bars 28 and 67), measurement by bars would be illogical. Further, the 4/4 sections obviously cannot be heard in terms of 3/8 groups. The logical course, as in 'Hommage à Rameau', is to take the lowest common denominator of pulse, which here is the quaver beat; and this introduces the problem. Bars 1–6 are in very free time ('Quasi una cadenza'), and it is only from bar 9 onwards that a regular quaver pulse is discernible. Is it then fallacious to count in terms of a nonexistent pulse in bars 1–8?

Not arithmetically, provided that some audible pulse is maintained all through the piece. Even if it is not the same unit throughout, provided there is no transition where more than one tempo relationship is possible, the piece's proportions are fixed. *L'isle joyeuse* meets this condition, since for its first 27 bars the basic articulation is provided audibly by the bar-lines, which provide continuity from the opening bars until after the quaver articulation has focused itself within the 4/4, from bar 9 onwards. Having heard the first 27 bars thus, the listener then hears bars 28–63 as 36 bars of 3/8. What is vital now is that these two blocks be related audibly where they meet – which they are by the clear quaver pulse running across this transition, marked ♪ = ♪ by Debussy. The same applies to the subsequent changes of metre at bars 64 and 67.[4] The relative proportions of those sections are then fixed unalterably, and measurement by quaver units is now merely the means of mathematical expression of these proportions. Units of 3/8, or indeed virtually any constant grouping, could equally be used, since the ratios yielded would be the same in every case. This reasoning will also apply, in Chapters 7 and 9, to some of the tempo modulations in the first two movements of *La mer*.

In *L'isle joyeuse* Debussy takes extra trouble to ensure we hear the metrical relationships in this way, by overlapping the metre at the first two metrical transitions. Thus bar 27, nominally in 4/4, is equally audible as $\frac{3+2+3}{8}$, anticipating the 3/8 of the next bar. Similarly bars 62–3 form a crotchet hemiola anticipating the ensuing 4/4.

In *L'isle joyeuse* these metrical transitions obviously mark principal musical nodal points; in Chapter 5 it will be seen that they also mark the principal proportional nodal points in the piece's architecture, counting the piece's dimensions as explained above. Structural reasons will then also be seen (pages 59–60) for the lack of rhythmic definition at the beginning of the piece.

In all other cases in the following chapters where metrical changes are accompanied by a specified tempo equality – for example the ♩. = ♩ linking the change from 6/8 to 6/4 at bars 44–5 of *D'un cahier d'esquisses* (Chapter 10), or the

4. Although the indication ♪ = ♪ is lacking at bar 64, this can only be because it is sufficiently obvious to be taken as read, since bar 64 brings back the theme of bar 9, and the quaver tempo has not changed since bar 9.

♩ = ♩ linking the change from 6/4 to 4/4 at bars 5–6 in the first movement of *La mer* (Chapter 7) – the principles outlined above apply equally logically, and the pulse will be calculated on the same basis. One further example of this – the ♪= ♪ transition at bar 32 of the *Prélude à l'après-midi d'un faune* (one bar after figure 3) – will, when treated the same way, be seen to have particularly curious repercussions later in the piece. This is discussed *in situ* in Chapter 10.

At metrical transitions where no tempo equality is supplied – for example at bars 83–4 in the first movement of *La mer* (two bars before figure 9) – procedure depends on the musical context. This problem concerns mostly the first two movements of *La mer*, and the principal criterion in such cases is always the nearest audible relationship of pulse carried across the transition. This will involve considering the tempo and metronome indications in the scores.

Suspension of pulse

The main impediment to measuring any piece by its pulse is, naturally, any suspension of that pulse. An example is the cadenza in Debussy's *D'un cahier d'esquisses* (Ex. 3), where the regular pulse of the rest of the piece is in a state of suspension. The top staff, indeed, gives a different rhythmic total from the bottom one in both cases, suggesting that Debussy wanted the passage free from literal rhythmic constraint. To read the note values literally, therefore, not only would be grammatically impossible, but also would contradict the music's expressive sense. So any attempt at relating the cadenza proportionally to what surrounds it must be musically realistic, accepting the cadenza's suspension of normal pulse.

Ex. 3: Cadenza of Debussy's *D'un cahier d'esquisses*

It helps if we remember that the cadenza's presence structurally provides a larger-scale temporal articulation in the music, from rhythmically defined sections to a unit-free one and vice versa. This is not dissimilar to the opening 'quasi-cadenza' of *L'isle joyeuse*, where the first 6 cadenza-like bars lead into, and are proportionally linked to, the regular 4/4 bars that follow. The cadenza of *D'un cahier d'esquisses* is not quite so clearly linked, and some alternative estimations are possible, although only within a small range. It could, as in *L'isle joyeuse*, be given the equivalent value of one of the surrounding 6/8 bars. But its internal articulation into two distinct phrases suggests that an equivalent value of 2 bars would be more apt musically, despite the lack of a bar-line between them. Or the bass notation – two tied semibreves tied to a dotted crotchet – might suggest 2½ bars. It will be seen in Chapter 10 that the last two possibilities provide the most accurate completion of the piece's proportional scheme, as well as being musically the most apt. (Unfortunately the autograph of the piece is lost, making it impossible to verify if Debussy notated the cadenza exactly as printed.) All this is not to say that the cadenza can be felt as a specific number of beats; a different type of temporal articulation is in force there and is most accurately expressed mathematically by this means, relative to the rest of the piece.

Not all cadenzas are out of tempo. In 'Poissons d'or' from Debussy's piano *Images* of 1907, the cadenza (Ex. 4) begins 'au dessous du mouvement' – that is, with the tempo attenuated but still active. (Two dotted bars later it is again 'au mouvement'.) It is strongly rhythmic, and if its notated value of 37 quaver beats is accordingly included in the calculation of the whole piece's dimensions (to be described in Chapter 10), the piece's proportional structure then completes itself with maximum accuracy – again suggesting that this was how Debussy either designed or intuited it.

Ex. 4: Cadenza of 'Poissons d'or'

Ex. 4 (contd)

Such a variety of rhythmic complications might suggest the argument that proportional systems are too fraught with possible ambiguities to be practicable or audibly effective. That, perhaps, is more the composer's problem. But if those systems are logically and consistently present in the music as a result of instinct, their presence speaks for itself. Alternatively, if applied deliberately, their function would have been to serve the music discreetly, not to force it into any rhythmic straitjacket. Debussy would have been the least likely of all composers to let the tail wag the dog in this respect. Likewise the difficulties of tracing those schemes in rhythmically complex scores merely indicate that composers notate their finished scores for the performer. There is no obligation to leave trails of clues for the analyst; Debussy's aim, if anything, would have been the reverse.

With this in view, the following chapters do not just choose the simplest works to 'unscramble', such as those with no metrical complications. Had they done so, the above ten paragraphs could have been omitted but the musical possibilities to be traced in the following chapters would have remained very restricted.

On the other hand, no extravagant claims are being made for the necessity of such systems to all 'good' music. Obviously proportional structure is only one of many ways of ensuring good formal balance, and even then only if it is well matched to the musical content; it could do little to help music that is deficient in its basic material or other formal processes. Its main importance in Debussy's music is its way of binding together other formal aspects, and thereby revealing logic that has not been traceable hitherto.

Works chosen for analysis

In selecting the works to be analysed here, a balance has had to be maintained. To study too many works would risk superficiality of analysis; yet one of the most remarkable trends to emerge from the analyses is the logical development of proportional systems from one work to another, in terms of sophistication and subtlety. With all this in mind, Debussy's most substantial instrumental score, *La mer*, has been chosen as the central work for analysis, and Part 3 of the book is devoted entirely to it. To prepare the reader for the complexity involved, Chapters 3–5 analyse some less complex pieces. Afterwards, Chapter 10 provides briefer indications of related structures in other works by Debussy. These last are not intended as thorough analyses: their sole purpose is to show relationships to, and development of, the schemes already analysed in detail.

Other general considerations

Before the analyses begin it is as well to clarify an issue which, though apparently simple, has been confused in many existing proportional analyses. If a piece is 34 bars long (all bars being of equal length), it finishes *after* 34 bars. Likewise its GS points come after 13 and 21 bars – that is, at the beginning of bars 14 and 22, not 13 and 21. In the following chapters the numbers given in the diagrams refer to *completed* units of measurement. Therefore, where the unit is the bar, the number 21, for example, will mean after the completion of 21 bars, that is, the beginning of bar 22. In cases where the unit is not the bar, bar references are also supplied in parentheses, for convenience.

GS, as seen in Chapter 1, is reversible: either the longer or shorter portion can come first. Evidently its aesthetic effect must be affected by this: for example, the short-plus-long type would be a risky position for a principal climax, since attention would be hard to sustain for the rest of the piece. The evidence of the following chapters reveals a distinct tendency – though this is not an invariable rule – for certain events to be associated with one particular type: points of maximum tension mostly with the former type (long plus short), and points of regeneration or growth more with the latter. Convenient names for the two types are evidently desirable, but in a musical context the most accurate terms – *major* and *minor* – would be confusing. Lendvai (1971) uses the terms *positive* (long plus short) and *negative* (short plus long); Pascoe (1973) chooses *active* and *passive*. Neither solution is very satisfying: what happens musically at a short-plus-long GS is often far from negative or passive. It has been decided here to use *primary* and *secondary*, logically the closest equivalent to *major* and *minor*, but without their musical ambiguity. Their one ambiguity is that, temporally, the secondary GS point (short plus long) arrives first; but the sense of 'primary' here attaches more to its predominating structural and dramatic role.

There is also the duality between GS and symmetrical division. It is widely recognized that GS is more characteristic of organic than of inorganic nature, its presence usually associated with growth or tension, whereas symmetry is more characteristic of inorganic forms (such as snowflakes), associated with stability. The same tendencies will be found in the following analyses.

As already seen in Chapter 1, GS division, involving an irrational number, does not normally produce whole numbers. In the following chapters most numbers are given to the nearest whole number, which is normally as near as the music can approach. When smaller musical divisions are involved, or when apt for any other reason, fractions or decimal places are supplied, the latter usually rounded off to the first one or two places.

Chapter 3

'Reflets dans l'eau'

The 'première série' of piano *Images* marks quite a decisive anchoring point in Debussy's development. Completed in the summer of 1905, after the completion of *La mer* in March that year, the three pieces share *La mer*'s breadth of architecture, and sum up well the innovations of the previous few years in Debussy's piano writing. (They were also the last work he was to finish until late 1907.) 'Reflets dans l'eau', though it opens the *Images*, was the last in order of composition, written in Eastbourne in August 1905 to replace an earlier version with which Debussy was dissatisfied.[1] It has been chosen for the first analysis here because it provides the most lucid exposition of the structural and proportional principles that recur throughout this book.

In orthodox terms the piece's construction is irregular, best described as an unusual species of rondo form built on two recurring motives, *A* and *B*, shown in Ex. 5. *A* begins and ends the piece (literally, as the bass line in the final six bars shows), defining a rondo outline with principal returns in bars 35 and 71.[2] It

Ex. 5

then returns in bar 81, marking the beginning of the coda. *B* is a more melodic development of *A*, beginning with *A* in retrograde (the minor third expanded to a major third in its first appearance). *B*'s appearances form contrasting episodes in the rondo scheme, with principal entries in bars 24, 50 and 78 – one in each of

1. According to Debussy's correspondence with Jacques Durand (Debussy, 1927, 31; and also an unpublished postcard in the Durand archives) the final version was composed in only three days. How much its form may have been based on that of the earlier version is not known, as the discarded version has never been found.

2. The London Peters edition gives wrong bar numbers because of its insertion of a spurious bar-line in the middle of the cadenza-like bar 23. This bar-line is not present in either the only known autograph copy (Music department of the Bibliothèque Nationale, Paris: Ms. 998) or the Durand edition.

the sections marked by the rondo returns prior to the coda. Of those three episodes the final one is very short and the central one much the most important: after its entry in bar 50 *B* dominates the entire climactic section until bar 70.

In itself this thematic *ABABABA* sequence is not indistinct; what blurs the form is that the tonal plan and dynamic shape, especially in the later part of the piece, follow a course quite independent of the thematic sequence, marking a series of separate musical turning points, particularly important at bars 43, 48, 56 and 69. This is the main reason why the term 'rondo' by itself is an inadequate description of the piece's processes. What is much clearer about the piece is its shape – dramatic and dynamic shape – as opposed to its more academic formal aspects.

This is dominated quite audibly by wave-like tendencies: the first section builds up in a wave, reaching its culmination in bars 30–1, followed by a second, much larger wave which leads into the piece's main climax between bars 56 and 61. Looking more closely, we can see that the intermediate events shape those waves precisely, grading the tension carefully before and after the peaks. For example, in the first section, the harmony modulates away in bar 17, having been largely tonic-based up to there, to prepare for the entry of motive *B* at bar 24, which then leads into the climax in bar 30. Similarly the next section starts, in bar 35, over a tonic pedal, modulating away in bar 43, before *B* enters in bar 50.

Conversely, after the main climax, Debussy's efforts seem to be concentrated on stretching the remainder of the piece out, delaying the expected return to the tonic key as long as possible, and making it as gradual as possible. The home tonality returns audibly enough at bar 69, with the return of the five flats and a dominant-ninth chord; but the expected tonic chord in bar 73 has the ground pulled from under it by an echo of the descending run that had dominated bars 67–70. Not until bar 77 is the tonic triad held steady, and even then it is immediately garnished with added sixths, sevenths and ninths.

Evidently the piece's formal layout is important in defining and giving maximum impact to its structural surge, also given maximum emphasis by the *pianissimo* beginning and triple-*piano* ending. In Chapter 1 above it was mentioned that the main climax here lies over the piece's overall point of GS. If the significance of that is to be evaluated now, not only does it have to be related to the rest of the piece, but also the climactic passage itself needs closer study. It begins obviously in bar 56, with the sudden modulation to E♭ major accompanied by powerful waves of arpeggios; and after a further crescendo from *fortissimo* in bar 57 (an instruction unfortunately contradicted, to the piece's detriment, in many performances), the climactic section reaches its dynamic focus in bars 59–60 with a dramatic collision of dominant-ninth and whole-tone harmonies.

As the piece has 94 bars altogether this dynamic focus, coming after 58 bars, is placed $^{58}/_{94}$ of the way through. This ratio cancels out to $^{29}/_{47}$, the significance of which is already known from the Lucas summation series 3, 4, 7, 11, 18, 29, 47... Therefore the piece's dynamic apex coincides to the nearest bar with its GS.

Motive *B* dominates this climactic passage; its first entry in the piece is after 23 bars, and its final appearance fades out after bar 80, marking the beginning of the coda. This is plotted in Fig. 3.1, which shows how the first entry and final exit of *B* – that is, the first episode and the coda – form intermediate points of GS between the beginning, climax and end of the piece. There is only one inexactitude – in the first entry of *B* which is delayed by one bar beyond the theoretical GS point (which would be after 22 bars). This is a relatively small inaccuracy (less than 2%), a possible reason for which will be seen later.

Fig. 3.1

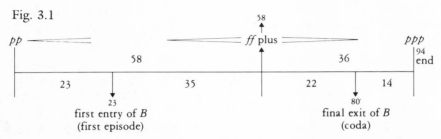

first entry of *B*
(first episode)

final exit of *B*
(coda)

If, as postulated in Chapter 2, the relation of two events by GS can produce a feeling of proportional correctness or inevitability, it will be clear that this would be perceived only when both events have occurred. If this hammers the obvious, the purpose is to clarify here that the GS relationship of the climax to the entire length would, by itself, give no sense of such 'correctness' to the arrival of the climax, but only at (and to) the end of the piece. Hence the significance of the intermediate events in Fig. 3.1: the entry of *B* in bar 24, itself proportionally unprepared, proportionally determines the position of the climactic focus at bar 59, and the combination of these two events then proportionally prepares the entry of the coda and finally the end of the piece. The piece's form is now demonstrably involved in its dramatic gradation, and this logic is reinforced in the following diagrams.

As already mentioned, the first rondo reprise occurs at bar 35 (that is, after 34 bars); this marks the primary GS point between the beginning of the piece and the onset of the climactic section at bar 56 (34:21 bars). Correspondingly, the remaining rondo return in bar 71 mirrors this by dividing the 39 bars remaining from bar 56 to the end in secondary GS of 15:24 (=5:8). The sequence is shown in Fig. 3.2. This second, slightly staggered structure, running in counterpoint

Fig. 3.2

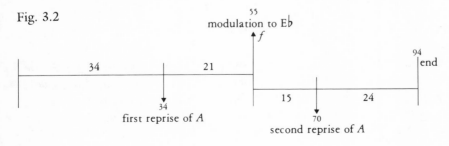

first reprise of *A*

second reprise of *A*

25

with that of Fig. 3.1, suggests a reason for the one inaccuracy seen earlier in Fig. 3.1. In Fig. 3.1 the division after 23 bars, instead of a theoretical 22, keeps the sequence as clear as possible of the number 21, which forms part of the Fibonacci series used in Fig. 3.2 – thus avoiding confusion of the two sequences.

It will be noticed that the ratio around bar 56 at the top of Fig. 3.2 is not GS. This is because the first two events in the sequence, unlike the last one after 70 bars, are important tonal centres, and are involved in a more comprehensive proportional tonal scheme, shown in the top part of Fig. 3.3. This divides the piece's 94 bars into another large-scale proportional sequence. The main point of tonal and harmonic departure, after 42 bars, marks the primary GS on the way to the final return to the opening tonality after 68 bars, and this latter point of return then subtends a symmetrical division of 26:26 bars, completing a sequence of 42:26:26 bars (=21:13:13) between beginning and end of the piece. These two divisions correspond exactly with the natural tendency, mentioned earlier, for GS to be associated with tension, and symmetry with stability. By the same logic the intermediate point of tonic return, after 34 bars of the piece, lies exactly halfway to the later one after 68.

Fig. 3.3

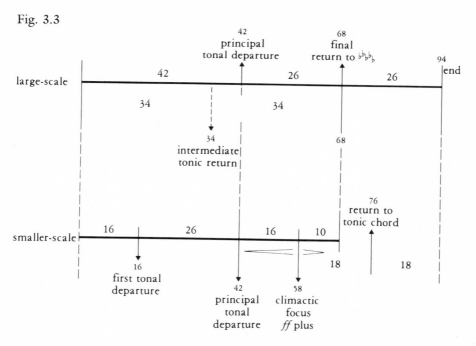

If the climactic focus in bar 59 (after 58 bars) is now added to Fig. 3.3, the dramatic function of the tonal sequence of proportions becomes apparent. This is shown in the lower part of Fig. 3.3. The first modulation away from tonic-based harmony, after 16 bars, forms the secondary GS on the way to the main tonal departure after 42 (a ratio of 16:26, or twice 8:13). Consequently this latter point now also marks the primary GS (26:16 bars) between the earlier tonal departure and the climactic focus after 58. In turn the climax then subtends a similar GS of 16:10 on the way to the final return of the home tonality after 68, completing a GS progression of 16:26:16:10 (=8:13:8:5). The piece's tonal organization, too, can now be seen as having a specific dramatic function of highlighting, and giving formal reinforcement to the piece's dynamic shape.

The remaining centre of tonal return, as already mentioned, is the unobtrusive but crucial return of the tonic chord after 76 bars; this is placed at the exact halfway point (18:18 bars) between the climactic centre and the end, again shown in the lower part of Fig. 3.3. This point has another proportional function. Effectively it is the piece's final tonic resolution, since the coda's deliberate plagal meanderings are merely decoration and confirmation of this, not a new tonal departure. It also marks the piece's fourth point of diatonic focus, the three previous ones having been bars 35 (tonic), 56 (supertonic) and 69 (dominant seventh). Taken together these four points form a Fibonacci sequence of 34:21:13:8 bars, linking all the sequences already shown in Figs. 3.2 and 3.3. This combination of sequences is shown as Fig. 3.4. The piece's large-scale diatonic sequence thus defined, I–I–II–V^7–I, can then account somewhat for the choice of E♭ as the diatonic key used to begin the climactic section.

Fig. 3.4

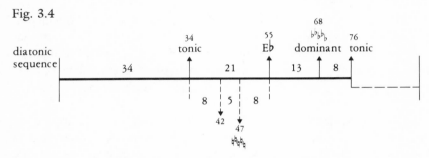

To the overall tonal plan in Fig. 3.4 we can now add the other important central harmonic transition, the change to completely whole-tone harmony after 47 bars. This completes a network of Fibonacci ratios of 5, 8, 13 and 21 bars within the 34 bars from bar 35 to bar 68 – that is, leading into and over the climactic section – so that the dynamic quality of this passage is emphasized by Fibonacci ratios in its internal bar-groupings.

The only exception to this grouping is the change to four sharps after 64 bars. This fits instead into the lower part of Fig. 3.3, forming a GS of 6:4 of the 10 bars between bars 59 and 68. (To avoid congestion this detail is omitted from Fig. 3.3.) It quite aptly does not form part of the Fibonacci sequence in the middle of Fig. 3.4: the dynamism of the climactic passage has by then subsided, and this point, placed as it is, provides instead a more apposite four-bar approach to the final change of key after bar 68.

A further confirmation of the piece's large-scale dynamic shape is supplied by the smaller dynamic peak in bars 30–1, bringing the piece's first section to its culmination. As this occurs over the tonal stability of a dominant pedal, it correspondingly forms a symmetrical division, its arrival after 29 bars defining the exact halfway point to the dynamic apex after 58 bars.

Finally the combined functions of Figs. 3.1–3.4 complete their convergence at the end of bar 94. At that point all the tensions generated by the structural counterpoint are resolved – in effect a structural cadence – and the piece, having fulfilled its structural plan, ends.

On a small scale, it has often been observed that the opening phrases of the piece follow a wave shape. To be more precise, the tops of these two-bar phrases give each a GS shape (5 quavers out of 8) anticipating in miniature the piece's dominating dynamic wave form of Fig. 3.1. These opening phrases also introduce motive A, which comprises a similar refracted sequence of 3:2 semitones, so that the geometric characteristics of the entire form are made quite plain to the listener, even if only intuitively, from the very beginning of the piece, using the Fibonacci numbers 2, 3, 5, and 8.

It has already been mentioned that not all the bars in the piece are the same length: bar 11 is in 3/8 instead of the predominating 4/8, and bar 23 is extended into a short cadenza. The missing quaver in bar 11, however, has a negligible effect (less than 0·25%) on the overall calculations; and, musically considered, the flourish in bar 23 is effectively an extension of the fourth quaver 'beat': at that point, as implied by the instruction 'quasi una cadenza' at bar 20, the larger bar-groupings provide a clearer articulation than the details of bars 20–3. (Debussy then carefully cancels the 'quasi una cadenza' with the precise instruction 'Mesuré' at bar 24.)

Might all those geometrical shapes reveal subtler shades of meaning in the piece's title? Not only are many of the sequences in Figs. 3.1–3.4 visibly reflected round some central musical turning point; but also their reflected portions (or images) tend to be compressed in size, giving an effect of refraction – another aspect of reflection (or deflection) in water. It is easy to pursue this parallel with the refractive compressions in Fig. 3.4, for example, as the music passes into different levels of harmonic density after bars 42, 47 and 55; or with the 3:2-semitone progression of the opening motive A. This last case is suggested by Debussy's own analogy: the pianist Marguerite Long, who studied 'Reflets dans l'eau' with Debussy, recalled that he likened this motive to a pebble dropping into water (Long, 1972, 25) – after which one's view of it would be refracted. Fanciful perhaps, but so is Debussy's music, and the beauty of those natural phenomena must have held a fascination for a composer who professed 'une religion de la mystérieuse nature' (Debussy, 1971, 302).

In this respect a precise literary parallel can be drawn, via Jules Laforgue. In his essay *L'impressionisme*, which Debussy must have known thoroughly, Laforgue defines 'the basic characteristic of the impressionist eye' as 'seeing reality in the living atmosphere of forms, decomposed, refracted, reflected by people and objects in endless variations'. Even regardless of proportional analysis, 'Reflets dans l'eau' is surely one of the most authentic translations of this philosophy into sound; and it could well have been Laforgue's reference there to 'seeing reality' that Debussy had in mind when he later described his orchestral *Images* as '*realities* – what imbeciles call "impressionism"' (Debussy, 1927, 58).

It may have been observed in this chapter's analysis that the lower part of Fig. 3.3 contains exactly the same shape, and follows the same type of logic, as Fig. 3.1, even though it concerns a different structural function. This proportional shape, obviously a particularly logical model structure, will be found again in *La mer*, in Chapter 7 below.

Mention of *La mer* leads to another specific connection between the title of 'Reflets' and its musical material. Since 'Reflets' was composed shortly after the completion of *La mer*, and also given the explicit aquatic connection between the two works, it is especially remarkable that they share not only the key of D♭ but also their thematic material: *B* here is also the cyclic motive of *La mer*, and *A* is the retrograde inversion (a reflection in two geometric senses) of the basic motive that forms the first and last climaxes of *La mer*'s first movement (bars 76 and 139). In the following chapters – with *La mer* in particular – more connections will be found between titles and and the formal processes defined by proportional systems. Again this is in the Symbolist tradition, as exemplified by Debussy's painter friend Odilon Redon, who was also a trained architect and a skilled musician: 'A title is justified only by its vague indeterminate nature, suggesting a double meaning' (quoted in Lockspeiser, 1973, 167).

PART 2

Earlier developments

Chapter 4

Early works – up to 1892

If the proportional intricacy of 'Reflets dans l'eau' is not just an isolated example but the result of accumulated expertise, the first question that arises is: how did it begin? As this must closely involve the more obvious aspects of Debussy's musical development, some discussion of this general musical development is apt.

Up to approximately 1894 (the year the *Prélude à l'après-midi d'un faune* was completed) Debussy's musical language underwent similar stylistic transformations in both vocal and instrumental genres, although the change effected itself much more slowly in the instrumental field than in the vocal one. Comparison between the opening melody of 'Chevaux de bois' of 1885 and the reappearance of virtually the same theme two years later in *Printemps*, as seen in Ex. 6, adequately demonstrates the disparity.

Principally this transformation – in part the Wagnerian legacy – introduced a broader, more fluid concept of tension and dynamics. His earliest pieces had generally static forms, defined by contrasts of thematic groups and of tonal centres, but with relatively uniform textures and harmonies inside them. In later works these are replaced by less conventional sequences whose outlines are still well marked, but marked rather by different types of harmony, different degrees of chromaticism and different types of texture, all of which also tend to change at independent rates. In the process, sustained or extended melody is progressively curtailed in favour of more compact and plastic motivic units.

The effect of it all, while blurring the conventional formal outlines, is to create, and define much more precisely, many levels of tension at various stages in the music. Bars 35–68 of 'Reflets dans l'eau', as seen in Chapter 3, illustrate this technique excellently. Connected with this is the introduction of undulating dynamic shapes that follow a course independent of the formal outlines, instead of merely labelling them, for example as they do in the *forte–piano–forte* ternary outline of the 'Prélude' of the *Suite bergamasque*, divided at bars 20 and 66. The outcome is dramatic: whereas in the earliest works any dramatic effect (there are few) is achieved by the momentary event – the sudden modulation, the *sforzando*

Ex. 6

(a) 'Chevaux de bois', bars 8–12

(b) *Printemps*, figure *31*

(for example, bar 18 of the song *Pantomime* of 1882, Ex. 7) – the mature works are dramatically conceived in the sense that moments of dramatic importance, even if their exact grammatical nature comes as a surprise, provide a fulfilment of anticipatory musical events and sequences – basic dramatic principles, in fact.

Ex. 7: *Pantomime*, bars 16–23

To borrow Schenkerian terms for this different context, the dramatic event has penetrated from a 'foreground' or surface position in the form to a more 'background' or fundamental one (while retaining, if necessary, its 'foreground' dramatic effect by means of its grammatical surprise value). A model example already seen is the modulation to E♭ in bar 56 of 'Reflets dans l'eau'.

Another way of putting all this is that clarity of dynamic and dramatic shape has taken precedence over conventional clarity of formal outline. The following chapters illustrate this with examples of pieces which have either similar forms but very different shapes, or similar shapes but very different forms. For this inherently dramatic concept of form and shape there is evident sense in ensuring that the focal events are well timed – again, just as in any dramatic plot.

Equally clearly this idea is less relevant to undramatic forms, such as the 'Passepied' from the *Suite bergamasque*. No large-scale dramatic tension accumulates there; accordingly there is little to resolve except the immediate logic of its modified rondo form. Whether this is done quickly or slowly is not crucial, so long as it avoids blatant large-scale imbalance.

This chapter covers the period of this transition in Debussy's style, with particular attention to two of the earliest works to show intricate proportions – the song 'Spleen' from the *Ariettes oubliées*, and the piano piece 'Clair de lune' from the *Suite bergamasque*. Limitations of space mean that the larger-scale scores of Debussy's early years cannot be studied in detail here. It would be unfortunate, though, to omit the *Prélude à l'après-midi d'un faune*, Debussy's first large-scale masterpiece, which moreover contains intricate proportional structure. It will be discussed instead, more briefly, in Chapter 10 (which correlates formal and proportional tendencies shared by different works), by which stage its structures can be demonstrated more compactly.

One exception to chronological order in this chapter is both inevitable and convenient. Most of the piano pieces published in 1889–92 cannot be dated exactly; it is even possible that one or two may have originated in the early 1880s. They are dealt with together after discussion of the songs up to the *Ariettes oubliées*, and this separation is musically apt, since they represent a much less advanced stage in Debussy's development than the songs of that time.

The works before 1885

In Debussy's earliest songs (up to 1885) there is virtually no sign of any proportional systems. Their forms vary widely, using ternary and strophic forms sometimes strictly, sometimes freely, and sometimes mixing elements of them with through-composed tendencies. They demonstrate that even then Debussy was no slave to procedure; in any case the poems provide an existing unified structure, allowing more freedom in the musical setting.[1] Their musical quality is variable; most of them are at least charming, and rarely does drama intrude. There would be little use for proportional systems: symmetry would make them too square, and GS might suggest an element of tension foreign to their stylistic nature. Of the small amount of instrumental music that survives from that time, a typical example – the *Danse bohémienne* of about 1880 – already shows a disparity between vocal and instrumental styles, with its eight-bar sequences plus a tonal plan and ternary form that firmly toe the textbook line. Again there is no sign of proportional systems.

Occasional occurrences can be found. The song *Beau soir* of probably 1882–3,[2] 41 bars long, begins and ends *pianissimo*, beginning its two-bar climax in bar 27 – just under a bar after its primary GS ($41 \times 0.618 = 25.34...$). But taking the dimensions of its arch form into account – 12:14:(2-bar climax):6:7 bars – adds no consistent proportional exactitude. it suggests intuition only,

---

1. François Lesure (1977) lists which of the early songs are published. The unpublished ones to which access has been possible are similar in formal style to the published ones of the time.

2. Margaret G. Cobb (1982, 61) points out that this song can date from no earlier than 1882, when its poem was first published.

since there is nothing to stop it from being more accurate, had it been consciously planned. GS occurrences in any other early songs are even more fragmentary, involving only one or two events in the piece concerned, and telling us nothing important about the forms (or the sensations). In only two cases – *Zéphyr* of 1881 and *Rondeau* of 1882 – do the circumstances draw attention: in both of them the GS is achieved by a change of metre, and the numbers involved catch the eye – 13 and 21 units of 2/4 (dividing the first stanza halfway and beginning the second) in *Zéphyr*, and 29 and 47 units of 3/8 (beginning the second and third stanzas) in *Rondeau*. Even so, for every one of these sporadic proportional correspondences just seen, there are numerous musical parallels in other early songs which show no such numerical relationships, and sound none the worse for it.

If the last two paragraphs therefore are hardly very positive, showing little proportional intrigue, and little musical significance in what proportions are visible, they nonetheless demonstrate a vital point by providing a control group, or backcloth, against which the results obtained, musically and proportionally, from specific other pieces (as already seen in 'Reflets') are going to stand in the sharpest contrast.

Ariettes oubliées: 'Spleen'

The *Ariettes oubliées*, composed between 1885 and 1888, represent arguably the largest evolutionary leap in Debussy's career, expressive chromaticism suddenly taking a dominating role in their forms, replete with tritonal and other chromatic relationships. 'Spleen' – the last of the set,[3] and tonally the most adventurous – opens with a splendid example of tritonal juxtaposition (Gb to C), and ends with a device unprecedented in Debussy's music – the withholding of the F minor tonic chord until the song's last bar, in the light of which the opening tritonal progression can be seen as neapolitan–dominant. (See the reproduction of the song on pages 201–2 below.) To describe the form, truthfully enough, as a tonally free rondo now does nothing to explain what is crucial to its expression, or how Debussy controls the tension between the neapolitan opening and the final, unique tonic chord. It is worth remembering, too, that whatever the form is, it has to be compatible with the logic and shape of Verlaine's poem. Such an essentially dramatic form suggests an apt context for proportional structure; and one can see immediately that its total of 34 bars (all in 3/4) are divided principally after 13, 17 and 21: that is, at its halfway and its two GS points, using Fibonacci numbers.

3. The only traceable autograph of this song, in the Bibliothèque François Lang, Royaumont, France, bears no date; both Trevitt (1973, 1001) and Lesure (1977, 60) estimate 1888 as the date of composition. The publication date of 1886 supplied by Lesure (1977, 60) for the six songs is an obvious misprint.

34

How is this influential in the form? Debussy controls the tonal tension by alternating the two principal returns to the neapolitan harmony, at bar 18 and bar 28 (the climax), with two contrasting modulations at bars 14 and 22. These modulations coincide with the more ruminative moments in the poem (lines 5 and 9), and act as a foil to the starkness of the G♭ harmony, the latter accompanying the poem's two peaks of despair, lines 7 and 12. In the first of those modulations (bar 14) the G♭ is turned into F♯, introducing a more warmly chromatic sequence of unresolved dominant ninths alternating between F♯ and A. In the second case (bar 22) a more diatonic alternation of B♭ and D major leads towards a strong anticipation of E♭ major in bars 25–6, before bars 27–8 wrench the music back into G♭ and despair. The strong qualitative contrast in these modulations is underlined by the way the transitions into bars 14 and 22 are effected with rising semitones in the harmony – from G to G♯ and D♭ to D respectively – whereas at bar 18 the return to gloominess is marked by descending semitones in the accompaniment.

Fig. 4.1: 'Spleen'

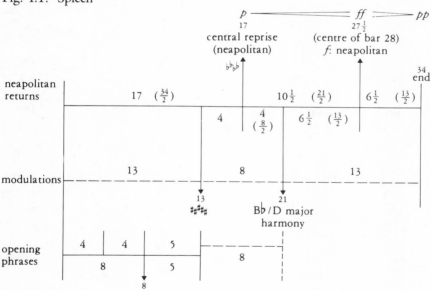

Fig. 4.1 shows how these powerful tonal oscillations are distributed. The two modulations away from the neapolitan–dominant harmony, after 13 and 21 bars, mark the song's two points of GS. The climax, introducing the final neapolitan return, lasts for all of bar 28. Taking the centre of this bar as the point of measurement, the earlier return to neapolitan harmony after 17 bars marks both the exact halfway point of the song and the primary GS on the way to the centre of the climax, forming a ratio of 17:10½ bars (=34:21). The centre of the climax forms another GS of 10½:6½ bars (=21:13) to the end of the song,

thereby completing a sequence of $17:10\frac{1}{2}:6\frac{1}{2}$ bars ($=34:21:13$) between beginning and end.

When this latter sequence is taken together with the earlier 13:8:13-bar sequence, their interaction produces further GS and symmetrical divisions, leading again to and over the climax, shown also in Fig. 4.1. On a smaller scale, the reprise of the opening motive in bar 9 divides the first 13 bars in GS of 8 + 5, simultaneously allowing the entire structure to grow spontaneously out of an opening 4+4-bar sequence, as shown lower in Fig. 4.1.

There could hardly be a greater contrast to what has gone before in this chapter. All the important structural events are involved here, and the resulting scheme is virtually an architectural model, the only compromise in its realization being that at the climax Debussy gives priority to the 3/4 metre and places the top note of the climax at the beginning, not the middle, of the bar. This does no serious damage to Fig. 4.1, since not only is the arithmetical amount involved small, but also the climax lasts audibly for all of bar 28 before subsiding in the next bar.

What is paramount here is that, as in 'Reflets', all these structural events are proportionally directed towards two objectives – emphasis of the climax on one hand, and mutual resolution at the end of the piece on the other. The system is less complex than that of 'Reflets' – not surprisingly in view of its date and its shorter length – but the logic it follows is of the same type, and the more remarkable here for being completely based on Fibonacci numbers.

The remaining five *Ariettes* take no tonal risks of the order just seen. Correspondingly they do not need, and do not have, any such comprehensively applied proportional schemes. But the two most tense – 'Il pleure dans mon coeur' and 'L'ombre des arbres' – both have their emotional climaxes situated at their primary GS points. In the former this is the passage marked 'plus lent' (bars 46–51), at the words 'Quoi! nulle trahison? / Ce deuil est sans raison', with the GS point after 49 bars, at the centre of these six bars. In itself this does not determine all the other formal details in the song; but it does cast light on the curious asymmetry of its ternary form, with its terse central section consisting only of these six bars. (The outer sections are then related by GS – 46:28 bars.) In 'L'ombre des arbres' the climactic placing after 20 bars is less accurate (GS of 31, the total, is 19·2); but, while still remaining within a bar of the theoretical point, this gives the song a nearly symmetrical formal sequence of 10:10:11 bars and allows the climax to be approached by a GS progression of 10:6:4 bars ($=5:3:2$), the second of these divisions being formed by the beginning of the crescendo. The *Ariettes* date from 1885–8, just the time when Charles Henry's theories on number and proportion in art were appearing in Parisian Symbolist journals. This is discussed more in Chapter 11 below.

Some later examples

As already noted, Debussy's musical evolution was not so linear that all his songs from this time on could be expected to conform to similar proportional systems; they do not. We should bear in mind, too, that if the scheme of 'Spleen' was applied deliberately, it may well have been one of various types of musical experiment; in 1888 he could not know what his music would be like ten or twenty years later. But proportional schemes thoroughly involved with the other aspects of structure now begin to appear more frequently.

One example is the 1891 setting of Verlaine's much less dramatic 'Clair de lune', with the principal divisions of its 32 bars, at the beginnings of the second and third stanzas, placed at the two points of GS to the nearest bar, after 12 and 20 (GS of 32 is 19·8). The much simpler ratio resulting here, 3:2:3, allows the song (aptly for the context) to unfold mostly within a four-bar framework. There is no dynamic surge comparable with that in 'Spleen'; the principal dynamic peak here (*mezzo-forte*) is placed at the halfway point, after 16 bars, and the preceding one is related by GS, coming after 10. The system here is less striking than in 'Spleen', and more notable for its overall symmetrical shape – in marked contrast to Debussy's earlier (1882) setting of 'Clair de lune', which was divided into a proportionally insignificant sequence of 10:20:23:31 by the beginnings of the three stanzas.[4]

A slightly peculiar, more asymmetrical example is 'L'âme évaporée' (Bourget), composed probably late in 1886.[5] Its ternary form divides the poem into 6:4:2 lines, and the music into 13:8:6½ bars, counting the bar of 2/4 (bar 25) at the climax as half a 4/4 bar. That is, the first and central sections are related by GS, and the recapitulation is exactly half the length of the first section, its bar of 2/4 also being placed at its own centre, with three bars on either side. This is shown in Fig. 4.2. The scheme's dramatic unsubtlety is evident: the climax in

Fig. 4.2: 'L'âme évaporée'

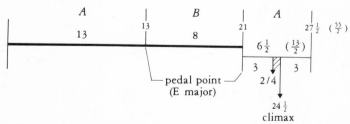

bars 25–6 has no proportional preparation, and the fact that the recapitulation is exactly half the length of the opening section means little in dramatic terms. It corroborates the song's early composition date, but – more important here – also

4. A comparative survey of the two versions (but not of their proportions) is provided by Roger Nichols (1967).

5. Margaret G. Cobb (1982, 85) has established this as the most likely date of its composition.

suggests contrivance, since it could not have been intuitable purely by a GS instinct.

It seems at first surprising that the *Cinq poèmes de Baudelaire* of 1887–9 make no significant use of GS–symmetrical systems (only a small amount in 'Recueillement' and 'La mort des amants'); in the *Proses lyriques* of 1892–3 there is also virtually none. But for all their Wagnerian chromatic turns the Baudelaire settings stay mostly on firm tonal ground; neither they nor the *Proses lyriques* take structural risks comparable with 'Spleen'. On the other hand GS plays a more important part in the three Verlaine settings of December 1891 ('La mer est plus belle', 'Le son du cor' and 'L'échelonnement des haies') – the second of which repeats the procedure seen in 'Spleen' of withholding the tonic chord until the final bar, although in a less dramatic context.

The examples of insignificant or absent GS are again important, as they make the logic and comprehensiveness of the system in 'Spleen' stand out in sharp relief.

Piano music

To judge Debussy's musical development in 1889–92 solely by the piano music published in those years would be unjust. Some of it, sold to the publisher Choudens at a time of financial strain, may date from much earlier, and some of the rest was produced hurriedly, as we know from Debussy's very sharp letter to the publisher Fromont, expressing disgust at Fromont's republication of the *Rêverie* in 1904 (Lesure, 1977, 69).

As in the earliest songs, proportional correspondences in the earliest piano pieces are sporadic and incomplete enough to be insignificant. As if to emphasize this, three of the most successful of them – the two *Arabesques*, and *Danse* (originally entitled *Tarentelle styrienne*),[6] all published in 1891 – are devoid either of any dramatic element (particularly, they lack any centres of dramatic focus) or of any sign of consistent proportional structure in their forms. To document this, their proportions are shown in Fig. 4.3; nothing significant is visible apart from one or two fragmentary correspondences that could easily be fortuitous. Again examples like 'Reflets' and 'Spleen' could hardly stand in sharper contrast.

The *Petite suite* (published in 1889, though some of its material dates from as early as 1882)[7] also has no proportional systems, except for 'Cortège' whose ternary form is symmetrically divided into 3 × 21 bars. But this movement

6. Ravel's fondness for *Danse* led to his orchestrating it in 1923, and Debussy had sufficient faith in it to recycle its thematic material in 1891, in the Verlaine setting 'L'échelonnement des haies'.

7. The 'Menuet' is an extended reworking of the unpublished song *Fête galante* (Banville) of 1882, a dated autograph of which is in the Bibliothèque François Lang, Royaumont, France.

Fig. 4.3

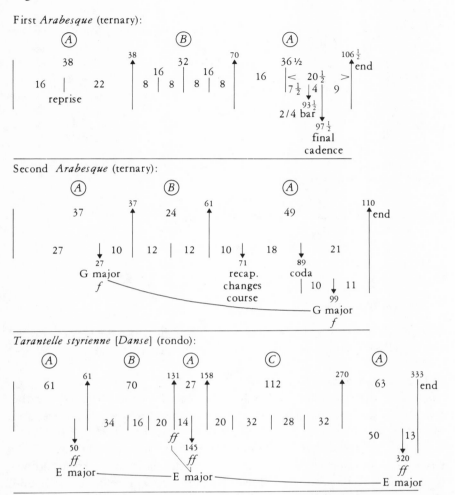

First *Arabesque* (ternary):

Second *Arabesque* (ternary):

Tarantelle styrienne [*Danse*] (rondo):

sounds no more or less coherent or dramatic than its companion movements, none of them dramatic. The number is perhaps notable, but it has no GS significance here and could easily be fortuitous.

The *Rêverie*, *Ballade* and *Nocturne*, published in 1891–2, represent progress in one respect, in having more undulating dynamic sequences. In the *Rêverie* these are of less interest, as the dynamic peaks coincide with phrase divisions (seven consecutive 8-bar phrases in the opening section); but in the rather better *Ballade* and *Nocturne* the opening sections follow a dynamic course independent of the phrase divisions. These dynamic sequences show GS and symmetrical tendencies, simple enough to be self-explanatory as shown in Fig. 4.4 – the end of the five-bar introduction in both pieces also being visibly important. But the proportions do not continue beyond the pieces' opening sections. In any case their

Fig. 4.4: Opening sections of *Ballade* and *Nocturne*

Ballade:

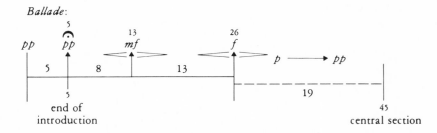

end of
introduction

central section

Nocturne:

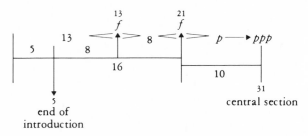

end of
introduction

central section

forms are clearly articulated in conventional terms; therefore the lack of consistent proportional schemes would not involve any structural risks.

Suite bergamasque; 'Clair de lune'

The *Suite bergamasque* (published only in 1905, though dated 1890 by the composer[8]) presents some curious contrasts. The 'Prélude', 'Menuet' and 'Passepied' mostly match the style of the *Petite suite* and *Arabesques*, if with somewhat greater strength (the 'Menuet' flexes some unexpected muscle in its last two pages). But their forms are not inherently dramatic, and correspondingly are not dominated by proportional systems. An exception concerns the first 34 bars of the 'Menuet', sufficiently simple for Fig. 4.5 to be self-explanatory, given

Fig. 4.5: Opening section of 'Menuet' (*Suite bergamasque*)

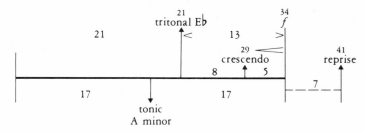

8. The date appears in Debussy's writing beside the title in the corrected proofs (Music department of the Bibliothèque Nationale, Paris: Rés. Vma. 286).

that the movement's tonic chord of A minor is not heard until after 17 bars. But the scheme ignores the reprise in bar 12 and does not continue past bar 34: the sudden jump to E at bar 38 disrupts the proportions just as it disrupts the harmonic line. The 'Passepied' also has some thematic entries at multiples of 29 bars; but this eventually leads nowhere, and connects with no other formal functions.

As suggested by its poetic title, contrasting with the dance-forms of the other three movements, 'Clair de lune' is very different (see the reproduction of the piece on pages 203–8 below). If it really was written at the same time as the other movements, it shows Debussy being more adventurous than ever before in his piano music. The contrast is amply illustrated by comparing its ternary form (with an added coda, derived from the central section) with that of the 'Prélude'. In the 'Prélude' the thematic ternary form is emphasized by simultaneous changes of texture, key and dynamics; in 'Clair de lune', however, these mask the ternary transitions (the central section begins in the tonic), drawing the listener's attention more to the piece's two-part dynamic wave shape – a feature the piece shares with 'Reflets dans l'eau'. Its flowing dynamic outlines are further emphasized by Debussy's subtle handling of transitions and harmonic tension (for example bars 37–42) – a marked contrast to the other three movements – so that within a smaller range of dynamics the piece achieves better dramatic definition than the *fortissimi* of the *Ballade* and *Nocturne*, with their more conventional outlines, could do.

Its main proportions are shown in Fig. 4.6. The principal two pillars of the ternary form, at bars 27 and 51, divide it into a tripartite, progressively dimi-

Fig. 4.6: 'Clair de lune' (*Suite bergamasque*)

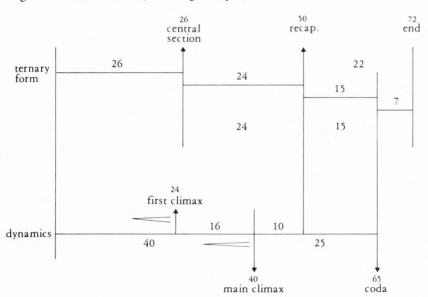

41

nishing sequence of 26:24:22 bars, these last 22 being subdivided 15:7 by the coda at bar 66. The first dynamic peak, after 24 bars, is within a bar of GS on the way to the principal climax, after 40 bars ($40 \times 0.618 = 24.72...$). (If this small inaccuracy has any effect, it would only be to heighten the tension in bar 40, making the listener wait a bar or so beyond the theoretical point.) The principal climax then forms two primary GS divisions: one of 40:25 between the piece's beginning and the onset of the coda, and one of 16:10 between the first climax and the recapitulation after 50 bars. The arrivals of both the recapitulation and the coda are therefore proportionally prepared by the dynamic sequence. In addition the recapitulation lies at the GS point (24:15 bars) between the beginning of the central section and the thematically related beginning of the coda, thus relating these three structural divisions proportionally.

By comparison with the rest of the *Suite bergamasque*, the tonal structure of 'Clair de lune' shows an enormous advance in subtlety. Although the opening section moves away from tonic-based harmony (bar 15 onwards), it avoids modulating, so that the entire piece contains only one modulation away from the tonic key, placed strategically, in bar 37, to lead into the main climax some bars later. How easily Debussy now moves within even such a small self-imposed tonal framework is indicated by the skill with which he grades the piece's subsequent points of progressive tonal resolution. Bar 43 takes the first step, restoring the home tonality over a dominant pedal. Eschewing the expected perfect cadence, the music first moves to a recapitulation on a mediant chord (bar 51) and then qualifies the eventual cadence to the tonic at bar 59 with the added seventh, before allowing the coda at bar 66 to complete the tonal resolution.

How all these points are distributed is shown in Fig. 4.7.

Fig. 4.7: 'Clair de lune' (*Suite bergamasque*)

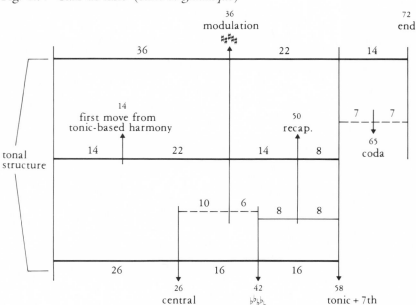

The focal point of development is clearly the modulation after 36 bars. This lies both at the piece's exact halfway point and at the GS point on the way to the eventual return to the tonic chord, after 58 bars, forming a GS sequence of 36:22:14 (=18:11:7) from beginning to end of the piece. Intermediate points of GS articulation within this are then provided by the first sustained move away from tonic-based harmony after bar 14, and by the recapitulation after 50, filling in a GS sequence of 14:22:14:8 (=7:11:7:4) up to the return of the tonic chord in bar 59. (This is the same proportional shape remarked upon twice in 'Reflets dans l'eau' on page 29 above.) Simultaneously these same 58 bars are divided 26:16:16 (=13:8:8) by the beginning of the central section after 26 bars and the return to the opening tonality at bar 43. Therefore the eventual return to the tonic chord in bar 59 marks the convergence of those two separate sequences. As both of them involve tonality they must interact: the modulation at bar 37 provides GS of 10:6 within the other sequence, and likewise the recapitulation at bar 51 forms a symmetrical division of 8:8. Finally the beginning of the coda, completing the tonic resolution, divides the piece's last 14 bars 7:7.

The scheme's numerical exactitude is certainly remarkable, and it involves all the important events; yet it is not as lucid an entity, architecturally, as the proportional shapes of 'Spleen' and 'Reflets'. For example, the dynamic shape, although it proportionally prepares later structural events, is not itself proportionally prepared by earlier ones, and is unrelated proportionally to the tonal sequences.

To this there are three logical answers. First, relative to 'Spleen', 'Clair de lune' is longer and deals with a greater complexity of musical material. Second, relative to 'Reflets', 'Clair de lune' was written by a composer with probably fifteen years' less experience. Third, again relative to 'Reflets', the less far-reaching structural role of dynamics in 'Clair de lune' also reflects its more restrained dynamics: to have made this more modest dynamic surge as formally crucial here as the much more powerful one is in 'Reflets' would have put the entire structure at risk.

But there are striking parallels between 'Clair de lune' and 'Reflets', apart from their being in the same key – the larger dynamic wave preceded by the smaller one, the main tonal departure preceded by the proportionally related smaller harmonic one, the symmetrically placed tonal return over a dominant pedal and its subsequent deflection from the expected perfect cadence. Their similarities of shape and sequence are shown in Fig. 4.8; but it also shows how much more space the main climax is given in 'Reflets'.

It is logical that, of the two structures, the one of fifteen years later should be more sophisticated yet simpler in concept. All this applies whether conscious or not on Debussy's part, being based on the tangible evidence of the musical scores.

If it was conscious, the affinities of mood and shape, and the identity of key, between 'Clair de lune' and 'Reflets' invite a further speculation. The *Suite*

Fig. 4.8

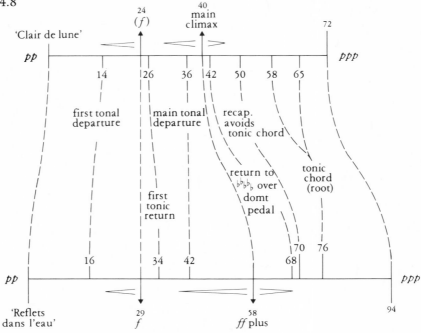

bergamasque was eventually published in 1905, and we know from Debussy's correspondence (Lesure, 1977, 74), and the proofs he corrected, that he revised it thoroughly just before this.[9] The dance movements, in an idiom he had long discarded, he could probably treat with objectivity; but might the imperfections he saw in the more forward-looking 'Clair de lune' have impelled him within the year to produce a more satisfactory solution of the same structural problems of shape and mood, this solution being 'Reflets' in its final form? Whatever the answer, it is notable that while Debussy made cuts at proof stage in the *Suite bergamasque*'s 'Prélude' and 'Menuet', neither of which contains consistent proportional systems, he left the proportions of 'Clair de lune' intact.[10]

The shape of 'Clair de lune' is also reflected by its positioning in the *Suite bergamasque*: as the third of the four pieces it lies over the GS of the entire suite, in general terms. This would hardly merit special mention were it not for this piece's stylistic contrast (yet not an incongruous one) to its three companions, making it prominently the lyrical climax of the suite. In this respect, too, its

9. The proofs must date from no earlier than 1904, since they have the title 'Clair de lune' printed; earlier in 1904 a rather premature *sous presse* advertisement from Fromont had still quoted the piece's original title, 'Promenade sentimentale' (again after Verlaine).

10. In the 'Prélude' two bars are scored out in the proofs after bar 31, and another two after the published bar 33. In the 'Menuet' seven bars are similarly deleted after bar 72, and a further 18 bars are cut after the published bar 96. The 'Passepied', incidentally, is still headed 'Pavane', as in the 1904 Fromont *sous presse* advertisement already mentioned.

44

structural surge is gently anticipated by the partial proportional system, with its small dynamic surge, at the beginning of the 'Menuet', already seen in Fig. 4.5. If Debussy was experimenting between GS and non-GS forms – a feasible hypothesis in view of the evidence of the rest of this chapter – he turned this structural duality to very precise advantage in the large-scale design of the *Suite bergamasque*.

The three piano *Images* of 1894, which there is not room to analyse here, show proportional coherence to approximately the same degree of thoroughness and logic as 'Clair de lune'. (These early *Images* are now published by Theodore Presser Co., 1978, as *Images (oubliées)*; the second of the three pieces is an early version of the 'Sarabande' from *Pour le piano*, with harmonic variants but identical proportions.)

'*Tout* est nombre. Le nombre est dans *tout*. Le nombre est dans l'individu. L'ivresse est un nombre.'   – Baudelaire

Chapter 5

L'isle joyeuse

Some pattern is now emerging in the way Debussy's use of proportion developed. At first relatively simple, as in 'Spleen', proportions become more complex in a larger piece like 'Clair de lune'. But by 1905, in 'Reflets dans l'eau', a more complex piece again, Debussy has managed to resimplify, as we saw in Chapter 3, fitting more processes into a more lucid architectural pattern than 'Clair de lune' has. Evidently Debussy's more obvious musical techniques developed enormously in the intervening years, culminating in *La mer*, completed shortly before 'Reflets'. Did he develop his proportional techniques concurrently?

To go through all the intervening works is not possible here, though some of them are investigated more briefly in Chapter 10 below. But *L'isle joyeuse* provides such notable answers to the question that it justifies a chapter to itself. Completed in the summer of 1904 while *La mer* was in preparation, it has symphonic breadth and unusually weighty textures (Ravel more bluntly called it 'an orchestral reduction for the piano') that reflect Debussy's preoccupation then with extended symphonic structure, and suggest that he may have been using it to rehearse structural techniques for *La mer*. It therefore fits aptly here, with the possibility that it might aid understanding of *La mer*'s symphonic intricacies.

Another immediate characteristic of *L'isle joyeuse* is its exuberant dynamic shape: beginning *pianissimo* on two notes a tone apart, and in an undefined rhythm and tonality, it finishes in A major splendour, triple-*forte*, the last two bars spanning virtually the entire keyboard and completing a coda of rhythmic vigour unsurpassed in Debussy's output. (See the reproduction of the entire piece on pages 209–21.) this overall wedge-shape could hardly be more pronounced: even the opening bar gives it in miniature (just as the opening phrases of 'Reflets dans l'eau' anticipated the overall arch shape of 'Reflets'). Evidently, though, the shape of *L'isle joyeuse* raises very different problems of dynamic and dramatic gradation from the dynamic arch shapes of 'Reflets dans l'eau' and 'Clair de lune'. The main difference in dramatic structure is that here climax and resolution are placed together in the coda, whereas in 'Reflets' they are in geometric opposition in the form, a fact obvious even without undertaking proportional analysis. In *L'isle joyeuse*, too, the open-ended dynamic shape is accompanied by an unusual complexity of structure that makes it very hard to define in any orthodox formal terms.

46

One reason for this is the piece's abundance of thematic and tonal returns. On a large scale there is a strong ternary tendency, with a long central section beginning in bar 67, whose second melodic strain (bar 75) returns in force to begin the coda at bar 220. In this respect the plan is similar to the ternary-plus-coda outline just seen in 'Clair de lune', where the coda was also derived from the central section. But in *L'isle joyeuse* the ternary model is complicated in various ways. An additional episode (bars 28–51) inside the first main part of the overall ternary scheme creates in effect a smaller ternary system within the larger one, with both of the central episodes marked by the two transitions to 3/8 metre at bars 28 and 67. There are also further returns of the piece's two opening motives – *A* and *B*, shown in Ex. 8 – in places where they appear to contradict the ternary logic: *B* appears in the central part of the main theoretical ternary form (bars 105 and 145), and *A* returns in the final bars of the coda (bar 244 onwards).

Ex. 8

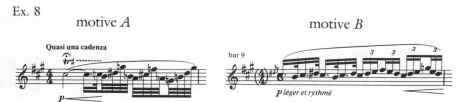

motive *A*   motive *B*

In view of all this why not call the piece a rondo? This is still inadequate: not only is it a most irregular rondo, with various themes recurring in a quite unpredictable order, but also those smaller-scale elements do not destroy the larger-scale ternary feeling, especially since the tonal recapitulation at bar 160, much more emphatic than any of the other rondo returns, strongly underlines the ternary aspect. For the moment it seems wiser to follow what the music suggests and think in terms of an amalgam of rondo and ternary elements. This is reasonable: in such a large piece both small-scale accumulation and large-scale formal stability are necessary: rondo elements logically supply the former and ternary elements the latter. In addition, the ternary-within-ternary sequence has another significance: if the element of departure and return inherent in ternary form is understood as a type of wave, this gives us here a smaller structural wave preceding a larger one, leading into the final culmination of the coda. A parallel might immediately be traced in this respect with 'Reflets dans l'eau' (and 'Clair de lune'); in *L'isle joyeuse*, however, this is a much more formal wave sequence, operating quite separately from the more immediately obvious sequence of dynamic waves which also lead cumulatively to the coda. Already, then, the structural counterpoint is well under way, with separate strands of rondo elements, ternary elements and dynamic waves.

The reference immediately above to the tonal recapitulation in bar 160 touches on another ambiguity. Tonally bar 160 is the main recapitulation, but thematically it has already been anticipated by motive *B* taking over completely from bar 145, in a sequence that overlaps the tonal return at bar 160. This is not the only place where the tonal movement is delayed or staggered: both the main central section and the earlier episode (bar 67 and bar 28) begin in the tonic key, modulating away only later. Indeed, the first part of *L'isle joyeuse* is remarkable for its unexpected absence of modulation, there being none at all in the first 35 bars. Correspondingly we are not told what the piece's tonic key is until bar 7. In sum, the piece's tonal movement is constantly made to lag behind the other formal aspects, thus shifting weight and tension towards the dramatic end of the piece, where this phase-lag is finally resolved with the arrival of the coda in bar 220.

Even to talk of a recapitulation is risky, convenient label though it may be. The piece's central section gradually becomes something of a development section from bar 105 onwards; but bars 145 onwards, all the way to the coda, also constitute as much a development as they do a recapitulation of the passage first heard in bars 20–7. Again this concentrates weight towards the coda by preventing too firm a sense of arrival at any stage before.

The recapitulation section, with its developments, focuses our attention on the oppositions of different modes that play a part both colourful and dramatic in the piece, an aspect already discussed in studies by Arnold Whittall (1975) and Jim Samson (1977, 38–9). The piece's main theme, motive *B*, is based mostly on a mode Debussy used on various occasions (as Ravel and Bartók did later), an amalgam of lydian and mixolydian modes characterized by a sharpened fourth and flattened seventh. Françoise Gervais (1971, vol. 1, 41) identifies it as the sixty-fourth of the Hindu 'karnatic' modes, the *Vachaspati*, and Chapter 11 below traces some sources where Debussy would probably have learned of these modes quite early in his career. This particular mode's peculiar physical quality is that it is the scale most closely corresponding, in terms of equal temperament, to the harmonic series, as shown in Ex. 9. (This is why it is sometimes called the 'acoustic scale', a useful label for it which is adhered to in the following pages.)

Ex. 9

Both Whittall and Samson observe that much of the tension in *L'isle joyeuse* is generated by the contrast between tonal stability and instability, the latter represented particularly by the whole-tone scale. A vital reason for Debussy's use here of the *Vachaspati* acoustic scale must be that, while in itself tonally defined, it needs only one substitution – an augmented fifth above the root in place of its fifth and sixth degrees, as shown in Ex. 10 – to become a whole-tone scale, and thus for the tonality to be immediately threatened. Bars 20–1, also shown in Ex. 10, illustrate this precisely, and are no doubt present in the music for that purpose, judging by the emphasis the new melody (motive *C*) gives to the pivotal f'.[1]

Ex. 10

[motive *C*]

Evidently in such a context the acoustic scale is a powerful dramatic weapon, holding the tonality constantly at the edge of a precipice, and this is indubitably one of the main reasons for the powerful sense of resolution at the beginning of the coda, when the arrival of the normal major mode finally pulls us clear of this tonal threat. The transition from the acoustic scale to the whole-tone scale shown in Ex. 10 is in fact the first glimpse Debussy gives us of this precipice. Although he then rescues the threatened tonality in bar 25, the point has been made, and the device is then exploited increasingly until the tonal resolution of the coda.

If we add to the above list of structural adventures the piece's duality between 4/4 and 3/8 metres, and the strangely asymmetrical distribution of the two types through the piece, it is evident what a structural tightrope Debussy is walking by throwing them all together, viewed from any orthodox formal standpoint. Exciting the piece is likely to be, but will it hold together as an entity? (And in its holding together of all these elements lies a major part of the musical excitement.) More precisely, how can all those strands of structural adventure be woven together without a complexity of construction too dense to be comprehensible or practically applicable? A basically simple system of logic provides an answer, and is shown in the following proportional analysis.

1. Confusion has often arisen because Debussy's habitual carelessness in correcting proofs resulted in the first edition of *L'isle joyeuse* lacking the necessary natural to g″ in bars 9, 15 and 16, a mistake arising from his having also omitted them in the autograph used by the engraver (Music department of the Bibliothèque Nationale, Paris: Ms. 977). They are present in that manuscript and in all editions at the parallel passages from bar 64 onwards, and were added to the earlier passages in subsequent Durand reprintings. Marguerite Long, who studied the work thoroughly with Debussy, confirms the authenticity of g♮″ in bars 9, 15 and 16 – but g♯′ in bar 10, thus making the only two full statements of motive *B* (bars 9–10, 160–5) a mixture of acoustic and lydian modes (Long, 1972, 38).

Proportions

How to measure the piece's proportions has already been discussed in detail on pages 17–18, where it was shown that any quaver grouping can be adopted here as a unit of measurement, provided it is adhered to throughout the piece. Units of 3/8 are used here for two reasons. The first is one of convenience: the resulting figures are more manageable than those produced by a quaver count. Moreover, since most of *L'isle joyeuse* is in 3/8, one unit of 3/8 also conveniently equals one of the predominating bars, although of course bar numbers will not be the same as unit totals. The second reason is connected with the first: one bar of 4/4 equals $\frac{8}{3}$ units of 3/8 (or 3 bars of 4/4 equal 8 units), and in *L'isle joyeuse* both of the 4/4 sections (bars 1–27 and 64–6) comprise multiples of three bars, or eight units, so that counting the work's dimensions in 3/8 units produces whole-number totals at all the metrical transitions, as well as at all the other major transitions. Apart from suggesting that the scheme may have been deliberately designed on this basis, this numerical coincidence will also be seen to have important connections with the preponderance in this piece of four-, eight- and sixteen-bar phrases in the 3/8 sections.

The reproduction of the piece on pages 209–21 is annotated throughout with unit references (the numbers are circled), referring always to units completed. In view of the ambiguity in defining the form, to avoid confusion the two central episodes in the ternary-within-ternary scheme are referred to from now on as the *first episode* (bars 28–51) and the *central section* (bars 67–159).

Clearly the transitions to these are two key points of symphonic growth in the large-scale form, and this feeling of growth is directly suggested by the subtle effect of propulsion produced by the 3/8 metre springing out from the preceding 4/4 at these two transitions. The piece ends after 305 units, GS of which is 188·5:116·5. The beginning of the central section at bar 67, after 116 units, thus marks the piece's secondary GS point to within a dotted quaver. In turn 116 × 0·618 = 72, which marks precisely the beginning of the first episode in bar 28, these two divisions giving the large-scale form the overall expanding GS pattern shown in Fig. 5.1.

Fig. 5.1

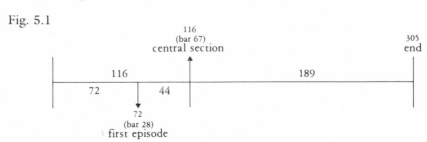

Even the half-bar inaccuracy just noted can be accounted for if one calculates instead up to the last actual note of the piece, a staccato quaver. This gives a total of 304 units, secondary GS of which is 116·1, so that the central section begins, now accurate to within a semiquaver, at the secondary GS on the way to the final note of the piece. This sequence of numbers, 72, 116, 304, when divided by 4, gives 18, 29, 76 – from the Lucas summation series 3, 4, 7, 11, 18, 29, 47, 76... – and the manifestation of the series here in multiples of four is again significant to the preponderance of four-bar phrases in the piece, discussed more below.

Within this large-scale GS framework the piece's dynamic shape follows a course logically related to the ternary-within-ternary scheme. A first peak in bars 25–7, *mezzo-forte* (peak I), leads into the first episode, and the first episode in turn completes itself with a *forte* climax (peak II) in bar 52, marking the first return of motive *A*, leading into the central section. The central section then builds up, this time more slowly, to a powerful symmetrical *forte* climax in C major (peak III) in bars 141–4, after which a steady stream of dynamic waves leads, via the recapitulation, to the sustained final *fortissimo* of the coda.

In contrast to the large-scale GS outline in Fig. 5.1, the smaller-scale articulation, incorporating these various peaks, follows at first a surprisingly symmetrical course. It has already been noted that each of the 4/4 sections of the work makes up a multiple of three bars (or eight units). More significant, their principal points of internal articulation also mostly follow this grouping. Thus the first emphatic event – the end of the introduction, where the tonality is first established, and the rhythm first clearly articulated (bar 7) – arrives after 16 units. The next emphatic event, peak I, arrives after 64 units (bar 25), and the first episode arrives eight units (three 4/4 bars) later, after 72 units. The piece's first modulation then occurs eight units after that (80 units), and peak II arrives after 96. Of these five events four occur at multiples of 16 units (or six 4/4 bars), and the remaining one – the beginning of the first episode, whose position is determined by the large-scale plan of Fig. 5.1 – manages to fit symmetrically within this in terms of 8-unit groups. This sequence, almost completely based on multiples of 16 units, is plotted in Fig. 5.2. One much less emphatic event – the reprise of motive *B* in bar 15 – departs from this sequence; it forms instead a GS division of 8:13 bars of 4/4 (or 21⅓:34⅔ units), also shown in Fig. 5.2. The other exception to this sequence, the modal transition at bars 20–1 quoted on page 49 (Ex. 10), has an entirely different significance, and will be returned to later.

Fig. 5.2

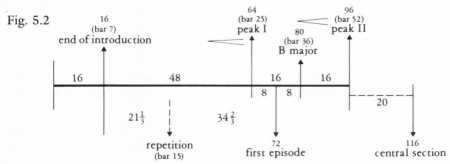

The predominant sequence of multiples of 16 or 8 is interrupted by the arrival of the central section 20 units after the beginning of peak II. Having broken the first sequence, the central section now begins a similar one. At first this follows an even more symmetrical course of 4 × 4-bar phrases. Motive D (bar 67), having opened the central section, is repeated an octave higher (and slightly varied) 16 units later; a further 16 units lead to the modulation to E major in bar 99, and another 16 to the cancellation of the key signature in bar 115 (164 units).

Events now take a different course, both musically and proportionally. Since the end of the introduction, when the tonic key was established, all the tonal movement has been firmly diatonic – and mostly over a tonic pedal (which anchors down the whole-tone harmony over it in bars 23–4). The only tonal excursions have been to the diatonically related keys of B major (bar 36), E major (bar 99) and C♯ major (bar 52), the last one the most adventurous, although even there the hegemony of A major was really not jeopardized, as the following bars show. This element of sustained diatonic movement, unusual for Debussy, is matched by the other stable element of four-bar phrases having dominated the 3/8 sections exclusively up to bar 99. Both these elements now change. The 16 bars after the modulation to E (bars 99–114) are subdivided 6+4+6 rather than 4 × 4; and, more audibly dramatic, at their completion diatonic movement is abandoned: the bass jumps the tritone from C♯ to G at bar 115, and the key signature is cancelled. The new departure is underlined by the way this harmonic leap of a tritone cuts into what had begun as a repetition of the diatonic C♯-to-G♯ sequence ten bars earlier. Correspondingly, instead of subtending a symmetrical 16:16-bar division, this point of tonal departure subtends a GS one of 16:26 bars, leading to peak III at bar 141 (190 units), thus completing a sequence of 16:16:16:26 units (=bars) from the beginning of the central section, as shown in Fig. 5.3.

Fig. 5.3

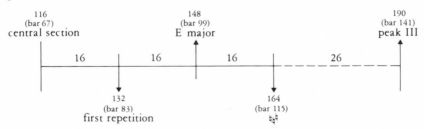

Peak III is the most powerful climax so far, the more so for its unexpected key of C, and its positioning marks the convergence of the sequence in Fig. 5.3 with other proportional correspondences, one dynamic, one tonal and one motivic. Fig. 5.4 shows this. As already mentioned, peak III is symmetrical, its centre placed after 192 units. The exact halfway point to this from the beginning of the

Fig. 5.4

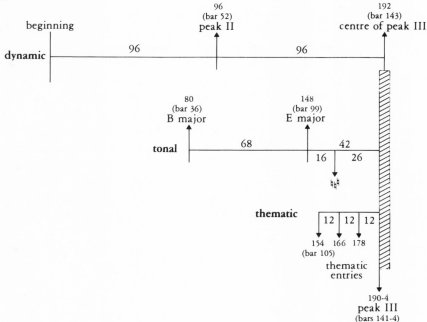

piece is after 96 units – the beginning of peak II, with the first return of motive *A*. Tonally, the two points of modulation from the tonic key, in bars 36 and 99 (B major and E major), form a sequence of 68:42 units (=34:21), leading to the beginning of peak III (the modulation to C); this is reinforced by the smaller GS division of 16:26 inside the sequence, at the intermediate tritonal modulation. Motivically, the three distinct entries in bars 105, 117 and 129 form a symmetrical sequence of 12:12:12 units (bars), leading again to peak III.

Peak III therefore is visibly a strong focus proportionally, as well as in the more ordinary musical sense that it introduces the piece's motivic recapitulation. From this point onwards the nature of events changes entirely. An indication of this change comes from the first phrase of thematic recapitulation following peak III (bars 145–7), now compressed to three bars – the piece's first departure from even-numbered bar-grouping in the 3/8 metre.

This new course of events grows out of a simple device. Peak III is preceded by a well-defined build-up of eight bars (four of them crescendo); then after the four bars of peak III, 13 bars follow, building up to the main point of impact of peak IV in bar 158. (Bar 156 is already marked *forte* and might be considered as the beginning of peak IV; but the change of register in bar 158, together with the bass movement in bars 156–7, ensures that bar 158 provides the more incisive point of impact. This point will be returned to later, as it has further structural significance.)

After the 13 bars leading into peak IV, peak IV itself is then followed by 22

53

bars (units), leading to peak V at bar 182; and after the four bars of peak V the longest crescendo preparation of all, leading to the final *fortissimo* plateau of the coda, lasts for 34 bars. This sequence of approaches to these peaks is one of 8, 13, 22 and finally 34 bars – an expanding Fibonacci sequence with only one small inaccuracy, 22 instead of 21. A reason for this inaccuracy will be seen later.

An important rhythmic reason for the tremendous sense of exhilaration in this part of the work is that the Fibonacci ratios in these crescendos are made up by juxtaposing asymmetrical phrase-lengths with four-bar sequences, the former first providing a degree of tense compression, the latter then adding an element of broader momentum leading into the dynamic peaks. This is shown in Fig. 5.5. Approaching peak IV, the four-bar series is preceded by a single three-bar phrase; that approaching peak V is preceded by two of them, this time with added jostling from the hemiola suggestions in the left hand; and in the final crescendo passage the 3/8 metre comes under more sustained attack, being turned into seven hemiola groups before four-bar phrases again take over from bar 200, continuing now without interruption right to the end of the piece.

Fig. 5.5

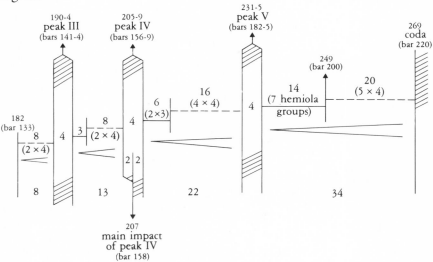

In each case the transition from asymmetry to symmetry underlines an important harmonic moment – in bars 148 and 166 a change from the acoustic and lydian modality to the whole-tone scale; and in bar 200 the arrival at E♭, the tritone from the home key, in the bass progression by whole tones. This is one of the best illustrations, on an intricate scale, of Debussy working in 'blocks' – in this case harnessing the opposed harmonic or modal blocks together with the opposed rhythmic blocks, for maximum dramatic power.

This terse combination of modes and of symmetrical and asymmetrical structure, with its dramatic results, also accounts for the unusual structure of peak IV already noted on page 53. Its two points of articulation in bars 156 and 158, both marked *forte*, evidently indicate that Debussy wanted a renewed articulation in bar 158. (None of the other peaks is given a differentiated internal articulation of this sort.) The *forte* arrival at bar 156 forms part of the four-bar series, which can then continue unbroken to the recapitulation at bar 160; whereas the 13-bar Fibonacci component of this sequence, as shown in Fig. 5.5, is marked by the sharper articulation inside this four-bar peak at bar 158. The modal structure of peak III accords precisely with this explanation: bar 156, articulating the four-bar series, changes to the acoustic scale, while bar 158, articulating the Fibonacci one, changes back to whole tones.

Peak III has been seen to be a central point of proportional convergence, as well as a main structural watershed. As one might therefore expect, it is carefully placed within the entire work. The primary GS of the piece's 305 units falls after 188·5 units, only 1½ units (bars) from the beginning of peak III. In the context of 305 units this inaccuracy is very slight (0.5% of the total length), but can in any case be easily accounted for by peak III's involvement in the various proportional sequences of Figs. 5.3–5.5, in which any inaccuracy would represent a much larger percentage error. Thus the piece's large-scale dynamic progression, shown fully in Fig. 5.6, represents a system divided principally round its primary GS, with the part before this division dominated by symmetry (mostly groups of 16 units), and the part after by GS, using Fibonacci numbers – another particularly logical model structure that reappears in the following chapters. In this example the transition from symmetry to asymmetry is stressed by the piece's first three-bar phrase in the 3/8 metre, entering at bar 145, immediately after this principal structural watershed.

Fig. 5.6

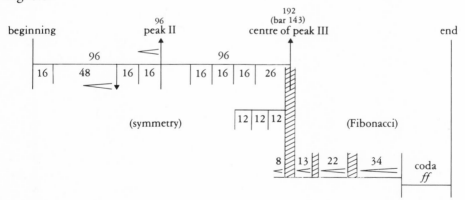

We have seen that the long passage just analysed is developed from the polarity between the acoustic and whole-tone scales first heard in bars 20–1 (Ex. 10 on page 49 above). On page 51 it was remarked that this early event, which also introduced motive C in bar 21, formed no part of the symmetrical sequence seen in Fig. 5.2 – aptly, as this event is quite foreign to the diatonic movement articulated in that symmetrical sequence. It is, however, strategically positioned. Beginning in the second quaver of bar 21, it comes after 54 units of the piece, and the piece's first entry of motive *B* in bar 9, introducing for the first time the acoustic scale, comes after 21⅓ units (to be precise), so that the introductions of the piece's two main modes, and with them the first entries of motives *A*, *B* and *C*, are related by near-GS. The slightly reduced accuracy of GS in this instance (instead of the exact Fibonacci numbers 21 and 55) can be accounted for by the need for this tonally subversive modal progression to infiltrate itself quietly within the 4/4 framework, without causing disturbance to the more obvious symmetrical diatonic sequence in progress. This more surreptitious sequence of 21 and 54 goes no farther for the moment – Debussy restores diatonic order in bar 25 – but the seed has been sown, proportionally as well as modally, and it is this same Fibonacci sequence that eventually returns with the same themes and juxtaposition of modes to take over after peak III.

Points of formal return

The large-scale formal framework between peak III and the end of the piece – including points of return like the recapitulation and coda – is still unaccounted for, proportionally. This is now traced in Fig. 5.7.

The central point of tonal return is the recapitulation (bar 160) after 209 units, which is led into directly by peak IV; this lies within 1½ bars of the halfway point between the beginning of the central section and the end of the piece, producing a division of 93:96 units (bars). Some necessary reasons for this inaccuracy – although only 1·6% of the distance measured – will soon be seen. (It can be pointed out immediately that to follow an exact ratio of 93:93 here leads to a point only three bars before the end of the piece, by which time the imminence of the end is obvious enough.)

By contrast to this symmetrically placed tonal return, the most accentuated point of harmonic tension and instability is peak V, the whole-tone climax, in bars 182–5. Accordingly the exact centre of this four-bar peak, after 233 units, lies at the primary GS (117:72 units) between the same two points – the beginning of the central section and the end of the piece. In the process a symmetrical division of 116:117 units is formed across the transition into the central section at bar 67, at which the tonic key was reaffirmed. (The apparent discrepancy here of one bar is inconsequential, as it is more than covered by the four-bar spread of peak V.) These last 72 bars (units), from the centre of peak V to the end of the work, are then symmetrically divided 36:36 by the beginning of the coda in bar 220, marking simultaneously the final return to the tonic key, the arrival of the diatonic major mode, the completion of the dynamic sequence from Fig. 5.6, and the closing of the piece's tonal phase-lag mentioned earlier. This positioning of the coda is given extra proportional weight by the placing of peak III: the 153 bars (units) from the beginning of the central section to the coda are

Fig. 5.7

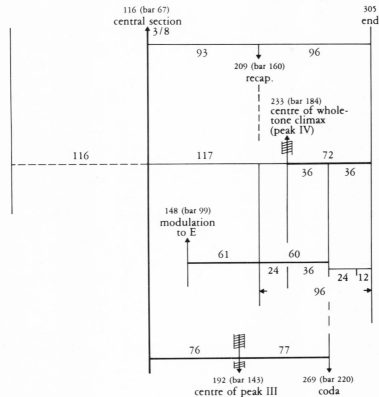

divided 76:77 at the exact centre of this strongly diatonic and symmetrically shaped peak, after 194 units (the apparent one-bar discrepancy again is more than covered by the four-bar spread of peak III).

The recapitulation point has one other important proportional function. The modulation to E major in bar 99 (148 units) is the principal point of tonal departure for all the subsequent harmonic adventures, which are finally resolved only at the coda in bar 220. From this principal point of tonal departure to the final large-scale point of tonal return there are 121 bars (units), and these are divided 61:60 by the intermediate point of tonal return – the recapitulation.

This division partly accounts for the inaccuracy in the recapitulation's other important 93:96 division in Fig. 5.7: to alleviate the latter would increase the inaccuracy in the former, and to a greater percentage degree. Similarly, to alter the 22 bars before peak V (Fig. 5.5) to the theoretically accurate value of 21 would again exacerbate the same small inaccuracy, making the ratio in Fig. 5.7 61:59 instead of 61:60. More immediately important, even if Debussy were to alter the same recalcitrant 22 bars to 21 (and thus also the 93:96 in Fig. 5.7 to 93:95), the only place he could do this, without disrupting the structurally vital series of 4 × 4 bars within that passage, would be in bars 160–5. This would mean compressing one of the two 3-bar phrases there to two bars, which would cause immediately obvious musical damage. The present positioning therefore provides the maximum possible accuracy in all the proportional sequences involved; and the inevitable element of inaccuracy that results from combining so many sequences is visibly spread as evenly, and as logically, as possible among the sequences involved. (This again, as arithmetical fact, applies whether or not Debussy was conscious of it.)

If we join these various points together, lower in Fig. 5.7, we see that from the recapitulation onwards all the divisions conform to groups of 12 bars, in Fibonacci multiples of 1, 2, 3, 5 and 8, providing a series of contracting ratios of 12 leading to the end of the piece. Why ratios of 12 are used cannot be proved with certainty. But it could reasonably be conjectured that the combination of GS and symmetry in these numbers might be present to combine the dynamism of all this section with a breadth of articulation necessary when using such a short bar length. Whatever the case, the choice of the number 12 has another significance: as already seen, the 3/8 sections of the work are articulated completely in phrases of either four, six or three bars, and 12 is the lowest common multiple of these three numbers.

To complete the proportional detail in the final parts of the work Fig. 5.8 traces events from bar 184 (the centre of peak V) onwards. (The significance of the 36:36-unit overall balance of this extract has already been seen in Fig. 5.7.)

Fig. 5.8

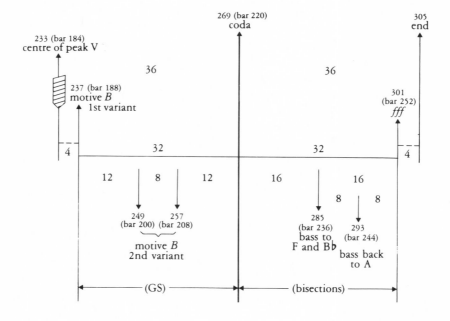

Motive *B*, in fragmented form, enters only in bar 188, four bars after the beginning of the extract. Those initial four athematic bars are matched by the four athematic bars with which the piece ends, leaving a balance, thematically defined, of 32:32 bars across the beginning of the coda. As part of the broad crescendo, the first of these groups of 32 bars is divided at its two points of GS (to nearest whole bars – a ratio of 12:8:12), the two *forte* entries of motive *B* in its most extreme metamorphosis, in bars 200 and 208.

Conversely, after the coda's return to the tonic, the 32 following bars are divided mainly 16:16 (bar 236, *più ff*), and these latter 16 are again divided 8:8 at the final bass return to A, in bar 244. This system of an overall bisection, balancing GS on one side against bisections on the other, forms the exact converse of, or complement to, the logic of Fig. 5.6 on page 55: there the overall GS division, at peak III, formed the watershed between a preceding predominantly symmetrical system and a following GS one. The two complementary systems of Figs. 5.6 and 5.8 are also linked geometrically: the central division of Fig. 5.8 – the beginning of the coda – is also the point where the dynamic sequence of Fig. 5.6 completes itself, so that the plan of Fig. 5.8 is really a logical offshoot of the final sections of Fig. 5.6.

All this is summed up in miniature by motive *A*, which begins and ends the piece. In bar 1 motive *A* begins to spiral after 5 of its 8 quaver beats (admittedly the pause obscures the exact numerical relationship, but it underlines the asymmetry). In the coda (bar 244), this is adjusted to a symmetrical division of 3+3 beats. In effect, at the beginning motive *A* gives the basic shape of Fig. 5.6 in miniature, and at the end it gives the shape of Fig. 5.8 in miniature.

What is most remarkable about the formal outline of Fig. 5.7 is that it makes absolute proportional sense by itself, all the points of growth and return being placed with obvious proportional logic relative to one another and to the whole. Yet all these points of return and culmination from the central section onwards have their positions precisely defined, quite separately, by the independent logic of the dynamic sequences in Fig. 5.6. Thus the movement's formal framework has visibly been generated by the combination of the large-scale expanding GS pattern of Fig. 5.1 (page 50) with the smaller-scale dynamic progressions shown in Fig. 5.6. Expressed in another way, each of the later points of return and resolution is defined from two different structural directions, by two quite separate courses of proportional logic. This phenomenon will be encountered again in *La mer*.

From Figs. 5.2 or 5.6 it can be seen that the entire geometric structure is set in motion by the end of the introduction, after six bars (16 units). This moment, determining the course of a strongly tonal and dynamic sequence, should ideally set these qualities of tonality and dynamism sharply in relief. A most effective way of underlining these is simply to withhold them beforehand – the catapult principle – which is precisely what Debussy does by beginning in an unarticulated rhythm and a tonally ambiguous whole-tone mode. Thus, apart from the more immediate dramatic reasons for this introduction's tonal and rhythmic vagueness, its presence as a 'quasi-cadenza', causing the complications of measurement discussed in Chapter 2 above, can also be justified in proportional terms.

Other relationships

The connections between the rondo and ternary elements of the piece can now be better understood. First, the relevance of the smaller ternary scheme within the larger one is evident from Fig. 5.1, since the first episode, introducing the first change to 3/8 metre, provides both rhythmic and proportional preparation for the larger central section, giving a palpable forward impetus to the form.

Of the rondo returns, the least explicable one in normal terms is that of motive *B* in bar 105, forming part of the sequence in Fig. 5.4 (page 53). Why *B*, in a section apparently intended as a complete contrast from what has gone before? The probable answer lies in bar 115, the proportionally and structurally important transition from diatonic to whole-tone harmony. Motive *B*, preceding it, is the theme based on the acoustic scale, emphasizing the last few bars of diatonicism, whereas the change to chromaticism is then underlined by the change to the whole-tone theme twelve bars later, the theme properly belonging to the central section. The other rondo return, that of *A* in bar 52, is more explicable in view of its role in defining the ternary-within-ternary sequence. The importance of its positioning together with peak II has been seen in Fig. 5.4.

All the rondo returns, then, are demonstrably highly influential in defining the piece's dynamic shape. But, as already pointed out, this same dynamic sequence itself generates and defines the framework of the entire ternary-plus-coda outline, especially the later part of it shown in Fig. 5.7. Therefore by logical extension, the rondo elements play a major part in defining the formal logic of the large-scale ternary-plus-coda outline. Far from undermining the large-scale form, as might otherwise have been concluded, the rondo elements, in a most original way, ensure its solidity.

It was suggested earlier that in general terms ternary elements in the form would tend to supply structural breadth, and the rondo elements a more continuous cumulative element. Proportional analysis confirms this, the ternary elements being connected predominantly with the large-scale framework of Fig. 5.7, and the rondo ones with the cumulative dynamic sequence of Fig 5.6.

Earlier, a structural overlap was pointed out between the tonal recapitulation in bar 160 and the thematic anticipation of this in bar 145, where motive *B* again takes over. The proportional logic of this can be seen from Figs. 5.6 and 5.7. Tonally the recapitulation is logically placed at a major halfway division in Fig. 5.7; but the earlier thematic recapitulation, entering immediately after peak III (that is, as near as possible to the work's overall primary GS), provides a proportional complement in the ternary scheme to the positioning of the central section, which began at the work's overall secondary GS.

More intricate modal relationships can be traced in the passage between peak III and the coda, whose proportions were shown in Fig. 5.5 on page 54. The precise modal sequence is shown in Fig. 5.9.

Fig. 5.9

approach to peak III	peak III	approach to peak IV	peak IV	approach to peak V	peak V	approach to coda	coda
	diatonic, but in foreign key		acoustic, whole-tone		completely whole-tone		diatonic major
whole-tone		acoustic, whole-tone,		acoustic, lydian, whole-tone,		chromatic, shifting harmony; then whole-tone bass movement	
		bass pedal C		bass pedal A			

Separating the dynamic peaks from their approaches, as in Fig. 5.9, reveals a marked divergence. Taking the peaks by themselves shows a progression of, first, diatonic major in a foreign key; then acoustic scale to whole tones; then uniquely whole tones; and finally the diatonic major in the home key. That is, the chromatic content increases progressively until it takes over completely in peak V, before giving way to the diatonic major in the coda. By contrast, the approaches to the peaks follow a course beginning purely with whole tones but then becoming progressively infiltrated not only by the acoustic scale but also by other modal elements, until in the final approach to the coda the entire apparatus gradually disintegrates under a welter of modal combinations, hemiolas, other rhythmic alterations and motivic fragmentation. (Motive *B*, here torn to shreds, disappears completely from the coda, as does the acoustic scale it first introduced.) This is not the only dissolution: as a result of the opposing tendencies within Fig. 5.9, the contrasts of mode between the dynamic peaks and their respective approaches also gradually dissolve on the way through this passage. This comprehensive disintegration is so thorough that the return of whole-tone and lydian elements, juxtaposed in the last part of the coda (but not the acoustic scale, as G♯ and E never occur together), can no longer threaten the outcome: the disruptive power of the chromaticism appears to have been completely exorcized in this piece's extraordinary version of a recapitulation.

If Debussy in this piece was deliberately 'playing off one type of mode against others, building forms from a delicate drama of tensions, oppositions and resolutions', as Arnold Whittall has suggested (1975, 264), there could hardly be a more dramatic example than this passage of how he achieves the dénouement.

But only through proportional analysis does an organic logic become visible by which these tensions, oppositions and resolutions are comprehensively organized and integrated with the other aspects of the music's form.

It is to the same passage that Debussy made one alteration at proof stage. In his final manuscript copy (Ms. 977: see page 49 note 1) bars 156–7 appear as in Ex. 11. In this version peak IV is entirely whole-tone, instead of the mixture of acoustic and whole-tone scales that the printed score has. Debussy's change at proof stage is logical for a number of reasons. First, the final printed version includes the change of mode in bar 158 that emphasizes the structurally important articulation there (relative to the dynamic sequence in Fig. 5.5 on page 54). Second, it provides a better gradation of the modal progression shown in Fig. 5.9. Third, by preventing peak IV from being whole-tone, it prevents it from harmonically pre-empting the impact of the whole-tone peak V.

Ex. 11: *L'isle joyeuse*, bars 156–8, final manuscript version

Perhaps Debussy was unaware of these considerations, and made the alteration simply because it intuitively sounded better; even if so it cannot invalidate the logic involved. But we have seen already, from the unusual construction of peak IV and its role in Fig. 5.5, that the spot is a slightly 'tight' one in the structure. All the more striking, therefore, that the manuscript should betray some indecision on Debussy's part at exactly this place.

One other manuscript variant is worthy of mention, not from Ms. 977 but from what was evidently one of the first sketches for the piece.[2] This consists of a rough draft of bars 117–44, corresponding structurally to the final version except that bars 123–4 are missing. In this form the passage is equally acceptable in linear terms, indeed in one respect more so, as the omission of bars 123–4 matches the surrounding bars as a sequence more logically to bars 127–36. The main justification for the added two bars therefore appears to be proportional (the immediate feeling of greater breadth they cause is also connected with local proportions, as traced in Fig. 5.4 on page 53) – a parallel case to the grammatically inessential bar Debussy added to 'Jardins sous la pluie', as discussed in Chapter 1 above.

2. Music department of the Bibliothèque Nationale, Paris: Ms. 17729, page 5; formerly from the collection of Mme de Tinan. Some other sketches for the piece are listed by Lesure (1977, 111), but they are only disjointed melodic and harmonic fragments, telling us nothing about how Debussy put the form together.

An ingenious type of polarity introduced in *L'isle joyeuse* involves two contrasted uses of four-bar sequences, placid and stable in the earlier parts of the piece and powerfully propulsive later. Those contrasted characteristics are separated, indeed to a great extent polarized, by the effect of the compressed three-bar groups between bars 145 and 166, and the resulting two types of polarity— symmetrical against asymmetrical, and symmetrically static against symmetrically propulsive— will be encountered again in *La mer*.

This is obviously the most complex structure seen so far in this book. Yet the basic plan – that of Fig. 5.6 in combination with Figs. 5.1 and 5.7– is in its essence simple: the definition of a logical large-scale framework by the use of a more fluid and small-scale dynamic one, both following the same proportional logic. Only in its detailed execution does the plan inevitably become more complex; but the complexity concerns detail, not principles. In this sense the structure is more lucidly organized than that of 'Clair de lune' (Figs. 4.6–4.8 on pages 41–4). As already mentioned, 'Reflets dans l'eau' then carries the process of simplification even farther, notwithstanding the sophistication with which the same principles are applied there. More continuity is now becoming apparent in Debussy's development of proportional techniques, and the following analysis of *La mer* amplifies this further.

PART 3

La mer

Chapter 6

Introduction

La mer provides both an ideal and a necessary central focus for this investigation. One reason is simply its symphonic complexity. Are devices and structures of the type already discovered in the previous chapters present, and influential, in such a large work as this? The answer is bound to have a crucial bearing on the importance of those devices to Debussy's musical language in general.

The other main reason for investigating *La mer* here is one by now familiar – the difficulty of defining exactly what its formal processes are and how the work achieves its coherence, both within its separate movements and as a whole. The problem is well demonstrated by the large number of different labels applied by different writers to the movements, and by the caveats that many of them even then feel obliged to append to their definitions.[1]

All this is compounded by the contrasts between the three movements. For example, the first movement is almost unique in Debussy's output for the sharp definition of its various large sections, achieved here by simultaneous changes of metre, tempo and key. The finale counterbalances this by holding a steady, if flexible, 2/2 metre throughout. Both movements, however, share a large-scale sense of tidal motion, moving broadly and powerfully; 'Jeux de vagues' provides another counterbalance by leaping along, at least for its first half, in an unpredictable series of short paragraphs and sudden dynamic explosions. Naturally such contrasts serve the obvious purpose of avoiding formal monotony, but might they also have more precise constructive uses? If they do, are the contrasts offset by other unifying devices? The composer Jean Barraqué, for whom *La mer* held a constant fascination, observed one strong suggestion of the movements' inter-dependence, at the end of the first movement, with the curious diminuendo on its final chord: 'However static, this doesn't give the impression of an end ... but

1. The traps that threaten unguarded definitions are illustrated by Max Pommer's attempt (1972, xx–xxi) to explain *La mer*'s finale as a rondo of alternating 'refrains' and 'couplets'. In the system he proposes, main themes in refrains I and III reappear in couplets I and II, making the hypothesis thematically inconsistent.

on the contrary of a door opening on to a new universe.'[2] The relationships inherent in those subtle aspects of continuity, as well as in the contrasts already mentioned, are an important aspect of the work, one which is elaborated in the next four chapters. Some of what emerges may come as a surprise, especially regarding the work's relationship to symphonic tradition – although it will be seen that this has nothing to do with the over-simplistic view sometimes taken of the first movement as an approximation to sonata form.

La mer holds particular interest here for another reason. This is that three complete autograph manuscripts of the work survive: the full score, the piano duet reduction and the complete draft in short score.[3] The first two were used for engraving the two corresponding Durand editions of 1905 and are identical with those editions except for very minor proof corrections and printing errors. They are also identical with each other in terms of the music's structure and dimensions. The third manuscript, however, which was not of course intended as a finished copy, presents a number of differences, including differences in dimensions – this last type almost all concerning passages which are slightly shorter there than in the two final manuscripts. The significance of these variants is discussed here after the analysis of each movement in its definitive form.

To add to the intrigue, this definitive form is not either of the published scores of 1905. After conducting a number of performances of *La mer* between 1906 and 1908, Debussy made revisions for a second edition, issued in 1909. Most of them are small retouchings of orchestral balance and colour, but two are more significant. Of these the more audible is in the finale, in the eight bars leading into figure *60*, where he excised some fanfares for the trumpets and horns.[4] The other, though, has stronger structural implications for the present analysis, as it involves the compression of two bars into one in the first movement, in the passage leading into the movement's central point of sectional transition shortly before figure *9*. The two versions are shown here in Ex. 12.

The following analysis is based on the 1909 text, and the significance of this one compression is discussed after (and in the light of) the analysis of the first movement. Bar-number references in the next four chapters, therefore, all follow

2. 'Tout ce statisme ne donne pas l'impression d'une fin ... mais au contraire d'une porte ouverte vers un nouvel univers.' The passage occurs in his notes for what was to have been a thorough analytic survey of *La mer* (Barraqué, posth.), a project left incomplete at his untimely death in 1973. I am grateful to the late G. W. Hopkins for allowing me access to these notes.

3. The full score and piano duet reduction are Ms. 967 and Ms. 1022 in the Music department of the Bibliothèque Nationale, Paris. The complete short score is in the Sibley Music Library of the Eastman School of Music, University of

Rochester; for convenience it is referred to here as the 'Sibley manuscript'.

4. Though not documented in any Debussy biographies, a story circulates that Debussy removed the fanfares in embarrassment at an unintended resemblance to Puccini's *Manon Lescaut*. Marie Rolf (1976, 239) mentions the story, which is plausible in view of the passage in Act 1 of *Manon* leading to figure *64* (pages 170–1 in the Ricordi full score). The fanfares were evidently a last-minute addition in any case, as they are not in the Sibley manuscript.

Ex. 12: 'De l'aube à midi sur la mer', bars 82ff

(a) 1905 edition

the bar-numbering of the 1909 edition, even later in each chapter when the earlier sources are under discussion, since any other method would cause confusion. For simpler reference, however, rehearsal numbers (for example, *9*) in the score are supplied instead whenever they coincide with the point being referred to.[5]

In the course of the following analyses, the musical motives are shown *in situ*, each as it is discussed for the first time; but for ease of cross-reference, they also are all listed together at the end of this chapter as Ex. 13.

It should be said immediately that the discussion of the Sibley manuscript in the following three chapters is in no way exhaustive, but concerns itself only with dimensional variants; to do more would be irrelevant to this book. Marie Rolf

5. The alterations for the 1909 full score have never been incorporated in the piano duet version, which as presently sold still follows the 1905 text. No trace is known of the corrected 1905 score presumably used by Durand to prepare the 1909 edition; but the authenticity of all the corrections is documented by their pre-sence, in Debussy's writing, in a corrected copy of the 1905 printed score that Debussy gave to Edgard Varèse in October 1908. Now in the possession of Mrs Louise Varèse, this score also contains a few further retouchings which have never seen print (none of them concerning dimensions, though).

(b) 1909 edition

(1976) has already examined the Sibley manuscript in great detail and undertaken a full comparison of the variants in the manuscripts, annotated scores and various editions of *La mer*.

As a gratuitous complication, Durand in 1938 issued a revised edition of *La mer* in which some passages, including Ex. 12, revert—undoubtedly through negligence—to the 1905 text. The scores now on sale appear mostly to follow the 1909 text again, though there are exceptions—a state of anarchy that will not surprise those familiar with French editions. (A recent edition by Eulenburg also wrongly gives the 1905 reading of Ex. 12.) As the variant shown here in Ex. 12 is the only one that affects the present proportional analysis, the reader is advised to check the score being used against Ex. 12 here, before annotating it, to avoid any possibility of confusion.

Ex. 13: Motives in *La mer*

(a) 'De l'aube à midi sur la mer'

(b) 'Dialogue du vent et de la mer'

E

F

G

(c) 'Jeux de vagues'

H

J

K

L₁

L₂ L

M

Chapter 7

'De l'aube à midi sur la mer'

One aspect of this movement unusual in Debussy's mature style has already been mentioned – that the main transitions, instead of being overlapped and ambiguous, here are set in sharp relief by simultaneous changes of metre, tempo, tonality, modality and thematic content. Five main sections result, shown below:

	Introduction	First Principal Section	Second Principal Section	Transition	Coda
				14	
bars	1—30	31—83	84—121	122—31	132—41
metre	6/4→4/4—6/4	6/8	4/4—12/8	6/4	4/4

Again, exactly what labels we use is less important than what the sections do musically. Some writers (for example, Jean Barraqué, 1972, 148) choose to group the above Transition and Coda together as the Coda, a minor difference of labelling; but reasons will be seen that make it more useful here to have the additional differentiation.

Each section is examined in detail in the course of this chapter; but immediately it can be seen that they are all constructed differently. The Introduction is a quite clear arch form, whereas the First Principal Section appears as a more idiosyncratic type of rondo; the Second Principal Section is largely strophic; the Transition is simply a repeated melody over a dominant pedal, returning the music to the home key of Db major; and the Coda is essentially an extended plagal cadence, incorporating some thematic returns.

But this overall sectional clarity only increases the problem of understanding what the movement is about. How do those distinct sections, with their different metres, keys and thematic contents, cohere as a unity? The problem arises particularly because of the movement's apparently deliberate obfuscation of any clear recapitulation towards the end. Tonally and thematically there is some in the Coda, because of the return to the tonic chord in bar 135 together with the motive which had initially been heard with the first arrival of the tonic key, at the beginning of the First Principal Section (bars 31–3). But this recapitulative element is not only sharply compressed but also obscured. The return to the opening tonality just before the Coda (bar 122) almost sneaks in over its dominant pedal; the subsequent move to the subdominant at *14* neutralizes

70

much of the tonal momentum towards the imminent tonic chord; when the tonic chord does arrive in bar 135, new material on trumpets and trombones relegates the reprise of the woodwind motive to an accompanying role; and overshadowing all of this thematically is the entry of an entirely new chorale-like motive in the brass to begin the Coda at *14*.

There are other unifying devices to counteract this, however. The most obvious thematic link between sections is motive *X* (Ex. 14), known generally as *La mer*'s cyclic motive, which appears in the first three sections (and returns in the third movement). But this theme is not an integral part of the symphonic tapestry here; rather it is a dramatic gesture, set on a pedestal – literally so in the Introduction, where it forms the crown of the arch form.

Ex. 14

motive *X*

In addition to the points of dramatic focus defined by the three main entries of *X* (at figures *1*, *8* and *12*), three others are marked by the movement's three climaxes, at bar 76 (*sforzando*), figure *11* (*fortissimo*) and bars 135–9 (leading to triple-*forte*), which link the sections in a broad, tidal three-part wave sequence. Although the action here is on a much larger scale than in *L'isle joyeuse*, this movement's progression is similarly cumulative, following the title's archetypal progression from pre-dawn obscurity to the splendour of midday.

More coherence is ingeniously hidden in some intricate motivic relationships between the sections, shown in Ex. 15, and in the large-scale tonal progression: the First Principal Section carries the tonality from D♭ to E (this is traced more thoroughly in the following pages, as Debussy deliberately obscures it in one respect), from which the Second Principal Section jumps the tritone to B♭ major, finally leading back to the D♭ tonality of the final two sections. Discounting for a moment the B tonality of the opening, which has a different purpose, this symmetrical sequence of D♭ to E to B♭ to D♭, with its pendulum effect, forms another large-scale tidal impulse, most strongly discernible at the tritonal jump between the two Principal Sections.

For all those unifying devices, though, the movement's ends are still not tied up as comprehensively as in *L'isle joyeuse*. Since in the case of *La mer* two more movements are to follow, Debussy's aim here appears to be a delicately judged polarity between unity and open-endedness (as we have seen Jean Barraqué observe): the chronological element in the title suggests a succession of the sea's varying moods portrayed through a display, or exposition, of different sensations and forms (to use Debussy's phrase), each set in relief by different themes, keys and metres.

71

Ex. 15: Motivic relationships in 'De l'aube à midi'

Although the final two sections have a fairly simple, mainly cadential role, the first three sections really need to be studied first as independent symphonic entities. This applies specially to the two Principal Sections, with their dynamic peaks, and their prominent entries of motive *X*, and they are therefore analysed first.

There is another vital reason here for beginning with individual sections. The very device that ensures the definition of the five sections – the changes of tempo and metre – causes a problem of pulse relationships not yet encountered. An immediate proportional analysis of the entire movement, based on what could not be proved as exact pulse relationships, would be logically vulnerable without a more detailed perspective. On the other hand the internal proportions of each individual section are fixed by a constant pulse within each section – crotchet, dotted crotchet and a combination of the two for the first three sections respectively.

First Principal Section

This is symphonically the most complex section, with a motivic variety and tonal range much greater than in the other sections. Its beginning and end are well marked; the enclosed structure, conversely, resists simple classification, mostly because of the complex thematic order. Motivic relationships can, however, clarify this considerably. The dynamic focus, at bar 76, highlights motive *A*, and the other dramatic focus of the section, the entry of motive *X*, occurs four bars earlier at *8*. The two motives are related (as just seen in Ex. 15): *X* begins with *A* in inversion and then contains it again in its last four notes – a relationship made explicit at the transition from *X* to *A* in bars 75 – 6. The first three motives in the section, *A₁*, *A₂* and *A₃* (bars 33, 35 and 43), are also obvious derivatives of *A*, as shown in Ex. 16. By contrast the remaining two motives, *B* and *C* (bar 47

Ex. 16

and figure *6*), have no such relationship either to each other or to *A* and *X*. If we group the derivatives of *A* together, we obtain an almost pure ABCBA arch form, the opening A segment consisting of the *A* variants, the B segment of motive *B* (bars 47–52, 64–7) and the central C segment of motive *C* (figure *6* to figure *7*). Motives *A* and *X* in their basic forms, though, are unconcerned with

73

the opening A segment; they appear only after the completion of the arch form, from *8* onwards. This completion of the arch form then serves to highlight the two points of dramatic focus – the entry of *X* and the climax – which follow immediately, and at the same time bars 75–7 explicitly relate *X*, *A* and *A₁* (as shown in Ex. 17) before the section finishes with ostinato echoes of *A*.

Ex. 17

A_2, with an additional entry at *5*, forms the one interruption to the arch form, introducing – as in *L'isle joyeuse* – a rondo element. As with *L'isle joyeuse* this exception does not destroy the strong arch-form tendency: the use of the more chromatic A_2 at *5*, also over chromatic harmony, rather than the pentatonic A_1, minimizes the disturbance to the arch form by reserving the return of the tonally more assertive A_1 until bar 68, its logical place in the arch form. The entry of A_2 at *5* has another formal consequence: its presence completes a smaller-scale ternary sequence up to bar 58, of which motive *B* forms the central part. And in turn the opening A segment by itself contains a ternary grouping of motives $A_1–A_2–A_1$, before A_3 enters as a transition to the following segment of the larger arch form. This is shown in Fig. 7.1.

Fig. 7.1

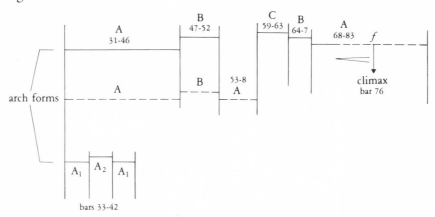

As already seen in *L'isle joyeuse*, a ternary or arch sequence is essentially a wave form, and in this case the large-scale wave of the complete arch sequence could be considered to have its impetus built up gradually by the formal momentum generated by the two preparatory ternary sequences – the whole section being an expanding sequence of three wave-like arch forms.

The *Vachaspati* acoustic scale, familiar from *L'isle joyeuse*, is prominent in this section, but here its relationship to tonality is necessarily different because this section has no whole-tone passages. The juxtaposition of motives A_1 and A_2, respectively pentatonic and acoustic, to open the section suggests that the acoustic scale's significance here is relative to pentatonicism (which, conversely, was almost completely absent from *L'isle joyeuse*). The two notes it adds to the pentatonic scale are the root and third of the tritone to the tonic, as shown in Ex. 18. With the A_1–A_2 progression in bars 33–7, also shown in Ex. 18, Debussy presents us with this relationship, just as he made the relationship between the acoustic and whole-tone scales clear to us in *L'isle joyeuse*.

Ex. 18

The appearance of this mode at bar 35 poses no tonal threat because of the security of the tonic pedal underneath; but just before the section's climax Debussy plays the logical follow-through. Having settled the bass on E at figure *8*, with acoustic-scale harmony above, he then quickly removes this incipient new tonic pedal at bar 73, but locks the music into the now unstable acoustic-scale harmony above, so that motive X and the climax are held in this tonal deadlock until its release in bar 84, the beginning of the next section. The move to B♭ major in bar 84 is thus the logical linear outcome of the modality of the preceding section, as shown in Ex. 19; but at the same time the removal of the root E from bar 73 onwards gives maximum impact to the bass F in bar 84.

Ex. 19

As this whole process is set in motion by the intrusion of C♭ into the pentatonic modality at bar 35, this offers an explanation for Debussy's use of B tonality to open the movement: in effect the B (enharmonically C♭) sets its seal in advance on the following D♭ tonality.

Within the First Principal Section, the overall transferral of the acoustic mode from D♭ (at the beginning of the section) to E (at the end of it) is related to intermediate tonal events. The first move away from the opening tonic pedal, at *4*, is introduced by motive A_3 (whose retrograde form of A symbolically turns its back on the preceding tonic pedal); the parallel chordal movement with which it makes this move suggests what we have already seen – that the preceding acoustic modality is not being abandoned but transplanted eventually to a new key. What this key will finally be (at *8*) is immediately suggested by strong dominant implications of F♭ (=E) major in bar 46 – though this expected new key is forestalled at bar 47, as explained in the next paragraph. And just as the entire section's large-scale move from D♭ to E precedes a tritonal shift to B♭ major at bar 84, the earlier small-scale shift from D♭ towards E in bars 42–6 is made via its tritone of B♭, at *4*. Having fulfilled this transitional role motive A_3 is no longer needed, and thus makes no reappearance at the end of the section, giving way instead to *A* and *X*.

As just mentioned, bar 47 avoids the expected arrival at E major by sidestepping into the dominant minor of A♭, which it holds to all intents and purposes until the turning point of the arch form at *7*. From there, after some chromaticism, the tonality tumbles down by a sequence of fifths as the music recovers its kinetic impetus (which had been attenuated in the central A♭ segment of the arch form) – via D♭ in bar 67 to G♭ at bar 68, C♭ in bar 69 and finally F♭/E at *8*, the key initially promised by the first modulatory passage in bars 43–6.

Proportions

As the section contains one odd bar of 9/8 (bar 67), units of 3/8 are best used here for measurement, avoiding fractions, and making a total of 107 units for the whole section. One of the most striking characteristics of this section is the regularity with which it opens – not only over an effective tonic pedal but also with its phrase sequence articulated uniquely in multiples of four units, or pairs of bars. Motives $A_1, A_2, A_1, A_3, B, A_2$ and *C* enter respectively 4, 8, 20, 24, 32, 44 and 56 units after the beginning of the section – all multiples of four. Figure *7*, the turning point of the arch form, breaks this sequence for the first time, bringing in the return of *B* ten units (five bars) after the preceding entry of *C*. This interruption of symmetrical phrasing is emphasized by the new chromaticism attached to *B*, and also by *B* now being given in a curtailed form. From then on the phrases are uneven or clipped (A_1 on its return in bar 68 loses its second bar). These opposed blocks of symmetrical and asymmetrical phrasing, balanced around *7*, underline the turning point there of the arch form, and this point divides the entire section's 107 units in GS of 66:41. The main structural event on the way there is the move away from the tonic pedal at *4*; this divides these first 66 units in the ratio 24:42 (=4:7) – the nearest possible to GS (within a bar of the exact value) without disrupting the four-unit sequences essential to the progression. Correspondingly the remaining 41 units after the main division at *7* are divided in GS of 25:16 by the climax in bar 76. This large-scale structure, based on the summation series 7, 9, 16, 25, 41, 66, 107..., is shown as the top part of Fig. 7.2. Its shape is identical with those of Fig. 3.1 and the bottom of Fig. 3.3 in 'Reflets dans l'eau' (pages 25 and 26), and the structural sequence is virtually identical with the latter of those two – marked in turn by the first move away from tonic-based harmony, then the transition to chromaticism (or stability to instability), and finally the climax.

Fig. 7.2

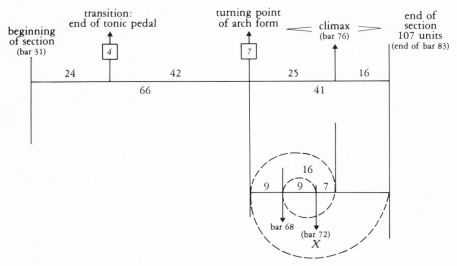

A new development follows in the last 41 units – the structurally unstable portion – stemming from their 25:16-unit division by the climax. These first 25 units are further divided in GS of 9:16 by the return of the A segment at bar 68 (this is underlined by the metrical distension at the end of bar 67); and, continuing the numerical series in reverse, the entry of *X* halfway through the bar of *8* divides these 16 units in ratio of 9:7 (9:7 is less accurate GS than 10:6, but adheres here to the summation series 7, 9, 16, 25, 41...). In this passage between *7* and the end of the section, the GS divisions surround and converge on the entry of *X* in a more centripetal action whose direction is most clearly represented lower in Fig. 7.2 by a broken curve: linking these points in a GS spiral, it completes itself in bar 72 at the entry of *X*. Whether Debussy intuited or designed this sequence, the spiral's formants are arithmetically there, and its circular character is in keeping with the asymmetry of these last 41 units of the section (one of the most mysterious passages in *La mer*), as opposed to the much more open regularity of the preceding 66 units. There is another reason for using a spiral in Fig. 7.2, which is simply that the music in this passage provides a strong evocation of a vortex, with the feeling of rapid descent from the plunging bass sequence in bars 67–72, followed by swirling textures and circular repetitions in the strings and woodwind in bars 69–75. Edward Lockspeiser's comments on 'symbols in *La mer* of vortexes and whirlpools' (1963, 60) are obviously relevant, and are discussed more in Chapter 11.

In case this seems far-fetched, it is worth digressing briefly to remark that the GS spiral is prominent both in organic forms and in art and mystical symbolism.

Among the many authors who take up this topic, Theodore Cook (1903; 1914) and Jill Purce (1975) have devoted whole books to it. In fact, probably the most common natural occurrence of this shape is in the shells of various sea molluscs and in other marine organisms – making the appearance of the same structure in *La mer* especially apt. This subject will be returned to at various later stages of this book. The overall shape of Fig. 7.2, incidentally, also recalls the opening motive of *L'isle joyeuse* which, as mentioned earlier, begins to spiral after 5 of its 8 beats.

Fig. 7.2's spiral construction simultaneously allows some bisections, marking two points of tonal arrival. The first, at bar 68 (75 units: the arrival at G♭ major), forms a 9:9 ratio leading to the entry of *X* (and thus provides another reason why the division formed by *X*'s entry is 9:7 rather than 10:6). The second bisection is at *8*, the bass's arrival at E half a bar before the entry of *X*, and forms a ratio of 8:8 units (4:4 bars) leading to the climax – so that the approach to the climax combines the tension of GS ratios with the momentum of four-bar groupings. (This gives a parallel to the mixture of GS and four-bar groups put to a similar purpose in the later parts of *L'isle joyeuse*.)

The other earlier divisions in the section's arch form produce more proportions, shown in Fig. 7.3, emphasizing those already seen in Fig. 7.2. They link the first two entries of motive A_2 to each other (GS of 36:22), the avoided modulation to E at bar 47 to the eventual arrival there at *8* (GS of 32:51), and the

Fig. 7.3

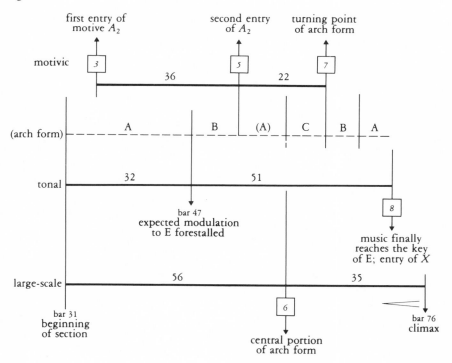

78

arrival of the central part of the arch form at *6* to the section's climax (GS of 56:35). These three relationships give proportional emphasis respectively to the turning point of the arch form at *7*, the entry of *X* in bar 72, and the climax. All the divisions of the arch form, and also the one exception to it, are now accounted for. In addition their geometry strongly focuses the entire structure on the section's two dramatic culminations, the climax and the entry of *X* – the latter in what appears an exceptionally esoteric geometric manner, particularly as it is a circular function used to define the positioning of the work's cyclic theme.

Second Principal Section

In contrast to the preceding complexity, this section opens with a simple strophic sequence on motive *D* (Ex. 20), developed from the two introductory bars (84–5), with three entries at *9*, *10* and *11* before motive *X* takes over at *12*. But motive *D*'s final entry at *11* also exposes a more hidden process of disintegration. Under the impact of the climax, *D* becomes fragmented and loses its tonic-key

Ex. 20

motive *D*

associations, which had been strongly present at *9* and *10*. Treble and bass then gradually drift apart until at *12*, with the music now completely chromatic, motive *X* breaks the strophic sequence, dominating the remainder of the section. This formal disintegration is reflected in other ways. The section opens with the most vigorous rhythm in the movement but ends 'Presque lent', with even the triplet rhythm collapsing in bar 121. It also begins with the only diatonic major scale in the whole movement (bar 87 contains all its degrees) and closes with one of the movement's only two whole-tone passages (the other one follows shortly in bars 128–31).

Dramatically the climax at *11* is prepared not so much by the strophic sequence as by more irregular tonal, dynamic and rhythmic punctuation. Like the preceding Principal Section this one begins over a pedal point, in this case a decorated dominant one. Bar 94 marks its abandonment, and between there and the climax the main dramatic punctuation is provided by the interruption of the 4/4–12/8 metre at the end of bar 100 together with the crescendo and ostinato which lead into the climax. (This interruption of the 4/4–12/8 metre is, of course, discernible as such only at the *end* of the 6/8 bar.)

Proportions
Because of this metrical digression in bar 100, and a later one in bar 110, the

proportions of this section are best counted in either minim or crotchet units (as before, either method yields the same proportions); crotchets are used here in order to avoid a complication later. The pedal point is abandoned after 40 units; a further 26 lead to the metrical interruption beginning the crescendo at the end of bar 100; and from there another 16 units lead to the climax at *11*. This is as near as is possible to a GS sequence (twice 20:13:8) without disrupting the 4/4 metre at bar 94, where the smooth continuation of the 4/4 is crucial in defining the sequence. The logic involved is almost identical with that of the approach to the climax in the preceding section (Fig. 7.2), the only difference being the quite acceptable logical variant that in Fig. 7.4 the move away from the pedal point subtends a primary rather than a secondary GS. Another parallel with Fig. 7.2 is that here again the GS approach to the climax is combined with the momentum of rhythmic groups of four, in this case a sequence of four 4/4 bars.

With the entry of *X* added, the proportions continue to the end of the section, completing a GS arch sequence of 40:26:16:26:40, whose turning point, after the 16 central units, is marked by the arrival of the climax, beginning the process of formal disintegration.[1] This is shown in Fig. 7.4. The entry of *D* at *10* reinforces this with a smaller GS sequence of 16:10:16, as also shown in Fig. 7.4 – again, a smaller wave within the larger one.

Fig. 7.4

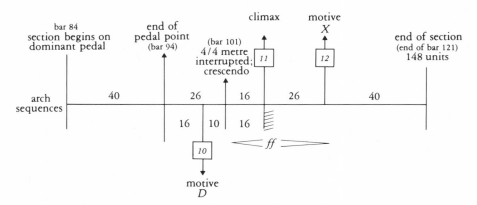

Other structural details add proportional emphasis, as shown in Fig. 7.5. Thematically they involve the first two entries of motive *D* (GS of 48:30, with a subdivision of 24:24) and, dynamically, the two lightly scored small peaks in bars 89 and 98–9 (GS of 23:37:23); both lead into the climax.

It might be contended that the distinction made here between the symmetrical arch sequence in Fig. 7.4 and the thematic one in Fig. 7.5 is musically arbitrary,

---

1. To make the exact reflection of the proportional sequence possible, a second bar of 6/8 is necessary, which explains its presence at bar 110. At that point, though, an interruption is not apt musically or proportionally, and correspondingly is not present.

Fig. 7.5

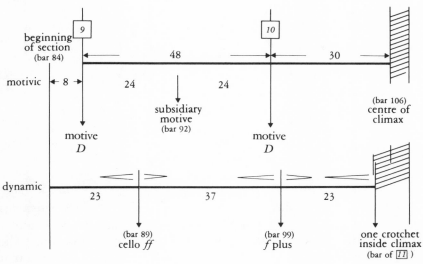

since both sequences are strongly articulative. The answer to this is the strong qualitative distinction between the two sequences. The strophic sequence marked by motive *D* is reiterative and representative of regularity, like the pedal point and regular metre that begin the section. The proportional arch sequence, on the other hand, comprises the points of interruption and discontinuity: the first division breaks the pedal point; the second one disrupts the metrical regularity; the third one, at the climax, breaks up motive *D* and its tonic associations; and the last division at *12* finally disperses the strophic sequence itself.

Introduction

Of all the sections the Introduction is formally the least ambiguous, consisting of an ABCBA arch form. Bars 1–5 correspond thematically to bars 23–30, bars 6–11 to 17–22, and the central portion (bars 12–16) consists of the work's first entry of the cyclic motive *X*. There is only one ambiguity, caused by the anticipatory trumpet and cor anglais entry in bar 9, which partly blurs the transition between the B and C segments.

In measuring the dimensions of this section the tempo relationship $\downarrow = \downarrow$ across bars 5–6 has to be taken into account. Counting the section by minim units avoids fractions, and this is done here. (This does not imply that bars 1–5 would be heard in terms of minim beats; the same logic applies as with *L'isle joyeuse* and has been discussed on pages 17–18.)

Fig. 7.6 shows the section's dimensions. The arch form follows an almost exactly symmetrical arch sequence of 15:12:10:12:16 units – the one small

81

Fig. 7.6

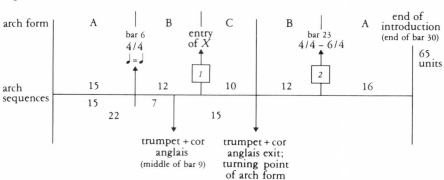

discrepancy being due to the different metre of bars 1–5. This change of metre is discussed more on pages 88–91 in connection with the variants in the Sibley manuscript, one of which is a different tempo relationship at this point. The other difference between Fig. 7.6 and the forms of the Principal Sections is that this nearly symmetrical arch avoids GS, bisection, or any other fixed geometrical ratio. Some of the significance of this will be seen only in the discussion (below) of the Sibley manuscript's variants, but there are also some immediate logical reasons for it. One is that bisections would be musically inappropriate, since the passage contains no points of tonal return and is mostly chromatic. The avoidance of bisections also necessitates the avoidance of any GS sequence, as a GS sequence by nature comprises bisections.[2] The other point is that this is the one part of the movement cast in a simple and recognizable conventional form, unlike the two Principal Sections with their involved structural counterpoints. Connected with this is the fact that the Introduction is mostly still and contains no internal dynamic focus, all its dynamic energy (generated in bars 23–30) being channelled into the following section.

The one ambiguity in the form – the anticipatory trumpet and cor anglais entry in bar 9 – has two effects on the arch form. The first is that, if taken together with bars 12–16 on textural grounds (which is reasonable), it marks another symmetrical progression of 15:7:15 units – again, a smaller wave within the larger one – leading to the turning point of the arch form (also shown in Fig. 7.6). The other is that, by being sited after 22 units, it is within one minim of GS on the way to the turning point of the arch form (where the trumpet and cor anglais exit again), after 37 units ($37 \times 0 \cdot 618 = 22 \cdot 87$). That is to say, the only incidence of near-GS in the entire Introduction is attached to the section's only formal idiosyncrasy in conventional terms.

2. For example, the sequence 13:8:5:8:13 contains two bisections of 13:13; likewise any sequence following a GS ratio.

The entire movement

Since the Transition and Coda sections are primarily cadential, they are best viewed together with what precedes them. It has already been mentioned that arch form is a type of wave form. As the first three sections of the movement are all articulated in different types of arch sequences, the entire movement can be viewed, from one angle, as a sequence of three such wave forms leading into the Transition and Coda. This is accompanied by other types of undulation. Tonally there are three areas of clear diatonic stability: the first parts of the First and Second Principal Sections respectively, and the final Transition and Coda. Taken together with the more chromatic sections leading to and from them, these form another three-part undulating sequence. The most clearly perceptible wave pattern of all is the dynamic one, again forming a triple undulation and completing itself at the final chord. The Transition and Coda sections therefore complete three different large-scale wave sequences, all of them tripartite. In view of those important large-scale structural rhythms, and of the strongly proportional basis of the sections already analysed, proportional links between them would seem logically probable.

In trying to link the tempi of the various sections, the main obstacle is the transition between the two Principal Sections, where ♪ = 116 is followed first by ♩ = 69 (bar 84) and then almost immediately by ♩ = 104 (figure 9). It would be easy to conclude that no continuity of pulse was intended here; but in fact the score tells us otherwise, with the instruction at bar 84 'Un peu plus mouvementé'. *Plus mouvementé* than what? It has to be relative to something, otherwise the instruction would be meaningless. It cannot be relative to the preceding quaver, which was faster, and therefore it must relate to the dotted crotchet of the preceding 6/8 metre, with its tempo of ♩. = c. 39. Although the increase from that to ♩ = 104 another two bars later at 9 is certainly drastic, the intermediate tempo in bars 84–5 acts as a distinct stepping-stone between the two, suggesting that Debussy was anxious to preserve a perceptible flow through this passage, even while using the change of tempo to emphasize the transition.

The other transitions are less extreme. That from the Introduction into the First Principal Section gives a continuity of compound duple metre, replacing the dotted minim of the former with the dotted crotchet of the latter, even though at an attenuated tempo. At the beginning of the Transition section (bar 122) the indication ♩ = 104 relates the crotchet directly to the ♩ = 104 of the preceding section, restoring the tempo after the rallentando in bars 109–20.[3]

3. The possible alternative here would be for this rallentando to be so extreme that the crotchet in bar 121 would equal the dotted minim of bar 122. This would require a tempo of ♩ = c. 35 in bar 121, which would be 'très lent' rather than the score's 'presque lent', as well as making the written-out rallentando in bar 121 stilted. ♩ = ♩ therefore seems more probable. This relationship is distorted by many conductors who play this entire section much more slowly than Debussy's indication, therefore finishing too slowly, as well as sentimentalizing the music and emasculating the climax at 11. Serge Koussevitsky's 1938 recording of *La*

Finally, in the Coda the nearest unit to this is the quaver pulse of $\flat$ = 80. Thus, for a continuous denominator of pulse, its fluctuations in speed notwithstanding, we may at least postulate relationships linking the movement's five sections as in Fig. 7.7.

Fig. 7.7

Introduction	First Principal Section	Second Principal Section	Transition	Coda
6/4→4/4–6/4	6/8	4/4 – 12/8	6/4	4/4
3→2 units per bar	2 units per bar	4 units per bar	6 units per bar	8 units per bar

and the total numbers of this common unit constituting each section are as follows:

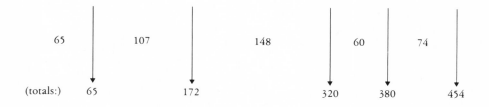

65	107	148	60	74

| (totals:) | 65 | | 172 | | 320 | 380 | 454 |

The number of units per bar increases steadily across the various transitions, from two to eight (not counting the exceptions of the metrical digressions in bars 1–5, 67, 100 and 110), again in keeping with the movement's general expansion. And the totals of units in the above diagram, when compared with the dimensions of Figs. 7.2–7.6, explain the choice of units made earlier for our analyses of the first three sections, for the units are common to all the diagrams, and the diagrams can now be fitted together as required.

From virtually all aspects, the movement's most emphatic transition is between the two Principal Sections, audibly the main point of regeneration in the form. Taking the movement's proportions as postulated above, the total of units, 454, yields GS of 281:173, so that this principal division in bar 84, after 172

mer (until recently available on an RCA record, VICS 1514) proves that ♩ = 104 is not impracticable between *9* and *11* and makes better sense of the later rallentando.

units, lies only one crotchet beat from the movement's secondary GS. 172 in turn produces GS of 106·3:65·7, placing the end of the Introduction, after 65 units, within one dotted-crotchet beat of the secondary GS on the way to the main division. This expanding sequence is shown in Fig. 7.8; there is an obvious resemblance to that of *L'isle joyeuse* in Fig. 5.1 on page 50 above. (The small inaccuracies are negligible in the context of such a large movement – 0.3% and 0.4% respectively of the distances measured; reasons for them will be seen later.) This also produces a balance of 65:66 units across the end of the Introduction (measuring up to 7, the turning point of the arch form) where the tonic key first arrives.

Fig. 7.8

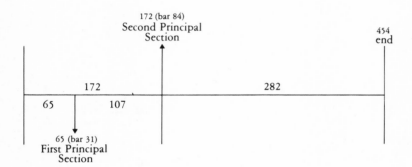

Independent of all this the dynamic shape follows a progressive sequence, the first climax marked *sforzando* (bar 76), the second one *fortissimo* (11), and the third one reaching triple-*forte* in bar 139. The first climax arrives after 156 units (65 units from Fig. 7.8 plus 91 units from Fig. 7.2 on page 77 – this method can be used to ascertain the unit total at any point in the movement); and the second climax arrives after 254 units (172 units plus 82 units, similarly calculated using Fig. 7.4 on page 80). GS of 254 is 157, relating these two climaxes again within one crotchet beat of GS.

It might be too naïve to expect an exact repetition of this with the final culmination, since the enormous tension accumulated in the final bars would be consistent with some more sophisticated procedure. Moreover, the final climax is stretched over five bars (135–9), and we should consider the comparative nature of the three climaxes. The first is sharply focused; the second, more lyrical, is symmetrically spread over two bars; and the third is powerfully cumulative, beginning in bar 135 and building up to its apex on the last crotchet beat of bar 139. With this in mind the placing of the final climax has visible logic: 254 units (the point of arrival of the central climax), when multiplied by 1·618, gives 411 units, and 411 units in the movement lead to the last quaver beat of bar 135. At

85

the beginning of this same bar the final climax begins, so that by the point of projected GS (411 units) this last climax is already under way; the listener, however, is now carried along for another four bars on this massive final wave until its triple-*forte* culmination.

In turn the final point of resolution after 436 units (bar 139) divides the 50 units between the beginning of the final peak and the end of the movement in the ratio 32:18 (=16:9 crotchets), giving GS accurate to the nearest crotchet beat—as near as is practicable in the context.

Taking this together with the sequence seen in Fig. 7.8 then defines the exact positioning of the divisions that lead the movement to its close. This is shown in Fig. 7.9.

Fig. 7.9

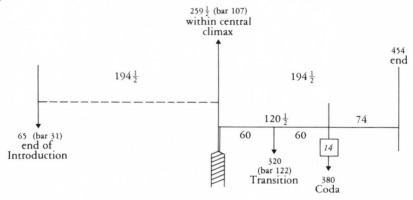

Between the first occurrence of the tonic key, at the start of the First Principal Section, and the similarly pentatonic close of the movement, the halfway division is marked by the central climax with the ratio 194½:194½ (taking the point of measurement as 259½ units, the second beat of bar 106, well within the central climax's two-bar spread). From this follow the remaining points of division. GS of 194½ is 120·2:74·3, defining to the nearest crotchet beat the beginning of the Coda at *14*. These 120½ units leading to the Coda are then divided symmetrically 60:60 (the extra ½ is inconsequential, being more than covered by the central climax) at the beginning of the Transition section, which restores the home D♭ tonality over the dominant pedal. All the movement's points of transition, and the sequence of five sections they define, are now logically accounted for.

The difference between Figs. 7.7–7.9—dealing with the entire movement—and all the preceding diagrams in this book is that in Figs. 7.7–7.9 the tempo relationships, and therefore the proportions, are not completely indisputable as they have been in the preceding examples. But the logic, the exactitude, and particularly the congruity with the proportional systems already seen in other works: these are all too consistent to be fortuitous, and suggest inevitably that this was how Debussy either intuited or designed the form.

The 1905 edition

Why did Debussy take the unusual step of shortening a score already in print by a bar (as seen in Ex. 12 on pages 66–7)? Perhaps his only conscious consideration was to tighten the transition rhythmically, as this compression does. But if so, it is an extraordinary coincidence in view of what has just been seen by way of proportional precision. Since Debussy allowed the 1905 version into print, it is reasonable to consider its proportions too, since the change affects Fig. 7.2 here (the First Principal Section alone) and also the movement as a whole, as in Figs. 7.7–7.9.

Fig. 7.2 (page 77), already as accurate as is musically possible, suffers geometrically by having the extra bar added. The effect on Figs. 7.7–7.8 is different, though. There the central division at bars 83–4 was seen to be one crotchet beat out from exact GS. With the additional bar of the 1905 edition, the movement's length becomes 456 units instead of 454, and the transition at bars 83–4 arrives after 174 instead of 172. GS of 456 is 281:174 to nearest whole number, making this main transition completely accurate in the 1905 edition. But it brings other disadvantages: GS of 174 is 107·5:66·5, so that the end of the Introduction after 65 units is proportionally less accurate in the 1905 edition. Similarly in Fig. 7.9, in the 1905 edition the central climax arrives after 256 units instead of 254; GS of this is 158, now two units away from the first climax which arrives after 156.

The 1909 version therefore seems the happier solution in terms of keeping percentage inaccuracy to a minimum. Given the lack of any comment from Debussy, reasons for all this cannot be proved. Perhaps he even made an error of counting in 1905, noticing it only after publication. Or perhaps it was all subconscious judgment, with no counting involved – which would make Figs. 7.2–7.9 remarkable indeed! Whatever the answer, it is equally remarkable to find a third case of a small dimensional adjustment (the others being, as we have seen, in 'Jardins sous la pluie' and *L'isle joyeuse*) that is linearly inessential but proportionally very significant.

The Sibley manuscript

This is a complete draft of the entire work in short four-stave score, containing instrumental indications and consisting of twenty-one numbered loose sheets, each written upon on one side only. In effect it is Debussy's definitive pre-orchestral draft, representing quite a late stage in a work he had been preparing for at least a year and a half. The last sheet is dated 'Dimanche 5 Mars à 6^h du soir'–the same date as at the end of the manuscript full score, Ms. 967, suggesting not only that the Sibley manuscript was used to prepare Ms. 967, but also that revision of it may have continued during the preparation of Ms. 967.

Although there are no dynamics marked in the Sibley manuscript, this is not crucial, since the musical context makes it obvious that the climactic moments have to be placed as in the final score.

As the Sibley manuscript contains many alterations in various colours of ink and pencil, including added and deleted bars, it would be tempting to consider it as showing two distinct stages of preparation – the manuscript as originally drafted and the same in its final form. That conclusion has to be resisted. The original form of the manuscript cannot be guessed: since the manuscript consists of loose sheets, some pages with few or no alterations may be replacements which postdate alterations on other pages. James McKay (1977) shows examples of this in the pre-orchestral drafts of *Pelléas*, and a letter from Debussy to Jacques Durand (Debussy, 1927, 24) identifies an instance in the Sibley manuscript. 'I've reworked the end of "Jeux de vagues"…', he wrote on 13 January 1905 – less than two months before he completed the full score of *La mer*. As the end of 'Jeux de vagues' appears on pages 12 and 13 of the Sibley manuscript much as in the printed version, and with no major alterations visible, these two pages are evidently the reworked version. In addition the music there is more sparsely and hurriedly notated than elsewhere, and is on 28-stave paper instead of the 30-stave paper used for the rest of the movement; all of which confirms that these two pages are a late insertion into the Sibley manuscript.

By the same logic, even the final state of the Sibley manuscript must be treated with caution, since some alterations there may have been made when the full score was already partly written, and thus would not relate to earlier, redundant parts of the Sibley manuscript.

The following paragraphs therefore must tread carefully. For example, it would be too risky to estimate what the original dimensions of a whole movement were before alterations were made. On the other hand, a smaller section like the first movement's Introduction can more safely be attempted, since it is all contained on one manuscript page. The only risk we have to take there is to assume that all the visible revisions were entered *after* the entire Introduction had been initially written out; and this assumption is given some security by the fact that the alterations are written above and below the staves, or on spare staves, and in different ink from the main draft. The same applies to the finale's Introduction, which runs over to a second page in the Sibley manuscript, but with equal and corresponding amounts of revision marked on both those pages.[4]

Page 1 of the Sibley manuscript, containing the first movement's Introduction, is shown in facsimile as Ex. 21. As (probably) notated there initially, the section comprised only 26 bars instead of the printed 30. Bars 8–11 of the printed version occupied only two bars and bars 21–2 were omitted. The other difference from the printed version is that the tempo relationship across bars 5–6

4. Marie Rolf (1976, 35–6) has studied the evidence of the different layers of ink and pencil in this manuscript. While she has been able to determine a chronological order for some revisions, she stresses that in most cases this cannot be certain.

Ex. 21: First page of the Sibley manuscript of *La mer* (reproduced by courtesy of the Sibley Music Library of the Eastman School of Music, University of Rochester)

is evidently bar = bar, since the violins' octave B in bar 6 (top staff) is notated in dotted semibreves, and the sign ⁒ is used for the bass in both bars 5 and 6. There is also no 4/4 written in bar 6. In this version the arch form's dimensions were 5:4:5:4:8 bars, as shown in Fig. 7.10 version 1, so that the A segments together comprised 13 bars, the B segments 8 bars and the C segment 5 – a familiar sequence. Also the two A segments were related by GS (5:8 bars) and

89

the two B segments symmetrically (4:4), giving a combination of GS and symmetrical construction surrounding the central entry of the cyclic motive X.

The published bars 10–11 were then added on the lower staves of bar 9, with numbers to indicate the bar sequence, and similarly the parallel bars 21–2 were inserted on the lower staves of bar 20. (The musical congruity between those two revisions tends to confirm that both were done at the same time.) In this final form the Sibley manuscript corresponds dimensionally to the full score, as

Fig. 7.10

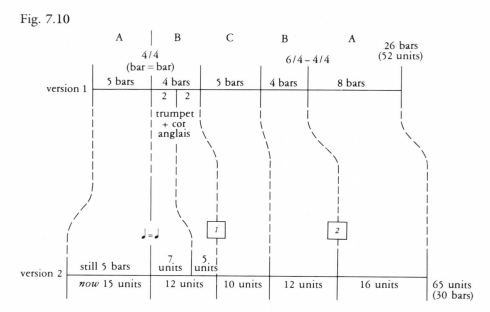

shown in version 2 in Fig. 7.10–except that the revised tempo relationship of ♩ = ♩ across bars 5–6 remains unmarked. Not much can be inferred from this, though, because Debussy may have had it firmly enough in mind not to have to write it in–or possibly even because he may by then have reached that point in the full score (Ms. 967) and notated the new tempo relationship there. (No significant proportions result from combining the expanded B segments with the original tempo relationship across bars 5–6.)

Why did Debussy change the proportions in exactly the way shown in Fig. 7.10? Presumably the main purpose was, consciously or otherwise, to match it proportionally to the movement's other sections (we shall see that there were differences there too). But there is another probable reason. On page 82 the avoidance of bisections in all of this passage was noted, and logical reasons were adduced for this. Version 1 in Fig. 7.10, however, contains one prominent bisection of 9:9 bars as well as two somewhat square blocks of 4 bars, all of whose effect is likely to be instinctively sedentary in the context of this arch form, and inappropriate to the large symphonic growth just beginning. The final version instead reserves the movement's first symmetrical division for the point

90

most apt musically, the arrival of the tonic key in bar 31, as already mentioned. All this means, incidentally, that if the evolution from version 1 to version 2 was accomplished purely by Debussy's subconscious, it must have involved complete intuitive resistance to any subconscious urge for GS or symmetrical division – that is, to the same urge as would then have organized the following sections with such GS and symmetrical precision.

The First Principal Section in the Sibley manuscript has the same dimensions as in Ms. 967 (that is, with one bar more than in the 1909 edition); but bar 80 is added only under the staff. If that addition was made after the section had been written out, as is probable, the section would previously have had the same dimensions as in the definitive 1909 edition; this will be returned to later.

The Transition and Coda sections in the Sibley manuscript again have the same dimensions as in Ms. 967 and the published scores, leaving only the the Second Principal Section to be examined. There are two differences here: bar 121 is in 6/8 rather than 12/8, and bars 115–16 were initially absent. This makes the section 10 units (2+4+4) shorter than in the published score – a total of 138 units. In this form the climax at *11* lies over the section's primary GS point, dividing the 138 units in ratio 85:53. The proportional sequence shown in Fig. 7.4 (page 80) remains unaffected by this up to *12*; only the end of the section does not fit the sequence of Fig. 7.4, and instead it has a logical place completing the dynamic GS arch just mentioned, of 85:53 units. Debussy then indicated bars 115–16 by repeat signs around bars 113–14; as these are in the same red ink as various other revisions, they were probably added later. He left bar 121 in 6/8, however, leaving the section two units shorter than in Ms. 967 and the printed scores – a point which will be returned to soon.

From all this it is evident that the music was not composed to fit rigid plans impervious to any subsequent modification. If Debussy was applying GS consciously, the plans could evidently be remodelled according to other musical demands, many of which may have been primarily instinctive ones, however consciously carried out and perfected eventually. The point again is that Debussy would never have set his intellect on the rampage without simultaneously applying his intuitive judgment. If, alternatively, he was completely unconscious of the proportions just seen, we are left with awkward logic. This is because the Sibley manuscript, even in its final state, does not have overall GS coherence, and the final score has. This would mean, therefore, that Debussy's proportional intuition failed him entirely with the large-scale dimensions in the Sibley manuscript, and then suddenly brought the form to virtually maximum accuracy in one fell swoop during the preparation of Ms. 967 – involving a changed tempo relationship that happily provided exactly the necessary dimensional adjustment.

It is notable that the Sibley manuscript's (probable) original versions of the Introduction and Second Principal Section are related by GS, the original 52 units (26 bars) of the former giving a match to within a beat of the 85:53-unit dynamic arch of the latter. But both are unrelated to the dimensions of the First

91

Principal Section. Might this suggest there was once an earlier version of the First Principal Section? If it comprised 85 units, for example, it would have resulted in an expanding GS sequence of 52:85:138 linking the first three sections. One can only speculate about what is not present. But the almost complete lack of alteration in the First Principal Section in the Sibley manuscript and the way it corresponds precisely to Ms. 967, unlike the sections on either side of it, do suggest that it could be a later draft.

We still have to account for the one discrepancy between the Sibley manuscript and the full score – the shorter unchanged version of bar 121 in the former. Although, properly, we can only hypothesize, there is a strong possibility. Had Debussy retained this shorter version in the full score, it would have brought the movement's overall length in Fig. 7.8 (page 85) down to 452 units instead of 454. GS of this is 279·4:172·6, so that the problem of proportional inaccuracy at the central transition (172 in Fig. 7.8) would have been lessened – but at the expense of greater inaccuracy within the Second Principal Section. The problem is precisely the same one that was involved in the extra bar's length Debussy added, probably at a late stage, to the Sibley manuscript (bar 80, mentioned four paragraphs above) and then effectively removed again in the 1909 edition by the compression at bar 83. All this is strong implicit evidence that Debussy was experimenting with alternative ways of obtaining maximum GS accuracy at the central transition (bars 83–4), and opted in Ms. 967 for adding a bar before this transition, rather than for keeping bar 121 two beats short – before scrapping both ideas in the 1909 score. Though this can be no more than hypothesis, it has considerable weight since it accounts for peculiarities in the Sibley manuscript, relates them to the exceptional alteration in the 1909 score, and makes sense of all that in terms of this chapter's proportional findings.

Chapter 8

'Dialogue du vent et de la mer'

'Jeux de vagues' presents particularly complex analytical problems, some of which will be more easily understood in the light of 'Dialogue du vent et de la mer'; the latter is therefore examined first.

This finale balances 'De l'aube à midi' in a number of ways: by restoring the Db tonality, the cyclic motive *X*, and the trombones and timpani, all of which were absent in 'Jeux de vagues'. It also ties some of the first movement's loose ends together, particularly by taking motives *E* and *X*, which in the first movement had been set somewhat on pedestals, and knitting them tightly into the symphonic structure, also using *E* again in the coda, at bar 258 (see Ex. 22).

Ex. 22

motive *X*

motive *E*

But this symmetrical tendency is double-edged: other characteristics of 'De l'aube à midi' are inverted in the finale. In the first movement the sections were thematically contrasted and firmly separated by changes of metre and tempo; the finale instead provides frequent returns of its main motivic material and maintains a constant 2/2 metre with only one sharp break in the music's flow. This break – a sudden silence – comes at the end of the movement's Introduction (*46*), whose equivalent in the first movement (bars 30–1) had given the smoothest of all the transitions metrically and texturally. In the first movement the idea of recapitulation was played down as much as possible; by contrast, in the finale the central focus in the entire form is a deliberately long-drawn-out perfect cadence to the tonic Db in bar 157 – the key's first occurrence in the major since the first movement. To underline this, the perfect cadence is given the stage completely to itself in the six bars after *54*, with not the slightest thematic activity to distract from it. No other movement in Debussy's output makes such an issue of the tonic key; here it is too large an event to be significant to this movement alone, and the purpose can only be to imply a recapitulative relationship, tonally at least, with the first movement.

If the movement is regarded in rondo terms, as it usually is, the main divisions come at bars 56, 157 (or 159) and 245, marked by the principal entries of the refrain theme *F* (Ex. 23), corresponding with returns to the tonic key or its enharmonic C♯ minor. But this way of labelling the movement runs into a musical difficulty, because it makes nothing of the important point of regeneration at bar 211, just after the movement's central climax. This point is the beginning of a sustained dynamic accumulation leading right to the end of the movement, and so dramatically it is illogical to separate bars 245 onwards (the final return of *F*) from what precedes them. If we look closer, we can also see that the order in which the themes reappear between bars 211 and 257 – *X*, *G* and *F* – is the exact reverse of their order of presentation in the section from bar 56 (figure *46*) onwards.

Ex. 23

motive *F*   motive *G*

By moving the last division accordingly (and thus retaining thematic consistency while recognizing the movement's dynamic shape), the main divisions are more logically placed at bars 56 (figure *46*), 157 and 211. More surprising perhaps, what this gives us is an entirely logical, if very unusual, specimen of sonata form, preceded by an Introduction up to *46*. The main themes of the exposition, *F*, *G* and *X*, are reversed in the recapitulation; *E* on the other hand first serves as a codetta to the exposition (bar 133) and then introduces the coda to the entire movement at bar 258. Whether or not Debussy thought consciously in terms of those labels, it is most noteworthy that the coda and codetta here are brought in with the same motive, *E*, as the first movement's coda. The sonata form's main outlines are shown below:

	Introduction	Exposition	Development	Recapitulation	and Coda
bars	1–55	56–156	157–210	211–57	258–92

Its main difference from the orthodox sonata model results from its exact reversal of traditional tonal procedure. The perfect cadence in bar 157 marks the beginning of the development section as the movement's tonal centre instead of the traditional tonic centre at the recapitulation. To balance this the recapitulation, led into from bar 211, avoids any immediate sense of arrival or tonal return. Instead it begins a chromatic sequence which gradually becomes diatonic at bar 245, but which is not cadentially resolved until well into the Coda, at *61*. Also, as the development section is concerned solely with motive *F* (the first subject), the Recapitulation sensibly avoids beginning with it, by reversing the Exposition's thematic order. The main results of all this are to 'earth' the central part of the movement tonally, and, conversely, to shift tonal and dynamic tension towards the end of the movement.

The prominence of bar 157 as the movement's tonal centre of gravity is further emphasized by the relative softening of the two tonic arrivals at the beginning and end of the sonata form, at *46* and *61*. Both are approached, like bar 157, via a dominant pedal; but at *46* the enharmonic minor tonality is given instead, and between *60* and *61* the Coda intervenes to prevent a perfect cadence, which is similarly avoided by the series of three cadences, from *61* onwards, that completes the work.

This view of the movement also corresponds with its dynamic shape: not only in the matter of a rhythmically animated Exposition and Recapitulation surrounding a warmly lyrical central Development section, but also as a sequence (following the Introduction) of three dynamic waves, the first breaking at *51* just before the Codetta, the second at *57* just before the Recapitulation, and the third building up all through the Recapitulation to the work's final chord. This is also the same type of sequence of climaxes – a sharply focused one, then a more lyrical one, and finally a cumulative one – as in the first movement. (True, the overall crescendo of the Introduction is extra to this, but as it is cut short at *46* without properly breaking, its momentum tends to be carried over into the Exposition.)

Proportions

By the sonata-form classification the movement's sectional dimensions are as below:

	Introduction	Exposition	Development	Recapitulation	Coda
bar totals:	55	101	54	47	35
				↘ 82 ↙	

There is no obviously significant proportional link between any two consecutive parts of the form; again, any other apparent relationships can mean little until the movement has been examined more closely. This continues the contrast with the first movement, where the sections were set apart by changes of metre but related proportionally; here the converse obtains. The sharp break between the Introduction and the following sonata form, however, suggests that the Introduction should be investigated initially on its own.

On a superficial level this Introduction serves as a transition from 'Jeux de vagues' to the main part of the finale, incorporating a steady overall crescendo. It begins by restoring the timpani (bar 1) which had been absent from 'Jeux de vagues', and ends after 55 bars by restoring (enharmonically) the work's main key. The remaining instrumental restoration, that of the trombones, is made in bar 35 – after 34, the primary GS point of the Introduction.

The other restoration – of the cyclic motive X – comes just before, and this leads into more complex aspects of the passage. In the course of the Introduction's gradual crescendo towards *46*, it strongly evokes the idea of passing through the eye of a storm, with its tonal clashes, occasional *subito* dynamics and uneven phrase sequences – a programmatic analogy brought to mind specially by the tensed stillness of bars 30–42, with their brittle orchestration, framed by the turbulent motion in the rest of the Introduction. The basic tonal motion (essentially a IV–V progression) is in fact very slow, enabling the tension to be controlled precisely by the harmonic changes at bars 22, 30 and 43, giving maximum dramatic prominence to bars 30–42, before the chromaticism channels itself into the dominant pedal between *45* and *46*.

These transitions also articulate the section motivically, dividing the Introduction's 55 bars into sections of 21:8:13:13 bars. If the divisions are linked in an order of increasing dramatic intensity, surrounding the central renderings of motive X, a GS spiral results, as shown in Fig. 8.1 – a return, this time even more thoroughly carried out, of the spiral shape already encountered in the first movement (Fig. 7.2 on page 77). As in Fig. 7.2 the focus of the spiral is again at the work's cyclic motive (in this case dividing the two statements of the theme), and musically the swirling textures and circular alternations of motives and registers are equally evocative of vortexes or whirlpools.

The possible symbolism of this shape, and its other artistic manifestations, are discussed more in Chapter 11. But it is worth mentioning here that spirals are recognized as a recurrent motive in many of J. M. W. Turner's seascapes, which also probably influenced many moments in *La mer*; Debussy once described Turner as 'le plus beau créateur de mystère qui soit en art' (Debussy, 1927, 58). This, too, is discussed more in Chapter 11.

Smaller subdivisions, shown lower in Fig. 8.1, again follow Fibonacci ordering. Bars 1–21 form the longest and most complex segment, constructed as $A_1B_1A_2B_2$ in the ratio 8:4:5:4. This means that $A_1:A_2 = 8:5$ (GS), $B_1:B_2 = 4:4$ (symmetry), and A_1+A_2 (GS) : B_1+B_2 (symmetry) = 13:8.[1] The music matches this, the turbulent bass in the GS-related A segments contrasted with

1. These are exactly the same numerical relationships as between the A and B segments in the early version of the first movement's Introduction (version 1 in Fig. 7.10), described on pages 89–90 above.

Fig. 8.1

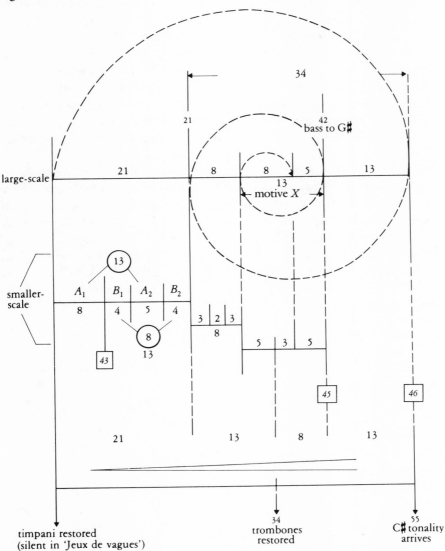

the forced stillness of the symmetrically related B segments. It is apt that the movement, with its title, should begin with such a dialogue between the dual elements of GS and symmetry, made musically very audible.

Exposition

Dramatically the Exposition is dominated by the chromatic climax at *51*. Coming as the culmination of undoubtedly the wildest passage in all of *La mer*, this tremendous eruption at *51* is prepared by two partly independent sequences.

One is thematic, introducing the Exposition's principal motives, *F*, *G* and *X*, at bars 56, 72 and 96. The other is tonal, and is a model of Debussy's use of block construction (as was the Introduction). Diatonic harmony from *46* to bar *79* (with no tonic pedal this time) is set against a completely chromatic passage in bars 80–93, which in turn gives way at bar 94 to whole tones, fortified by ostinatos – with just one chromatic twist in bar 113 to open the way for the chromatic explosion five bars later in the repetition of the same phrase. This block construction, is emphasized by substantial dynamic increases at the two divisions. Only after the climax does tonality gradually reassert itself, via the Codetta in bar 133 and then the dominant pedal, established decisively in bar 145, leading to the perfect cadence that closes the Exposition.[2]

Both tonally and dynamically, then, the Exposition forms a powerful arch, whose proportions are shown in Fig. 8.2. The climax, breaking halfway through the bar of *51*, defines the GS of the entire Exposition, accurate to the nearest half bar, and the two harmonic–dynamic turning points at bars 80 and 94 (after bars 79 and 93) mark the two intermediate points of GS on the way, accurate to nearest whole bars. The Codetta enters at the GS between the climax and the end of the section (14½:24 bars) and these last 24 bars are then divided 12:12 by the diatonic arrival of the dominant pedal at bar 145, completing this virtual model of a comprehensively articulated GS dynamic arch.

Fig. 8.2

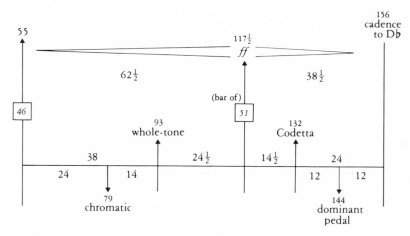

Motivically, the entry of *X* at bar 98, completing the Exposition's main thematic sequence (apart from the Codetta), comes 68 bars after the segment of

2. It could reasonably be argued that the Exposition should include the cadential resolution, thus finishing only with bar 158. This would be merely a variant of labelling, which leaves the proportions between the musical events – crucially, here, the perfect cadence – unchanged.

the Introduction, at bar 30, where X made its earlier entry.[3] The two other main themes between them, F and G, entering at *46* and *47*, mark the two GS points of these 68 bars, forming a sequence of 26:16:26 bars (=13:8:13).

Development

Both musically and proportionally, the Exposition is a particularly self-contained structure, and by its completion with the cadence at bar 157 the music, exhausted, virtually comes to a standstill – now the most static moment in all of *La mer*. Having arrived at D♭ major the music makes no further move for two bars, until motive F re-enters in bar 159, leaving 52 bars of actual development before the Recapitulation. These form a smaller ternary scheme, divided first by the point of tonal departure at bar 179, where the tonic pedal is abandoned and the key signature cancelled, and secondly by the subsequent tonic return, *forte*, at *56*. The first of these, the tonal departure, marks the secondary GS point of this ternary form (20:32 bars), and the second, the tonal return, divides those remaining 32 bars 16:16. The final 16 bars are then divided 8:8 by the arrival of the climax at *57*, so that the approach to this climax gathers its momentum from a series of four 8-bar phrases leading into it from *55*, and subsequently into the Recapitulation eight bars later. This part of the movement, traced in Fig. 8.3,

Fig. 8.3

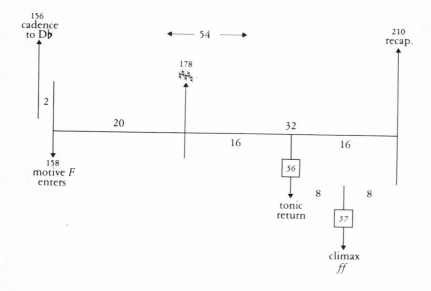

3. Although X itself enters only in bar 31 rather than bar 30, it obviously dominates the passage; the *sforzando* in bar 30 is the dominating dramatic moment with which the listener would associate the immediate entry of X. The reason for this piece of proportional poetic licence will be seen later in this chapter; in the Sibley manuscript X originally entered in the same bar as the *sforzando*.

forms another architectural model of GS and symmetrical combination – the third one encountered in this movement – its relative simplicity in keeping with this section's musical simplicity.

Incidentally, the prominence of four- and eight-bar groups in this section underlines (or underlies) the more lyrical effect of the climax at *57*, with no heavy brass or timpani, after the much wilder climax at *51* whose approach, however sequential, had avoided any such regular phrase lengths.

Recapitulation

Taken on its own the Recapitulation section forms no logical proportional pattern. This should come as no surprise if we consider its musical context. Unlike the Exposition and Development it enters as a harmonic interruption, tonally unstable. With its rhythmic intensification ('en serrant peu à peu') and the following reversal of thematic order, bar 211 takes on the aspect of a structural pivot, balancing the two surrounding sections. That is one reason for viewing the Recapitulation together with what precedes it. Another reason is that each of the earlier sections, though forming a self-contained system, is nonetheless based on a different set of numbers, so that taken together they do not form a proportionally continuous sequence. Given their internal proportional exactitude, it would be odd were this aspect to be ignored now with the movement's larger outlines. Since the Recapitulation musically binds together the contrasted preceding sections, it could logically have a similar proportional role.

Fig. 8.4 traces the Recapitulation's thematic sequence, taken together with the Development section. Motive *X* returns first in bar 215, four bars after the beginning of the Recapitulation section. Motive *G* follows 10 bars after the recapitulation point; motive *F* arrives 34 bars after the recapitulation point; and

Fig. 8.4

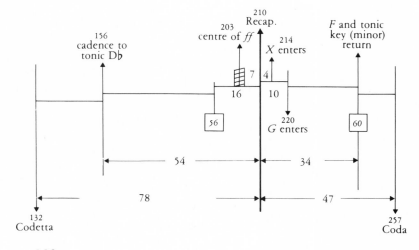

the Coda 47 bars after. These four main events in the Recapitulation complete four GS balances across the recapitulation point: 7:4 bars from the centre of the central climax; 16:10 bars from motive *F*'s entry at *56*; 54:34 bars, linking the main tonic cadence at bar 157 to the Recapitulation's enharmonic tonic return at *60*; and finally 78:47 bars, linking the beginning of the Codetta to the beginning of the Coda. In short, the thematic sequence in the Recapitulation, up to the Coda, provides an exact mirroring, refracted by GS around the recapitulation point, of the proportional spacing of the most prominent events leading up to it from the Codetta onwards – just as the thematic order of the Recapitulation also mirrors the thematic order of the Exposition.

These last two divisions, of 54:34 and 78:47, give slightly less than maximum GS accuracy (55:34 would obviously be more ideal, and GS of 125 is 77·25:47·75). Both, however, provide GS division of the overall distance involved accurate to within three-quarters of a bar (within 1%); reasons for the marginal inaccuracy will be seen shortly.

Fig. 8.5 supplements Fig. 8.4 by tracing tonal and dynamic relationships between the Development and the Recapitulation. As already mentioned, the Recapitulation accumulates dynamic intensity all the way to the end of the

Fig. 8.5

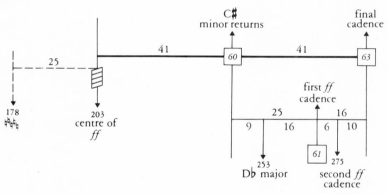

movement, reaching its final triple-*forte* via a sequence of three *fortissimo* cadences to the tonic, at *61*, bar 276 and *63*. The central tonic return before these is at *60* (enharmonically, before moving to the major at bar 254) – the first diatonic moment since the movement's central climax at *57*. This tonic return at *60* lies exactly halfway between the centre of the central climax and the final cadence (41:41 bars), and the intermediate points of progressive tonal resolution subdivide the latter 41 bars in GS of 25:16, 9:16 and 6:10. The earlier tonal departure in the Development section (bar 179) forms an additional GS balance of 25:41 in this sequence.

101

The entire movement

Fig. 8.4 has already extended itself back inside the Exposition. Fig. 8.6 now shows the formal outlines of the entire movement. The movement's central point of tonal focus, the perfect cadence at bar 157 that ends the Exposition, is situated exactly halfway (101:101 bars) between Introduction and Coda. The Codetta, at bar 133, forms the secondary GS of the same 202 bars (77:125) on the way to the Coda. Smaller symmetrical divisions then result (all accurate to the nearest bar) around both the central cadence and the later tonic return at *56*; these tonally stable symmetrical divisions form the logical counterpart to the cluster of GS divisions around the Recapitulation, already seen in Fig. 8.4. Around this framework, the Introduction and Coda form a GS balance of 55:35 bars. (The small inaccuracy here is inevitable, since to remove it would either distort Figs. 8.4–8.5 or else make the movement's last chord too short.)

Fig. 8.6

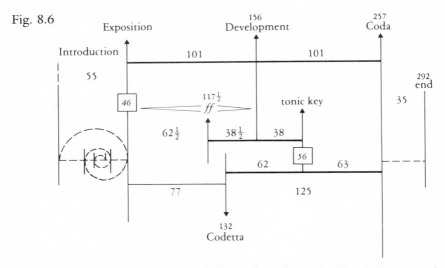

The dynamic sequence is equally logical, as shown in Fig. 8.7. Just as the first climax breaks at the primary GS of the Exposition, the second one breaks within a bar of the primary GS of the whole sonata form, dividing it 147:90 at figure *57*. As already mentioned, this is a more lyrical climax than the other two; accordingly the exact centre of its two-bar spread gives a symmetrical division of 85½:86 bars between the first and third climaxes. (The apparent half-bar inaccuracy is more than covered by the two-bar spread of the climax.) The beginning of the Coda then divides the 90 bars from the onset of the central climax to the movement's end in near-GS of 55:35 bars, and those first 55 are subdivided 34:21 by the subsidiary *forte* at bar 237.[4]

4. This intermediate peak in bars 237–44 was made more prominent in the 1905 edition by the fanfares for trumpet and horn (discussed on page 65 above) that Debussy removed in the 1909 edition.

Fig. 8.7

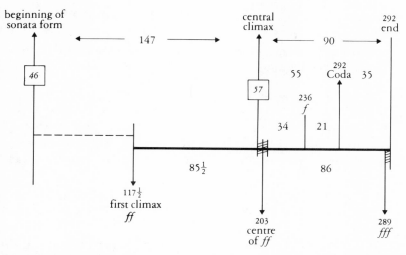

The ratio of 147:90 subtended at the beginning of the central climax is again not maximum GS precision (GS of 237 is 146·4:90·6); nor is the 55:35 ratio from there to the end. Once again, to remove the one inaccuracy would exacerbate the other. Therefore the small degree of inaccuracy inevitable when combining so many sequences is spread as logically as possible among the various sequences concerned, reserving maximum accuracy for the most important proportional divisions, and with no inaccuracy exceeding one bar. In fact there is no proportional detail in Figs. 8.2–8.7 that could be made more accurate than it already is without causing greater inaccuracy elsewhere. (The reader is encouraged to try.)

Another strong numerical tendency worth mentioning in passing is that the movement's final cadence, the last of a sequence of three cadences (*61* onwards), brings to its completion the third dynamic wave in a sonata structure based on three themes and forming the last of three movements, the first of which also contained three different types of tripartite wave sequence.

The entire movement provides some striking parallels with the first movement:

(1) Both are divided into five sections (counting the Coda as a distinct section in each case).
(2) Both contain a tripartite dynamic sequence with the same progression of climaxes (sharp; more lyrical; and finally cumulative).
(3) In both movements the central climax relates the dynamic sequence proportionally to the formal outline – characteristics 1 and 2 above – as well as marking the convergence of other proportional sequences.
(4) In both movements the Coda, with the same theme, begins at the primary GS between the central climax and the end of the movement.

103

(5) Both movements contain a circular type of construction – the spirals of Figs. 7.2 and 8.1 – in each case contained within clearly defined areas of musical asymmetry and tonal instability.

Simultaneous with this are two direct inversions, in addition to the tonal and metrical ones already mentioned on pages 93 and 95:

(1) In the first movement the central climax is placed symmetrically in the form – between the end of the Introduction and the end of the movement – but by GS in the dynamic sequence. In the finale these roles are reversed: the central climax forms the GS between the end of the Introduction and the end of the movement, but the halfway point between the other two climaxes.

(2 – more abstract, but nonetheless geometrically present) The GS spiral's reappearance in the finale is in mirrored form. In the first movement (Fig. 7.2 on page 77) the spiral is closed at the beginning and open at the end – reflecting that movement's expansive, open-ended form. In the finale (Fig. 8.1 on page 97) it is open at the beginning and closed at the end – this time visually reflecting its independence from the following sonata form.

In another tonal (non-proportional) respect the finale mirrors the first movement. As mentioned before, the finale's Introduction leads to the tonic at *46* by a IV–V–I sequence. This mirrors the V–IV–I sequence that was used to soften the final tonic return in the first movement (bars 122–35), and thereby emphasizes the finale's recapitulative aspects, played down in the first movement. The later return to D♭ in the finale (bar 157) repeats this IV–V–I sequence in a slightly elaborated version, the dominant pedal of bar 145 being approached via the subdominant F♯/C bass of the climax at *51* and their relative of E♭ in the Codetta.

In a number of ways, then, the finale not only balances the first movement but also recapitulates its sequences and geometrical characteristics. That in doing so it returns many of these in mirrored form is itself reflected on a smaller scale by the mirroring of thematic order in the finale's own internal Recapitulation. This relationship between the movements is returned to in Chapter 9.

The finale's proportional framework remains in one respect mysterious. Fig. 8.6 (on page 102) shows a large amount of proportional attention given to the beginning of the Coda. This point is visually more prominent, too, in the Sibley manuscript, where the brass chorale enters at the Coda with no other accompaniment – the string parts having been notated only at the full score stage. From this point of view one could describe the movement's overall proportional outlines as defining most strongly an Introduction and Coda related by GS (55:35), enclosing a main portion of 202 bars, divided principally 101:101. That is to say, the GS-related Introduction and Coda (55:35 bars) are separated by the 101:101-

bar division in Fig. 8.6 which bears no such relationship to them. Figs. 8.2–8.6 have shown various sequences linking them all through internal events. But there is another connection, involving the spiral structure of Fig. 8.1. As mentioned earlier, this is a particularly esoteric type of geometric structure to find in music, yet the strong evocations of vortexes or whirlpools in this passage suggest that Debussy was at least instinctively aware of the shape involved, and that our using a spiral in Fig. 8.1 is more than just a fanciful abstraction. This is corroborated further by the spiral's centripetal motion, which follows the well-defined gradation of tension in the passage.

The enigmatic way Debussy 'captures pictorial associations of sound in the identity of space and time' (Eimert, 1961, 9) in this passage suggests that more intricacies might lurk; and indeed they do. It is possible to measure the circumferences of such spirals, following an equation known for centuries. The calculation is supplied on pages 183–5 below as Appendix 1, and yields the information that the logarithmic curve of Fig. 8.1, with its 900° circumvolution, would measure in length within one unit of 202 of the units by which the radii are measured. As these units here are bars, this means that the spiral's length, if unrolled, would occupy, to within a bar, the 202-bar length of the movement's main portion between the Introduction and the GS-related Coda.

It is not impossible that this more abstruse correspondence is simply fortuitous; but the musical context and other structural patterns involved make it more than extraordinary if it is. If it is not purely fortuitous it must have been planned; since the spiral itself is not part of the music's temporal sequence, this correspondence could not possibly have been intuited by a temporal instinct. (And even if this particular numerical correspondence is fortuitous, it leaves the importance of all the other proportional relationships unaffected.)

The Sibley manuscript

Perhaps the most surprising evidence from the Sibley manuscript in the finale is that the Introduction appears not to have been originally written out there by Fibonacci proportions. Ex. 24 shows it in facsimile. Instead of the printed bars 22–9 Debussy wrote six quite different bars of 3/4, whose contents indicate that the tempo relationship must have been ♩ = ♪ of the 2/2 sections (a parallel to the metrical sequence in the piano *Prélude* 'Ce qu'a vu le vent d'ouest', which has many affinities with this Introduction). The other three differences are that the printed two bars 13–14 were initially written as one bar, likewise the printed three bars 30–2 (motive X entering immediately – cf. note 3 on page 99), and that the printed bar 55 was absent, the previous bar finishing on G♯ instead of G♮. This gave the passage a total of 52 units (the six 3/4 bars at half speed count as equal to nine 2/2 bars). While this did not invalidate the logic of Fig. 8.1 either musically or proportionally, as Fig. 8.8 shows, the proportional accuracy was

Ex. 24: Introduction of 'Dialogue' in the Sibley manuscript of *La mer* (reproduced by courtesy of the Sibley Music Library of the Eastman School of Music, University of Rochester)

much weaker at the centre of the spiral, mainly because the 3/4 passage could not be made to give the exact dimensional equivalent of eight 2/2 bars.

Fig. 8.8: (Probable) original dimensions of Introduction in the Sibley manuscript

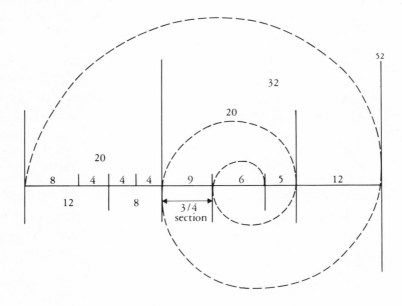

Evidently, then, Debussy did not write the passage down from a pre-planned Fibonacci 'map'. On the other hand this does not preclude the possibility that he might initially have intended it to comprise 52 units, a possibility lent extra weight by the probability that the Introduction to the first movement also initially comprised 52 units in the Sibley manuscript (version 1 in Fig. 7.10 on page 90). (It will be seen in Chapter 9 that the units are connected.) When the first movement's Introduction was changed, there would then be no point in preserving the same unit dimensions in the finale's Introduction, and the more apt Fibonacci numbers could be used. Whether or not Debussy was conscious of those factors, that is what happened. (Or, in view of how completely logical the proportional system is in its final state, might even the 52-unit version of the Sibley manuscript have been a compromise from an original Fibonacci model which Debussy finally was able to realize?)

The alterations from the 52-unit version to the final 55-unit (55-bar) one are written in the Sibley manuscript, above and below staves and in various colours of ink and crayon, with the number of deletions and re-alterations indicating considerable trouble taken over this section's revision.[5] Apart from the replacement of the 3/4 passage, though, the changes are merely slight extensions of the material already there – not a complicated process, which makes the enormous trouble visibly taken seem difficult to account for in ordinary musical terms. It would, however, be consistent with the idea of Debussy carefully accommodating the existing music to an amended dimensional framework – with the exception of the 3/4 passage which could not be made to fit and so was discarded.

In its final form, rather oddly, the Exposition in the Sibley manuscript remains two bars shorter than in the printed score: bar 103 is present but scored out and bar 109 is absent, reducing the Exposition's length there to 99 bars. This is hard to account for immediately, as the remainder of the movement in the Sibley manuscript's final form corresponds dimensionally to the printed score. The Sibley manuscript does, however, contain some visible changes later in the movement, and it is not impossible that those were made *after* the longer version of the Exposition had been written in the full score. Most notably, bars 189–94 initially occupied only two bars and bars 211–14 likewise, before being altered. The resulting (probable) shorter version of the main part of the movement matches the original shorter version of the Introduction, so that the spiral length relationship would still apply. Such ideas can only be tentative for reasons already discussed; but the most striking evidence there is that bars 189–94 are notated only in pencil and squashed into the space of two bars that had initially been left blank, with the music inked in on either side. Therefore at least in that passage Debussy appears to have decided the dimensions (provisionally, since he later changed them) *before* writing in some of the music.

The manuscript evidence now seen suggests a general hypothesis about working methods. Although it has been most logical here to trace the proportional systems, already present and fixed, by considering the smaller formal units before the larger ones, this would not necessarily have been Debussy's order of construction if he did plan them consciously. In the outer movements of *La mer* the most feasible strategy would have been to plan the large-scale outlines first, even if smaller-scale exigencies within this (such as the important eight-bar sequences

5. Among the changes in the Sibley manuscript, the later version of bars 25–6 is marked to be repeated, but this idea was abandoned in the full score. Possibly it was meant as an alternative to the final version of bars 27–8.

in the central section of 'Dialogue'), might later have necessitated large-scale adjustments to maintain the overall proportions. This would be exactly in keeping with the dimensional alterations seen in the Sibley manuscript.

Chapter 9

'Jeux de vagues'

In many respects the boldest of Debussy's creations up to 1905, this movement is one of the most elusive to intellectual comprehension. The main difficulty is that although it can easily be divided into sections, these, unlike the sequence of 'De l'aube à midi', are small and numerous. They also contain thematic cross-references, but in an unpredictable order that defies any consistent traditional classification.

This is compounded by the way those fragments merely touch on, rather than commit themselves to, clearly definable formal centres. There are brief thematic returns – of motives *H*, *J* and *K*, for example (see Ex. 25) – but they follow entirely different courses on each occasion. Extended periods of tonal stability of the type seen in the outer movements are similarly eschewed. Although the most clearly defined tonal centre is E major, first established at *19*, it is questioned even then by C♮s; these are given just time to resolve, in bars 38–9 and 42–3, before the music swings away from E and the harp's whole-tone glissandi at *20* sweep the board tonally clean. Not until *33* do the same figure and tonal centre return briefly, but now even the resolution is withdrawn: the C♮, now a B♯, moves upwards instead to C♯, and the music swerves off, after only eight bars of near-reprise, on a new course leading to the movement's main climax at *38*. Not until the Coda is a stable E major established, and then only at the movement's final cadence, at *41*.

Ex. 25

motive *H*

motive *J*

motive *K*

110

Logically we have to acknowledge this enigmatic mixture of open-ended and closed formal aspects (rather than opt solely for one aspect, as many analyses tend to do); a type of architectural counterpoint, it is one of various dualities that make this movement such an intriguing one. But the question remains: can this sequence of mostly short segments be viewed more coherently in terms of a larger framework? Among all the transitions, four stand out as main points of reference, or cross-reference. At *16* the movement's main recurring motive, *H*, first enters, underlined by the change to 3/8 time; at *19* the main key of E is first reached and the 3/4 metre returns; at *25* the themes start to return, again beginning with motive *H*; and at *33* comes the movement's nearest approach to literal reprise, already described.

These main transitions point out another important duality in the movement. As *H* is the most frequently recurring motive (it also ends the movement), in thematic terms the main part of the movement begins at *16* and the reprise at *25*. (All the material from *25* onwards either repeats or develops motives heard between *16* and *25*.) Tonally, however, the main part of the movement begins at *19*, with the reprise (as near as can be called one) at *33*. This is why most existing analyses of the movement disagree as to whether the Introduction ends at *16* or *19*, depending on whether their priority is thematic or tonal. The other peculiarity arising from this duality is that the movement's main recurring motive, *H*, is dissociated from the tonic key right until the final cadence, at *41* – a complete contrast from pieces such as 'Reflets dans l'eau' or *L'isle joyeuse*, or indeed 'Dialogue du vent et de la mer'.

This duality can be kept in focus if we view the movement as two overlapping binary systems, the thematic one divided round *25* and the tonal one round *33*. This is shown in Fig. 9.1.

Fig. 9.1

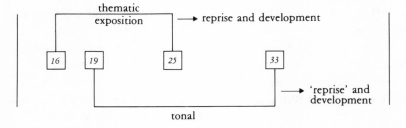

The thematic reprise at *25*, in A major, also forms a tonal midway point between, and a relative key to, the F♯/C polarity of the related opening section up to *19*. After *25*, though, the thematic order changes: motive *J* and the harp glissandi (originally the portion from figure *19* to bar 49) are taken out of the sequence and moved, much expanded, to between *33* and *40*, the harp glissandi now introducing the Coda at *39*.

111

There are other ways in which the movement's segments are linked. A device found often in Debussy's music, but never used so consistently as in 'Jeux de vagues', is that of overlapping two consecutive musical segments texturally. That is, the rhythmic and orchestral texture of the new segment enters before the phrase of the previous one has finished. A model example occurs at *21*: it is hard to define whether the new segment begins at *21* itself or two bars later, and Debussy undoubtedly intended the ambiguity. Other examples are the ten bars of violin trills leading into *33*, and the A♯ harp ostinato leading into and over *29*. In the latter case the ambiguity is doubled as the new theme does not enter until four bars after the harmonic change at *29*. To a less marked degree this operates at *16*, by means of the previous bar's sextuplet semiquavers which antipicate the new rhythm, and also in the four bars preceding *19*, where the trills in the descending bass line anticipate those of the violins at *19*.

The resulting conciseness is specially apt to this mercurial scherzo. But Debussy has a more definite purpose. After a sequence of smooth transitions effected thus, any subsequent sharp break will obviously stand out in relief; and Debussy plays this card twice. The first occasion is at *25*, emphasized by the complete interruption of harmonic and melodic flow, with an accompanying reduction of speed and dynamics. The other sharp break follows quickly at *26*. Evidently Debussy wants to draw our attention at those two points: on the first occasion he seems to be saying 'Now the themes return'; and on the second, 'but not in the same order'.

Three transitions sit texturally on the fence. At *20* the legato violin line prevents a break in texture, but the harps still disrupt the tonality in an unexpected way. Similarly at *39* the legato bass ensures continuity, despite the unexpected return of the harps. At bar 118 the transition is smooth, but there is no overlap of any special textural or rhythmic figure beyond the 3/4 metre.

In fact all the movement's transitions between segments have now been listed. (The double-bars at *17* and *18* have not been counted, as they are linked by motive *H* on all sides.) What has emerged is still enigmatic: no consistent purpose is evident except for the underlining of events at *25* and *26*, nor is the sequence consistent with the divisions in Fig. 9.1. With this ambiguity added to the others, Debussy's aim appears to be to ensure that the movement never falls into any simple recognizable pattern.

A further way of grouping the segments comes from the dynamic sequence. As not all the segments lead to a dynamic culmination, there is obviously a greater sense of renewal after those that do – affecting the segments beginning at *19*, *23*, bar 118, *29*, *33* and *39*. (For convenience they are defined here mostly by the thematic entries, but the ambiguities caused by textural overlaps have not been forgotten.) In this sense the movement also breathes in a series of dynamic paragraphs. Again this system does not specially favour the main pillars in Fig. 9.1; and it is further complicated by the way *25* and *26* jump the gun, dynamically. To be specific, *25* cuts in to prevent an incipient culmination, and *26* conversely supplies one without any preparation (unlike all the other dynamic peaks in the movement).

If this complexity of processes still leaves us with little understanding of what this movement's purpose is, expressively or architecturally, it is reassuring to remember that one crucial aspect still awaits attention. The reshuffling of thematic order after *26*, postponing the reprise of motive *J* until after *33*, is quite plainly directed towards the movement's dominating event, the final climax at *38*, and the long approach to it that imparts it most of its force. This is clear from the long pedal point, the sustained melody in the strings, and the constant four-bar phrases from bar 171 onwards – all in contrast to the fragmentariness all through the first half or so of the movement. (This technique of avoiding sustained melody until late in a piece is a speciality of Debussy's, taken to its extreme in 1912 in *Jeux*, which avoids sustained melody altogether until more than three-quarters of the way through a twenty-minute score.)

One large-scale tendency does emerge from the dynamic sequence in 'Jeux de vagues'. Up to *25* there are only two dynamic culminations (an incipient third one is forestalled at *25*). After *25*, however, they suddenly become more frequent, arriving suddenly in an unpredictable sequence, until from *29* onwards the dynamic shape broadens out again, now with long sustained crescendos to the final two peaks at *32* and *38*.

This provides the movement's most dynamic duality. All the climaxes up to *29* erupt with little warning and with a minimum of crescendo preparation. By contrast the final two, at *32* and *38*, are irreversibly led to by the entire content of the longer segments preceding them, building up their tension through pedal points and ostinatos. In convenient terms, borrowed from Schenker (as in Chapter 4 above), dynamics clearly move from a foreground (surface) role in the form before *29* to a background (fundamental) one after *29*.

Fluctuations in the movement's tempo emphasize this duality. After the rapid motion at *16*, the climax at *18* is followed immediately by a strong rallentando leading into the $\downarrow$ = 138 at *19*. By bar 62 this is already giving way, and the second peak, at bar 72, pulls the tempo back further to $\downarrow$ = 112 at *23*, a tempo which dominates until after *31* – that is, until the movement begins to breathe in a much broader way.[1] Various dynamic peaks in between are introduced by spurts of speed that immediately dissipate themselves in the peaks (as at bars 115 and 126), letting the music then return to the slower tempo. The slowest stretch of the movement, between *23* and approximately *31*, thus corresponds exactly with the highest density of dynamic peaks.

1. The instruction $\downarrow$ = 112 at *23*, present in the manuscript full score, Ms. 967, is missing in all the Durand editions; it was probably overlooked because Debussy marked it only over the first violin stave. The recent Peters edition restores it. Although it is surprising that Debussy overlooked it when proof-reading, it is not the only case of his carelessness with proofs (another example, the missing accidentals in *L'isle joyeuse*, has already been described in Chapter 5). Its presence is necessary to make sense both of the 'Cédez' four bars earlier and of the later instruction 'au Mouvement $\downarrow$ = 112' at *25*.

There are also quite precise thematic connections with this, an aspect Laurence Berman remarked upon in a paper given in 1974.[2] Noting the dominance of the final climax at *38* over the movement's shape and form, Berman pointed out how various events on the way there set up an alternation of impediments and forward impulses, before the final forward sweep towards *38* gets properly under way. He singled out the passage between *26* and bar 117 (motive *K*) as representative of forward motion, in contrast to the surrounding entries of *H* at *25* and bar 118, both of which obstruct forward impetus, pulling the tempo back to ♩ = 112 after prior spurts of increased speed.

This can be developed in more detail. Motive *K*'s legato line and longer note values, as against *H*'s uneven rhythm and triplet semiquavers, obviously account for their contrasting effects on the music's flow. Similarly motive *M* which, in a number of variants, dominates from bar 171 until *38*, has an even broader sweep, encouraging the gradual accelerando towards *38* – in contrast to *L*, whose first entry at *23* marks the first attenuation to ♩ = 112, and whose last appearance, from *38* to *39*, applies the brakes again after the headlong propulsion up to *38*.

L has another precise connection with tempo: the slowest portion of the movement, at ♩ = 112, from *23* to bar 146, is bounded by L_1 at the beginning and L_2 at the end (cf. Ex. 26). Motive *J* has a similar relationship to the faster tempo ♩ = 138: its first entry at *19* sets this tempo for the first time, and the tempo is not exceeded again until *J*'s only other entry in the movement, at *33*, is over. But here subtler aspects of context are involved. At *19*, motive *J*, with its attendant E major, ushers the music into a steady 3/4, to be followed by further reduction of speed, and other obstructions. But by *33* the return to ♩ = 138 has come about by an accelerando, not a rallentando as at *19*. The tide has turned, and *J*'s relationship to its context is now reversed: instead of calming the agitation as at *19*, it is now swept away, its attempts to re-establish E major being brusquely diverted to the new G♯ minor, and the speed now continuing to increase.

Ex. 26

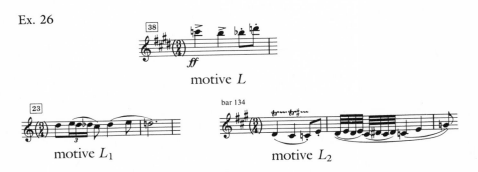

motive *L*

motive L_1

motive L_2

bar 134

2. Berman (1974). The paper remains unpublished, and I am grateful to Dr Douglass Green for drawing my attention to it.

H's role is equally affected by its environment. It has two relationships to the movement's metre: the first one is heard between *16* and *19*, and again from bar 191 onwards; the second one is effectively in rhythmic diminution, relative to the metre of three in a bar, and operates at *26* and bar 118. Rhythmically it is much clumsier in the second form, and this effect is presumably deliberate, emphasizing the element of delay at the entries at *25* and bar 118. At its next appearance, though, in bars 149–52, it is fragmented, and now it fails to prevent the tempo from beginning its resurgence to $\downarrow = 138$ at *32* (as indicated in bar 147).

It is tempting to deduce that this fragmentation is there expressly to illustrate that the surge towards the faster speed and the climax at *32* is now too powerful to be checked – an interpretation encouraged by what happens at *H*'s remaining appearances. First, it literally suffers a reverse with its appearance in retrograde, as the melodic outline of the climax at *32* (in its original key), the exact point where $\downarrow = 138$ is re-established. Its other entries (bars 191–7 and bar 227 onwards) are then made in rhythmic augmentation, its relationship to the metre restored to what it had been at *16*.

What all this suggests is that it is not so much to a motive itself that we need to pay attention as to what happens to it on each appearance. In Roger Nichols's apt phrase, 'they are signposts, not the road itself' (1980, programme 9). Effectively, the different settings and consequences of the main themes, each time they recur, act as a barometer of how and where the movement is progressing dramatically.

Returning to Laurence Berman's observations about the alternation of obstructions and forward surges, his example – the passage between *25* and *28* – appears as the central point in a larger-scale tendency. Up to *26* the music became progressively slower and denser, the delaying influence uppermost. *26* marks the first reversal of that tendency, being the first dynamic paragraph not to bring in a slower tempo; the forward-moving elements then gradually take precedence, leading the music steadily into the long-striding approach to the final climax. In this regard the delays in the central part of the movement provide a catapult-like impulse to what emerges from it. To take the formal sequence from the beginning: first of all motivic action starts, then the key is defined, then thematic recapitulation begins (emphasized by the interruptive effect of *25*); then, with all the ingredients assembled, the momentum is stepped up progressively at *29*, bar 142, bar 147, *32*, *33*, bar 171, *35*, and finally bar 199. Timing is obviously crucial to such a finely judged sequence, and thus also proportions.

Discussion of this movement has been particularly necessary before measuring its proportions. With this movement's density of events, numerical coincidences are bound to appear; but they can mean little unless they involve significant musical relationships – in this case, the counterpoint of the various levels of musical action just discussed.

Proportions

From *19* to the end of the movement there is no problem of measurement: despite the tempo fluctuations, the crotchet pulse and 3/4 metre are clearly continuous. Before this, though, the two changes of metre, to 3/8 at *16* and back to 3/4 at *19*, present a complication. This is because those two metrical transitions are not as complementary as they might first appear. At *16* the preceding crotchet pulse of ♩ = 116 runs directly into the following 3/8 at ♩. = 72, with no preparatory slackening or increase of tempo. This produces a virtual equality of quaver speed: at ♩ = 116, ♪ = 232; and at ♩. = 72, ♪ = 216. This quaver continuity across *16* is made audible in two ways – first, by the trumpet's sextuplet semiquavers in bar 8 which anticipate the cor anglais's triplets in bar 9; and second, by the following 3/4 hemiola groups which dominate between *16* and *17*. By contrast the transition at *19* is approached 'En retenant'; consequently a quaver equality across *19* is impossible in terms of musical flow, and here the very audible relationship is that the 3/8 bars leading into *19* are continued one-for-one by the 3/4 bars afterwards, so that in terms of pulse, bar equals bar across the transition.

This means that any bar between *16* and *19* has the same pulse value as each bar after *19*, but that bars 1–8 each have the equivalent pulse value of two of the later bars. Once again, this is not to suggest that bars 1–8 would be heard as units of two; the logic explained on pages 17–18 applies again. If one unit is taken as the value of a bar from *16* onwards, *16* occurs after 16 units, *19* after 43, *25* after 99, *33* after 170, and the movement ends after 269, giving the formal outline of Fig. 9.1 (the overlapping binary systems) the dimensions shown in Fig. 9.2.

Fig. 9.2

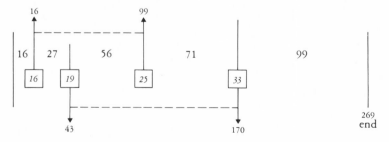

The first two transitions are linked by GS (16:27 units), and from the 'recapitulation' to the end is the same distance (99 units) as the portion up to *25*. But it is uncertain what to make of that, since the overall sequence, unlike the formal outline of 'De l'aube à midi', avoids any consistent pattern of GS or symmetry.

Fig. 9.3 adds detail to the outline with the movement's sequence of smaller motivic segments, measuring for the moment from each of the motivic entries.

Figure *20* is slightly ambiguous, as it could also be viewed as a continuation of the segment beginning at *19*. It is therefore marked separately below the line in Fig. 9.3, leaving both interpretations possible in the diagram; the same applies to bar *171*.

Fig. 9.3

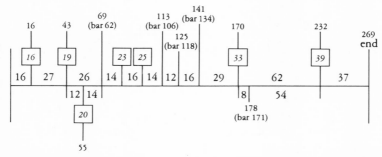

Again no consistent proportional sequence emerges, except that the first three main segments (if we pass over the entry at *20*) are related by GS and symmetry, there being only one inexactitude, of 27 units against 26. This discrepancy apart, the pattern relates the first thematic and tonal departure points by GS (16:27) and provides a near-symmetrical balance (27:26) around the arrival of the tonic key at *19* – all of this musically logical. (The 'recapitulation' at *33* – where E major is *not* re-established – correspondingly is given *no* symmetrical positioning.) The proportional sequence is then interrupted; while a careful search may reveal more correspondences, they mean little until they can be shown also to define special musical relationships. The most marked overall tendency in the succession of segments is that it becomes increasingly compressed between *25* and *29*, before broadening out from *29*, corresponding with the same characteristic in the dynamic sequence.

The state of affairs changes, though, if the textural overlaps, discussed some pages earlier, are also taken account of. This is shown in Fig. 9.4. Apart from setting the break at *25* in strong relief, the sequence of smooth transitions also reinforces this by forming a number of symmetrical and GS progressions – 30:30, 16:16 and 12:20 – all converging on *25*. But from then on the remaining textural overlaps do not focus proportions on any point in that way (the later part of the movement is omitted from Fig. 9.4 to avoid congestion). That is, this proportional system stops firmly at *25*, its point of convergence.

Fig. 9.5 follows proportions from a different aspect, the arrivals of the dynamic peaks. *25* and *26*, which have been seen to have a different structural significance (not being culminations), are included, but lower in the diagram, so that the sequence can be viewed either with or without them. (The less prominent peak in bar *99* is included as one of the culminative dynamic peaks, peak III, since it comes in the middle of a segment. Reasons for its lesser prominence will be seen later.) Again in contrast to the outer movements, this sequence by itself

117

Fig. 9.4

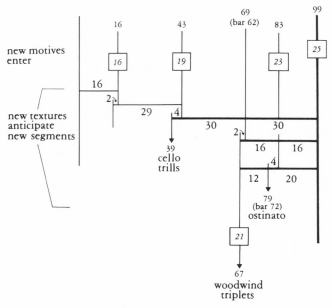

Fig. 9.5

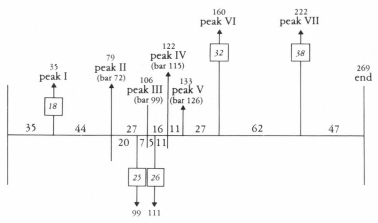

yields no exact or consistent proportional logic, except for the general tendency already noted of greatest density between *25* and *29*.

It is this general parallel between Figs. 9.4 and 9.5 that suggests what to do next, remembering that the segments have already been seen to be grouped into larger paragraphs by the position of the dynamic culminations. Fig. 9.6 shows the arrivals of the dynamic peaks, together with the beginnings of those larger paragraphs, one of which begins after each culmination. *25* and *26* are also taken as beginning new paragraphs in this sense, as that is obviously their audible effect; as will be seen, this has very specific consequences. Before following Fig. 9.6, it should be noticed that some of the peaks are momentary (for example, peaks III and V, at bars 99 and 126), whereas peaks I and II are spread, and also symmetrical, with the centre of gravity at the centre of the spread. Peak VI is more complex, covering at least eight bars after *32*, and with two twin points of *fortissimo* impact in bars 155 and 159.

The centre of peak I (beginning of bar 30) is placed 37 units after the beginning of the movement; similarly the centre of peak II (bar 73) is placed 37 units after the beginning of the second paragraph. This repeating pattern is then broken by the intrusion of the fourth paragraph at *25*, after only 16 units (bars) of the third paragraph. From then on, obviously, the distances between paragraph beginnings and culminations are much shorter, and are irregular.

25's interruptive effect therefore works on yet another front, breaking the earlier dynamic periodicity. But in doing so it begins a new development. The third paragraph, beginning at *23*, is denied a culmination at *25*; therefore the first culmination after *23* is peak III, which arrives 23 units (bars) after the beginning of paragraph III. By this time paragraph IV has already begun, at *25*; peak IV arrives 23 units after this. Again paragraph V has already begun, at *26*; peak V arrives 22⅓ units after this. Peak VI, at *32*, then arrives 23 units after the beginning of its paragraph at *29*. Only the paragraph beginning at bar 118 has no such follow-up, this being obviously to avoid interference with the build-up to peak VI which has already begun at *29*.

This hidden new pattern of repeating groups of 23 (with only one inaccuracy,

Fig. 9.6

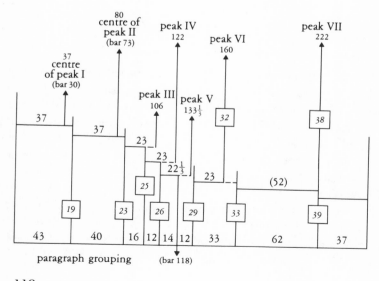

paragraph grouping   (bar 118)

119

of less than a bar) is remarkable enough by itself; but its particular significance to the larger surrounding context, with the earlier 37-unit repeating pattern, is that GS of 37 is 23. The sequence is achieved by a new variety of structural overlap – in effect a stretto of dynamic sequences – which begins at the exact point, *25*, where the earlier overlapping system, in Fig. 9.4, stopped. The stretto itself then ceases, as Fig. 9.6 shows, from *29*, and peak VII remains entirely independent of this numerical pattern.

Peaks I to VI, at least, can now be seen as having been logically introduced to the movement in proportional terms. Once there, they proceed to set up a further wave pattern, based on an intricate hierarchy of dynamic momentum. This is logically determined by a combination of their own dimensions and the amount of dynamic preparation preceding them. (This is just a very intricate application of the same logic that distinguishes the important peaks VI and VII from the preceding smaller ones.) Fig. 9.7 illustrates this system.

Fig. 9.7

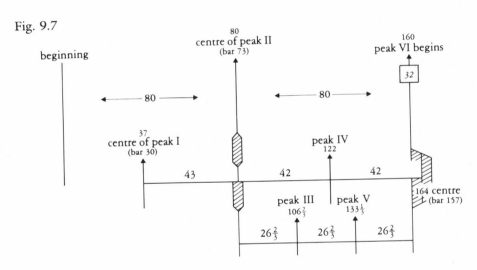

Peak VI, as already mentioned, is of a different order from the five preceding peaks, with its long preparation from *29* and its eight-bar spread following *32*; it accordingly forms the culmination of this proportional system. Of the preceding five climaxes, peak II (bars 72–3) audibly carries the most momentum, partly through its full scoring, but mostly through its two-bar spread and through having the longest preparation of these five climaxes – six bars of crescendo, from bar 66. It therefore takes a principal position, its centre forming an exact 80:80-unit division between the beginning of the movement and that of peak VI at *32*. It then sets off a second sequence in conjunction with peaks I and IV, the next two in order of momentum. (Peak I, more thinly scored, is spread over four bars and is given harmonic preparation, if little marked crescendo, between *17* and *18*. Peak IV lasts for a full bar and is prepared by three bars of crescendo.)

This second sequence is again a symmetrical one, of 43:42:42 units, leading to the exact centre of peak VI. (The apparent inaccuracy of one unit is more than covered by the spread of peaks I and II.)

Peak II finally sets off a third symmetrical sequence, this time passing via peaks III and V, the most momentary peaks, with also the shortest preparation times – less than a bar and $2\frac{1}{3}$ bars respectively of crescendo. (The *fortissimo* and fuller orchestration of peak V are presumably to draw attention to the imminent change of mood at *29*, without affecting the criteria of duration and preparation involved in Fig. 9.7.) Taking the point of measurement in peak III as the third (and loudest) beat of bar 99, the sequence is one of $26\frac{2}{3}$:$26\frac{2}{3}$:$26\frac{2}{3}$ units, and it again completes itself at the beginning of peak VI. One could give no apter name to the events shown in Figs. 9.6 and 9.7 than 'games of waves' – as Debussy has done in the title. This time the proportional games are all directed towards peak VI and stop on reaching it.

In various ways proportional coherence is beginning to crystallize. Yet it is tantalizingly incomplete: none applies to the whole movement. In particular, peak VII, the most crucial one, remains aloof from them all as, indeed, does the entire later part of the movement. What Figs. 9.3–9.7 do show is how logic gradually evolves, apparently spontaneously, out of events that first appear unpredictable and almost random.

This sense of inconsequential frolic in the earlier parts of the movement is apt to the movement's programmatic context. But in the course of those diversions Debussy, whether consciously or not, has taken us by stealth, using all the fragmentary sequences of events to define focal points of tension and qualitative change. Figure *25* is prominent as the focus of Fig. 9.4, as a centre of linear interruption generally, and as the central turning point in Fig. 9.6. Figure *29* marks the sudden end of the inconsequential frolics (and of the dynamic stretto in Fig. 9.6), replacing them with large-scale dynamic accumulation – the crucial point where dynamics move from a 'foreground' (or surface) role in the form to a 'background' (or fundamental) role. This is made audible exactly at *29*: instead of bringing in a playful new theme, as he had done at earlier parallel points like *23*, Debussy now turns the end of the preceding segment into an ostinato, delaying the expected thematic entry for another four bars, and adding harmonic tension by the bass's tritone leap to G. Peak VI then marks the completion and convergence of all the sequences (Figs. 9.6–9.7) set up by the 'foreground' dynamic events; it also marks the first 'background' dynamic culmination.

Taken in order, these three points define progressive focal points of increasing structural tension on the broadest scale; and since the various sequences of Figs. 9.6–9.7 are all set in motion by the impulse and positioning of peak I, peak I itself counts as a primary point of generation in this progressive definition of structural impetus.[3]

3. The relationship is also reflected tonally, the last two climaxes occurring on dominant-ninth chords on B♭, the tritone from the tonic E, which quickly follows each of them. The only

These points are shown in Fig. 9.8 as Sequence A. Peak I, centred after *37* units, as the generative point of growth, lies within one bar of secondary GS on the way to *25*, after 99 units.[4] *25* itself, as the main centre of interruption and compression, forms a primary GS of 99:61 units up to the beginning of peak VI at *32* (160 units). This last point, marking the centre of dynamic convergence at peak VI, then gives a symmetrical division of 61:62 units from *25* leading to *38*, the movement's final climax (peak VII), after 222 units (the apparent discrepancy of one unit is more than covered by the spread of peak VI). *29*, beginning the approach to peak VI, forms an intermediate GS of 38:23 between *25* and peak VI at *32*. In the process it also completes a further GS around *25* of 62:38 units. But most important, as the moment at which the movement's dynamics step out to a dominating dramatic and structural role, *29* lies at the primary GS of Sequence A itself, dividing the 222 units up to the final climax 137:85.

Fig. 9.8: Sequence A

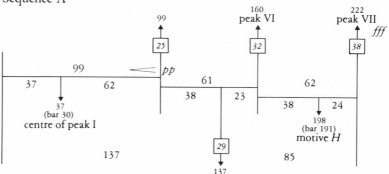

Sequence A's progress involves it particularly with motive *H*, which dominates Sequence A's first division, at peak I. The next division in Sequence A marks motive *H*'s first return at *25*, with a strong delaying effect. The reversal of this tendency (literally, with *H* in retrograde) occurs at *32*, again in Sequence A, where the tempo re-attains ♩ = 138, with no further delays before *38*. *H* makes one remaining appearance before peak VII, at bar 191 in rhythmic augmentation, its original relationship to the metre restored, as already described. This re-entry divides the final 62 bars of Sequence A in GS of 38:24.

Motive *L* is also involved. Most obviously, it dominates the final climax at *38*. The primary GS on the way there, at *29*, is the segment introducing *L₂*. The only preceding entry of *L*, in the form of *L₁* at *23*, is, correspondingly, within two

other peak that does this is peak I, which similarly leads the bass directly to E at *19*. The last intermediate peak, at bar 126, provides both a stepping-stone and a symmetrical balance to this, by being given on a dominant ninth on C♯, leading the bass immediately to the tritonal G.

4. GS of 99 is 37·8:61·2, so both 37:62 and 38:61 are within one unit of the exact value, although 38:61 is the closer approximation. A reason will be seen later for the use here of the marginally less accurate option.

units of the secondary GS of Sequence A after 85 units. (A reason for the small inaccuracy in the latter case will be seen later.)

The interruption at *26* (as opposed to the one at *25*) has had no part in either the proportional or the musical logic of Sequence A. What is its significance, assuming that Debussy's sudden *forte* is designed to bring it to our attention? It has three clear musical relationships. First, it is a point of tonal disruption, dispelling the preceding tonal stability rather as the harp glissandi at *20* had dispelled their preceding E major. In that sense, therefore, *26* and *20* are related. Thematically *26* is associated with the earlier entry of motive *K* at bar 62. And by giving the first indication of sustained forward flow after the earlier progressive reductions of speed, *26* starts the forward impetus that eventually leads through to the final climax.

These four points are proportionally related. The halfway point of the 111 units up to *26* is marked, to the nearest whole bar, by the earlier tonal disruption at *20*, after 55 units. The earlier entry of motive *K*, after 69 units (bar 61), in turn forms the GS on the way to *26* (69:42 units). And *26* itself marks the exact halfway point to the final climax at *38*, after 222 units.

Between *26* and the final climax at *38*, two more events in particular set the music irreversibly on its forward surge towards *38*. One is the nature of peak VI. The use of a double climax there, with two points of impact four bars apart, pushes the music on, preventing the ritardando which had followed each of the previous dynamic peaks; and this second point of impact in peak VI (bar 159) also sets in motion the sequence of four-bar phrases that runs unbroken to *38*. In particularly subtle ways, therefore, the presence of the second impact in peak VI, at bar 159, exerts a special influence on the movement's impetus. The most decisive turning point of all follows soon after – the shift to the G$\sharp$ pedal point at bar 171, which then continues all the way to *38*.

Fig. 9.9 shows all those points together, as Sequence B. The second point of impact of peak VII – with its dominant ninth on B$\flat$ also a centre of chromatic tension – continues the symmetrical part of the sequence, dividing the 111 bars between *26* and *38* in the ratio 55:56 (again as near as possible in whole bars, or 55½:55½ if one measures to the centre of bar 159). The other turning point – bar 171 – divides those same 111 bars 67:44 – as near as possible to GS without disrupting the four-bar groups that run to peak VII. (GS of 111 is 68·6:42·4; therefore the inaccuracy is less than 1⅔ bars out of a total of 111 – the minimum possible in the context.)

Therefore Sequence B comprises two main strands, both involving *26* and *38*, one of them GS and the other symmetrical; the former connected mostly with forward-moving melodic impulses, and the latter with tonal departure or disruption (*26* involves both). And the entire sequence develops by GS out of the movement's first two points of growth at *16* and *19*, whose GS relationship was noted in Fig. 9.2 (page 116).

The final part of Sequence B, from bar 171 to *38*, contains two more transi-

Fig. 9.9: Sequence B

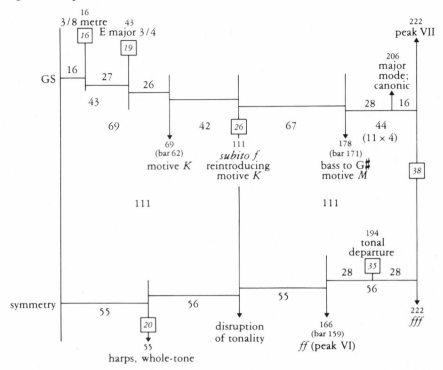

tions. At *35* ('En animant beaucoup') the G♯ tonality gives way to chromaticism above the bass; as a further point of tonal disruption this associates itself with the symmetrical part of Sequence B, dividing its last 56 bars 28:28. At bar 199 tonality is defined again with the change to the major mode, and *M* enters in canonic augmentation with itself, giving a final increase to the breadth of stride leading into *38*. This point is logically associated with the GS part of Sequence B, and correspondingly divides its last 44 bars 28:16 (=7:4) – again as near to exact GS as the four-bar groups permit.

It may appear odd that the part of Sequence B associated with tonal departure and disruption is based completely on symmetry, rather than GS. A logical reason is that tonal instability in this movement has a different dramatic and structural effect than in the outer movements, simply because here it is not set against a background of firmly established tonality. In this movement focal points of tension are defined more by the contrasts between different types of structure, and oppositions of delay and propulsion in the dramatic pacing; these form predominantly GS divisions in Sequences A and B. This is the same logic as already seen in Fig. 9.7; there the smaller-scale dynamic peaks before *29* – momentary events that do not have the structural weight of peaks VI and VII, or of the climaxes in the outer movements – also formed symmetrical rather than GS sequences.

124

The opposition between stability and tension in this movement appears, therefore, to have been shifted to different musical parameters from those operating in the outer movements – a logical continuation, in fact, of how Debussy's other works up to 1905 had shifted their architecture from conventional diatonic and thematic parameters to less usual ones like dynamic shape, forward impetus and recession, and degrees of chromatic tension. 'Jeux de vagues' now defines and exploits contrasts and layers within these new fields – such as differentiated types of dynamic 'weighting' (Fig. 9.7), or contrasts of delay and propulsion. One of the main results is greater freedom from dependence on conventions like sustained tonic stability for the music's anchoring points; the form can now be organized with even less obvious sign of what holds it up. In this way the movement's large-scale formal framework can avoid any proportional regularity in its gradual expansion (Fig. 9.2), while the smaller-scale events within it gradually build up weightier tensions and oppositions that guide the movement into a progressively more inevitable course.

Indeed it appears, from the polarity between 'foreground' and 'background' dynamics in 'Jeux de vagues', that Debussy is ingeniously exploiting within one movement, consciously or not, a process that had gradually evolved in his musical style over the previous fifteen years.

Smaller musical details reflect the proportional logic of Sequences A and B. The contrasted dynamics at the two interruptions at 25 and 26 are an example. 25 introduces a sudden compression of dynamic level and of subsequent dynamic pacing, corresponding to the geometric compression of its primary GS divisions in Sequence A (page 122). Conversely, 26 brings a sudden expansion in dynamic level, corresponding to the geometric expansion of its secondary GS divisions in Sequence B (page 124).

Peak VI embraces both Sequences A and B; it is within its eight-bar spread that their previously diverging paths begin to draw together again prior to converging on peak VII. (The way the beginning of peak VI at 32, which marks Sequence A, is pulled into the two following points of impact could be viewed as reflecting the approaching convergence of Sequences A and B.) As the culmination point also of all the smaller-scale dynamic sequences of Figs. 9.6–9.7, peak VI therefore binds together *all* the movement's dynamic sequences; it aptly lies over the movement's primary GS, after 166 units.

The diverging paths of Sequences A and B at the beginning of the movement also offer an explanation of why, in Sequence A, 37 units are taken as the secondary GS of 99, rather than the marginally more accurate 38 units (as mentioned in note 4 on page 122). The choice of 37 helps to keep Sequence A clear of Sequence B, whose course is defined only six bars later at 19.

The last part of the movement has still been discussed little. At 39, the beginning of the Coda, the bass returns to E, but the harp glissandi again intervene, introducing submediant harmony that prevents the re-entry of H in bar 227 from resolving itself harmonically with the bass E. Only at H's final entry in bar *243* does the now whole-tone chromaticism subside, reconciling the E major tonality with *H* at *41*, after which the movement logically can, and does, close.

Fig. 9.10 traces motive *H*'s complete entries in the movement (excluding the fragmentary ones in bars 149–52); the last two entries in the Coda complete a series of symmetrical and GS ratios linking them all – 99:99, 109:109, 125:125 and GS of 83:135. In addition, the entries of *L₁* and *L₂* accommodate themselves within this larger sequence, as shown lower in Fig. 9.10. (Hence the small inaccuracy of *L₁*'s entry relative to sequence A, mentioned on page 123.) Therefore the movement's final thematic entries are carefully placed to complete the earlier sequence logically.

Fig. 9.10

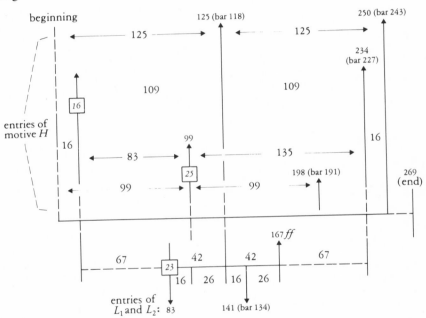

The positioning of events up to the end of the movement then mirrors that of events with which the movement began – but also with a reversal of the musical functions concerned. This reflects the reversal of effect which various of the motives and musical functions have undergone in the course of the movement. Thus the movement's first 99 units up to *25*, the important dynamic turning point, are matched by the final 99 units from the movement's formal 'recapitulation' (at *33*) to the end. The first dynamic focus (peak I) is centred 37 units from the beginning; the final formal segment division at *39*, beginning the Coda, is 37 units before the end. The movement's first formal paragraph finishes at *19*, after 43 units; 43 units before the end of the movement the dynamic

126

recession from the final climax begins, at bar 220. Slightly less accurate, the start of motivic action, 16 units after the movement's beginning, is matched by its final tonal resolution at *41*, 17 bars before the end. The positioning of every segment of the movement (shown in Fig. 9.3) has now been accounted for, and with the mirroring of events and functions just noted, the movement draws to a symmetrically matched close: the symmetrical formal aspects complete themselves, and the reversal of structural roles just described lets the purely forward-moving dynamic sequence run unhindered to its apex at *38*.

The synthesis

After all this intricate logic, the movement is left with a proportional discrepancy not encountered in any of the earlier analyses here. Sequences A and B lead to the main climax at *38* and the movement then recedes to a triple-*piano* conclusion. So did 'Reflets dans l'eau' and 'Spleen' (Chapters 3 and 4 above); but in those cases the end of the piece marked exactly the completion of the main proportional sequences which had led via the piece's climax. But in 'Jeux de vagues' the 47 bars from *38* to the end of the movement give no proportional connection whatever to anything in Sequences A and B. Similarly the final tonic resolution at *41*, 17 bars before the end, has no proportional relationship to Sequences A or B, and forms no other apparent proportional logic.

It is most surprising that the thorough proportional continuity throughout the rest of *La mer*, quite apart from the momentum of Sequences A and B, should suddenly be left unresolved at the end of 'Jeux de vagues'. An explanation might be that a sense of unresolved momentum is apt in this context: *La mer* does not finish after 'Jeux de vagues', and the unresolved momentum of Sequences A and B here corresponds with an instinctive feeling that the music has not come completely to rest at the end of 'Jeux de vagues'. (The response is admittedly subjective, but was present before proportional analysis of the movement was even contemplated, and is one shared by many listeners.)

Even so, for Debussy to allow (whether consciously or not) the preceding proportional exactitude just to collapse after *38* seems arbitrary; or might some new device be involved? If so, it would be likely to concern the idea of the accumulated momentum of 'Jeux de vagues' running on into the finale. To be more precise: is the apparent proportional disintegration at the end of 'Jeux de vagues' simply left, or could it lead to an eventual resolution?

An answer comes from Debussy's metronome indications. 'Jeux de vagues' finishes at ♩ = 138; that is, bar = 46. 'Dialogue' begins at ♩ = 96, or bar = 48 – a virtual equality of bar speed across the two movements. Since in each case one bar equals one of the units used above for the proportional analyses of the two movements, the same numbers can be used again to show the proportions of the two movements together in sequence.

127

It should be added that doing this carries no suggestion that 'Dialogue' should follow 'Jeux de vagues' in performance without any break. Within reasonable limits the gap between the two movements does not matter in this way since, being rhythmically unarticulated, it just represents a pause over the double-bar. 'Dialogue' then continues the motion, taking over at virtually the exact tempo at which 'Jeux de vagues' had finished.[5]

Fig. 9.11 puts the two movements together in sequence; to help clarity, 'Jeux de vagues' is represented by bold lines, and 'Dialogue' by broken lines. To avoid confusion between the two sets of number references in use (one for each movement), the bar (unit) references for 'Dialogue' are circled. These again refer to bars of the finale completed, and are the same as in Figs. 8.1–8.7.

Fig. 9.11: 'Jeux de vagues' and 'Dialogue' in sequence

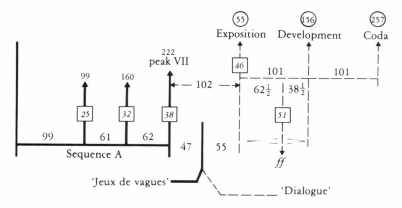

The most immediate result is that the 47 concluding bars of 'Jeux de vagues' (from *38*), added to the 55 which comprise the Introduction of 'Dialogue', make up a total of 102 bars from *38* to *46*, that is, from the final climax of 'Jeux de vagues' to the beginning of the sonata form of the finale. These provide, to within a bar, a symmetrical balance to the 101 following bars (after *46*) of the finale's Exposition. Therefore the finale's enharmonically related points of tonic arrival – at *46* and bar *157* – now both subtend symmetrical divisions, forming a

5. A curious detail at this point in the manuscript full score, Ms. 967, is that at the end of 'Jeux de vagues' Debussy omitted to ink in a double-bar, as he had inked in at the end of 'De l'aube à midi', leaving only a pencilled barline (Ms. 967 is otherwise all in ink). An oversight, no doubt, but it perhaps betrays at least a subconscious reluctance to ink in a visual barricade where the music had not properly come to rest. This idea receives support from a letter of 13 January 1905, from Debussy to Jacques Durand (Debussy, 1927, 24): 'I've reworked the end of "Jeux de vagues", as it would neither stand up nor lie down [*tant elle ne tenait ni debout, ni au reste*]' – a comment that sums up what we have seen proportionally. While the fact remains that Debussy then changed the passage, it is reasonable that in doing so he would retain any aspects of that state of affairs which could be put to precise musical purpose, as they are in the final version. (In his next symphonic triptyque, *Ibéria*, he made the structural and rhythmic connection between the second and third movements explicit.)

sequence of 102:101:101 bars from *38* to the finale's Coda. GS of 102 is 63; the 102 bars from *38* to *46* thus also provide a GS balance, to within a bar, of the 62 bars of Sequence A leading to *38*. (The slight inaccuracy of one bar in each case is covered by the spread of peak VII at *38*; other reasons for its presence will soon be seen.)

Therefore this entire sequence, including the central 101:101-bar division of 'Dialogue' (as in Fig. 8.6), forms the continuation and completion of Sequence A. As part of this, the end of the finale's Introduction at *46*, where the sustained crescendo is cut short, now forms a GS of 102:62½ bars between the final climax of 'Jeux de vagues' at *38* and the first climax of 'Dialogue' at *51* – a connection that obviously has some bearing on the tremendous animation of the section leading from *46* to *51*, and the explosive force of the climax itself at *51*.

Fig. 9.12 traces proportional continuations of Sequence B, again representing 'Jeux de vagues' by bold lines and 'Dialogue' by broken ones. Although its resulting points of continuation in the finale have not such powerfully defined musical connections as Sequence A's continuation – they hardly could have – it is remarkable enough that those projections of Sequence B (all accurate to within a

Fig. 9.12: Other continuations of 'Jeux de vagues'

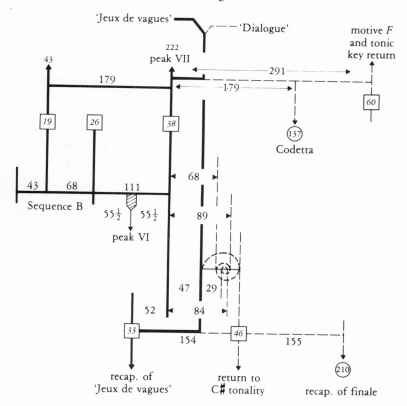

bar) all define important points of the finale – the remaining subdivisions of the Introduction, the Codetta, and the return of motive *F* with the tonic key in the Recapitulation.

Some additional links are shown lower in Fig. 9.12. Most notably, the 309 bars from the 'recapitulation' of 'Jeux de vagues' at *33* to the recapitulation of 'Dialogue' at bar 211 are divided symmetrically (to the nearest whole bar) 154:155 by the tonic key's return at *46*, where the finale's sonata form begins.

With the relationships seen in Figs. 9.11 and 9.12, all the main points in the finale's formal outline, including all the divisions of the Introduction's spiral, are now accounted for in terms of proportional continuation from 'Jeux de vagues'. (The reader who believes that such consistent connections could be found using any ratio, if one tries hard enough, is encouraged to try doing so with any ratio other than the two used here.)

The slight stretching of Sequence A's proportions, as it continues into the finale, can now be explained by Sequence B's simultaneous projection: as the musical relationships defining Sequence A are stronger, they can better afford to take this small amount of distortion (no more than one bar, or approximately 1%, at any division), whereas the less obvious connections of Sequence B's continuation would more easily be lost by small inaccuracies.

This linking of the two movements also clarifies larger-scale tonal relationships. The sequence of 102:101:101 bars in Fig. 9.11 from *38* onwards links the four points that end the four G♯/A♭ pedal points between *33* and the end of *La mer*. The central two of these four divisions mark the perfect cadences to C♯ and D♭, and accordingly subtend the sequence's symmetrical divisions. The outer two divisions, which conversely mark interruptions of the pedal points to B♭ (at *38*, and bar 258 of the finale), logically have no symmetry around them.

Obviously the G♯ pedal in 'Jeux de vagues' strongly anticipates the finale's home key; Debussy emphasizes this by adding a seventh to the G♯ harmony from bar 199 onwards in 'Jeux de vagues', giving it as strong a dominant implication as possible. One result of this is that by the final cadence of 'Jeux de vagues' at *41* the long-awaited resolution there to E major is already undermined by the implications of the preceding G♯ pedal. This is one logical reason why, despite its being a perfect cadence, it forms no symmetrical divisions within 'Jeux de vagues'. In larger terms it represents only an intermediate tonal centre, between the beginning of the G♯ pedal at bar 171 of 'Jeux de vagues' and the eventual resolution from G♯ at *46*. Those two points are separated by 146 bars; the perfect cadence to E at *41* divides them 74:72 – as near halfway as possible without interrupting the two-bar groups which preserve a broader momentum from *38* until after *42*.

The Sibley manuscript

This shows fewer visible alterations in 'Jeux de vagues' (although we know that at least the last two pages are a late replacement) than in the outer movements. Bars 148 and 150 are not written out in full but are indicated only by the instruction 'deux fois' above bars 147 and 149 – probably a later alteration, as Debussy normally entered repeated bars in sequence on the staves.[6] Omitting these bars has little effect on Figs. 9.3–9.7 (that is, leaving out Sequences A and B): where proportional systems exist there, the points of measurement at peak VI could reasonably be taken as the two points of *fortissimo* impact, rather than the beginning and centre of the climax. But when Sequences A and B are taken into account, accuracy suffers, particularly in relation to the finale.

The other differences are that bars 223–4 are entirely absent from the Sibley manuscript, and that the movement's final bar, although inked in, is scored out again in pencil. (It is then restored in the later scores.) Though these last differences, coming after *38*, leave Sequences A and B unaffected in Figs. 9.8 and 9.9, their significance becomes apparent when the relationship to the finale is considered. It has already been mentioned (page 109) that in its final state the Sibley manuscript rather mysteriously gives only 99, rather than 101, bars as the finale's Exposition. 'Jeux de vagues' supplies an explanation: because of the absence of bars 223–4 and the deletion of bar 261 in 'Jeux de vagues', the final form of the Sibley manuscript gives three bars fewer between *38* and *46* than in Fig. 9.11 – that is, 99 bars. In this state Sequence A and its continuation are given almost maximum accuracy from the beginning of 'Jeux de vagues' to the central part of the finale, with a sequence of 99:61:62:99:99 units (compare with Fig. 9.11 on page 128). As Sequence A is musically the most important, it is of interest that, according to the Sibley manuscript, it appears to have been Debussy's main concern at first, whether consciously or not, before Sequence B was catered for.

His order of proportional adjustment thus appears to have been (again whether consciously or not), first, the smaller sequences in 'Jeux de vagues' (the Sibley manuscript without its visible changes), then Sequence A (the changes visible in the Sibley manuscript), and finally the accommodation of all those together with Sequence B (the full score and editions).

The other result of the missing and deleted bars in the Sibley manuscript is to make the final perfect cadence of 'Jeux de vagues', to E major at *41*, subtend a division of 72:71 between bar 171 of 'Jeux de vagues' and *46*, instead of 74:72 as in the printed scores. If the deletion in pencil of bar 261 was made at a very late stage, as is likely, the ratio prior to this deletion would have been 72:72. Again, to have maintained maximum accuracy here would have caused greater inaccuracy elsewhere in Fig. 9.11.

6. Bar 33 in the Sibley manuscript also has a rough vertical line through it, implying that Debussy contemplated making it two bars; he evidently abandoned this late idea again in the full score.

Other observations

The initial marginal inaccuracy of Sequence B seen in Figs. 9.2 and 9.9 – the 27 units between *16* and *19* instead of a theoretically ideal 26 – can similarly be accounted for. Had Sequence B followed exact bijugate Fibonacci numbers (16, 26, 42, 68...), figure *26* would have had to arrive after 110 units instead of 111, and figure *38* after 220 instead of 222. Sequence A would then have had to be compressed correspondingly, resulting in worse inaccuracy later as it continued into the finale. The inevitable inaccuracies, therefore, are again distributed as evenly as is musically feasible. Once again, of all the slight inaccuracies seen in the proportionally significant parts of Figs. 9.2–9.11, there is not one that could be removed without causing either worse inaccuracy in another proportional sequence or else obvious musical damage.

Might the relationship between the last two movements have a bearing on the title 'Dialogue du vent et de la mer'? If the first movement has all the weight of the sea's tidal pull, and if the second movement's airier waves can be associated with the action of the wind, then structurally the finale provides a dialogue of the two, combining a recapitulation of structures from the first movement with a completion of the dynamic sequences from the central movement.

This also has specific numerical rapports. The form of 'Dialogue' is built up proportionally of a combination, or dialogue, of the number system seen in Fig. 8.5 with that of Fig. 8.6 (pages 101–2). Fig. 8.6 has now been seen as a structural completion of 'Jeux de vagues'. Fig. 8.5, more independent, is based on the summation series 9, 16, 25, 41, 66, 107, 173, 280, 453... – the same series that forms the basis of the main outline of 'De l'aube à midi' (to within a unit in the higher numbers) and most particularly its First Principal Section (Figs. 7.1 and 7.9 on pages 74 and 86). Debussy's original title for the finale – 'Le vent fait danser la mer' (Debussy, 1927, 14) – provides the same structural analogy: the momentum carried over from 'Jeux de vagues' makes the structures recapitulated from the first movement dance, in the exact sense of inverting their shapes and transposing their sequence.

Perhaps the most surprising point of all follows from this. It has already been noted that 'Jeux de vagues' is built up by exploiting and developing fine distinctions and layers within the broader structural principles which were seen to govern the first movement. The finale then recapitulates the original structures, but in a transposed sequence that integrates them more thoroughly. In this sense the three movements make up the three parts of a sonata form – not built, of course, on the conventional thematic and diatonic argument, but instead moving the process below the surface and using defined shapes and structures as subjects or motives, developing their musical implications, and finally recapitulating them. Since the finale itself aptly sums up the whole process by forming its own sonata form, it seems likely that Debussy also thought along those lines.

Whatever the answer, what we have seen proves that sonata form, used with such originality, is not incompatible with the spirit of Debussy's music.

This interpretation is substantiated by other formal characteristics of *La mer*. One is the sharp distinction between the sections in the first movement, unusual for Debussy, corresponding to the distinctness of separate subjects in an exposition (which literally means a display). Another is the reversal of traditional tonal use of sonata form in the finale, using the central section as a tonal focus for the entire movement and thus emphasizing the movement's recapitulative function in the entire work. A third is the more emphatic structural close of 'De l'aube à midi', corresponding to the traditional exposition's double-bar, whereas 'Jeux de vagues' carries its form and sequences over into the finale in the same way that the traditional development section needs the recapitulation to complete its logic.

It is worth adding that such unorthodox treatment of sonata form is no bolt from the blue. One notable forerunner of Debussy's ideas in this respect is Schumann's Fourth Symphony – an apt example, since Cyril Scott among others (1924, 103) has documented Debussy's enthusiasm for Schumann. In this symphony Schumann similarly deprives his first movement of the expected sonata recapitulation, and instead the finale recapitulates the first movement's irregular material, again making its own sonata form out of it. Schumann also links the introduction of the finale to the preceding movement, just as we have seen happen, though in a more hidden way, in *La mer*.

Precise connections with 'De l'aube à midi'

Though the form of 'De L'aube à midi' is more self-contained than that of 'Jeux de vagues', it has already been seen to compress and play down its recapitulative aspects. For this reason it is logical that its final returns to the D♭ tonic chord, in bars 135 and 139, avoid any symmetrical positioning within the movement. At the same time these are massive events musically, and one might expect their influence not to be completely cancelled by the end of the first movement. Jean Barraqué's remarks quoted on pages 64–5 above lend support to this view. Moreover, the score invites us to explore the idea, because the metronome marks indicate a rhythmic continuity into the next movement. 'De l'aube à midi' closes at ♪ = 80, or ♩ = 40; 'Jeux de vagues', opening at ♩ = 116, or bar equal to *c.* 39, continues this pulse almost precisely. Each of those – the crotchet pulse at the end of 'De l'aube à midi' and the bar pulse at the beginning of 'Jeux de vagues' – equals two of the units used for measurement in the above analyses of those two movements, so that the numbers used for the above analyses are again compatible for measuring the movements in sequence. (Indeed, this means that the units found most convenient for the above analyses of the three movements have turned out to form a common unit running all through the work, which is surely significant. One aspect of this has already been mentioned on page 108, linking the outer movements' Introductions.)

Fig. 9.13 puts the first two movements together in sequence, 'De l'aube à midi' represented by bold lines, and 'Jeux de vagues' by broken ones. (To avoid confusion between the two numbering systems there, the unit references for 'Jeux de vagues' are circled.)

Fig. 9.13: 'De l'aube à midi' and 'Jeux de vagues' in sequence

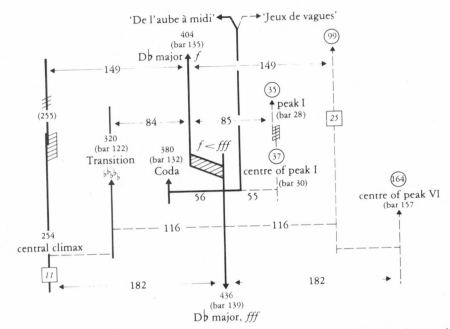

Each of the two final tonic returns in the closing bars of 'De l'aube à midi' forms symmetrical divisions from earlier important points in the movement, completing themselves, with no inaccuracy greater than one unit, at important focal points of 'Jeux de vagues'. The largest of these divisions is probably the most notable one, linking the central, or penultimate, climax of the first movement with its structural equivalent in the second movement, peak VI, via the final tonic chord of 'De l'aube à midi'. Therefore not only is the formal outline of the finale generated by the impulse of 'Jeux de vagues', but also 'Jeux de vagues' has its outlines determined by the first movement's final events – an extraordinary piece of hidden organic continuity and transformation linking all three movements. This process, viewed in terms of *La mer*'s overall sonata form, provides another close parallel with classical sonata form – in the common device of building a development section thematically out of the closing bars of the exposition (one example of many being the first movement of Schubert's String Quintet).

Connections with *L'isle joyeuse*

Viewed in the light of *La mer*, *L'isle joyeuse* takes on added significance. Its expanding GS framework (Fig. 5.1 on page 50) has already been remarked upon as anticipating the similar large-scale expanding GS sequence of 'De l'aube à midi' (Fig. 7.8 on page 85). At the same time its more complex dynamic sequence (Fig. 5.6 on page 55) bears a greater similarity to that of 'Jeux de vagues', especially in the way that in both movements a powerful double climax, placed at the primary GS of the entire movement, acts as a centre of convergence for all the preceding dynamic sequences, after which a larger-scale sequence takes over completely to carry each piece through to its culmination.

Debussy's structural *tour de force* in *L'isle joyeuse* was to have used small-scale dynamic sequences, which by themselves form a coherent logical pattern (Fig. 5.6), to define in the later stages of the piece a firm formal framework (Fig. 5.7 on page 57) that on its own then makes complete structural and proportional sense. What Debussy has done in 'Jeux de vagues', apart from its greater complexity, is to push the achievement of *L'isle joyeuse* two stages further. The first stage is a withdrawal of even the type of proportionally consistent expanding formal outline that had defined the overall GS proportions of *L'isle joyeuse* and 'De l'aube à midi'. The second stage follows logically: with such a self-contained formal scheme withdrawn, the dynamic sequences built up in 'Jeux de vagues', instead of defining points of return and resolution within the same movement, now project them beyond the end of the movement and into a following one – one that also makes complete sense on its own.

As with *L'isle joyeuse*, the relationship between the last two movements of *La mer* is in essence simple, becoming complex only in its detailed working-out. If Debussy designed the system consciously, many of the basic ideas probably sprang from intuitions, and his instincts must have been constantly alert towards the musical validity of what resulted.

PART 4

Other evidence

Chapter 10
Brief studies of other works

A clearer picture is now possible of how Debussy's use of proportions developed along with other aspects of his musical development. Above all, the technique never becomes a *formule*, is never used exactly the same way twice: any parallel between pieces is offset by some other sharp contrast between the structures of the pieces concerned. This chapter demonstrates more parallels of proportional logic, between the works already examined and a number of others – again showing that no system is used the same way twice. The following examples are not analyses in any thorough musical sense; rather their object is to chart the subtle network of structural cross-fertilization linking the various works.

'Jardins sous la pluie' (*Estampes*)

This piece is of immediate interest because of Debussy's addition of bar 123 at proof stage, and his accompanying *divin nombre* letter, quoted in Chapter 1 above. On a large scale the piece comprises four sections, the central (second) section (bars 75–99) and the coda (bar 126 onwards) dominated by the melody of the song *Nous n'irons plus au bois*. The third section (bars 100–25), which links the central section and coda, is related to the opening section but is drastically compressed, forming (as in *L'isle joyeuse*) a cumulative approach to the coda and the piece's exhilarating conclusion.

The first main section, the longest one, has its central dynamic focus, the section's only *fortissimo*, at bar 47, introducing D♭ major, the enharmonically equivalent key of the following central section. This *fortissimo* divides the opening section in GS of 46:28, as shown in Fig. 10.1. Between there and the end of the piece, the penultimate climax at bar 116 forms a GS of 69:42 bars; the beginning of the coda, at bar 126, similarly forms a GS of 51:32 bars between the beginning of the central section and the end of the piece (GS accurate in both cases to the nearest bar). These interact to complete smaller GS and symmetrical balances, leading from before the central section to the coda, which are shown in broken lines in the central part of Fig. 10.1.

Fig. 10.1: 'Jardins sous la pluie'

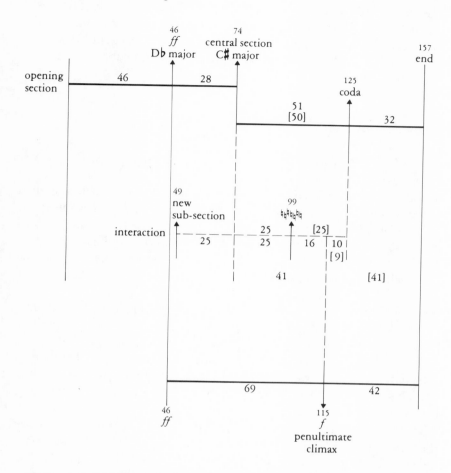

If the piece is measured *without* the bar that Debussy added to the proofs (bar 123), the numbers are as given in brackets in Fig. 10.1. Two symmetrical divisions are made exact (41:41 around bar 116 and 25:25 around bar 100); but two of the three large-scale GS divisions – now 50:32 and 69:41 – are made more than a bar inaccurate from GS. Bar 123's presence is evidently preferable in proportional terms.

Even if one insists that this proportional evidence might not be what Debussy was referring to in his *divin nombre* letter, one then has to ask what it was he was referring to. A less far-reaching alternative might be something smaller-scale, such as four-bar groups: with bar 123 present a 4+4-bar group leads into the coda. But this is not very convincing because four-bar sequences are infrequent in this piece; it contains many other asymmetrical phrases at comparable points that Debussy left as they were (for example, leading into the *forte* at bar 71). Smaller-scale proportions elsewhere in the piece tend to confirm the large-scale proportional tendencies – for example, GS balances of 15:9 bars and 26:16 bars, both measured from the beginning, or the 7:7:7:11-bar sequence of the coda. Above all, no other numerical plan is evident; and even if there is one we have overlooked, the chances that some other such design would simultaneously allow the GS and symmetry seen in Fig. 10.1 here to happen subconsciously are virtually negligible.

D'un cahier d'esquisses

Dating from late 1903, just as work on *La mer* was beginning, *D'un cahier d'esquisses* is particularly rhapsodic and free in form. Essentially it consists of two main episodes, beginning at bars 11 and 29 with the same theme but then developed differently, framed by an introduction and a long coda (beginning at bars 1 and 45) which are also thematically related. The piece's formal freedom comes from the way each of the sections is allowed to follow a quite independent course, until the coda steers the piece to a firm conclusion, quoting from the cadenza (which in turn was derived from an earlier accompanying figure in bar 34).

The problem of how to measure the cadenza proportionally has been discussed already on pages 18–19 (with Ex. 3), where two alternatives were suggested. One of them is to consider the cadenza as equivalent to two and a half of the surrounding bars, or five units, taking the unit as the dotted crotchet of bars 1–42, which becomes the crotchet from bar 45, as Debussy's instruction $\downarrow. = \downarrow$ indicates. This produces a total of 149 units for the piece, and the resulting proportions are shown in Fig. 10.2.

The coda and the second episode begin exactly at the primary and secondary GS of the piece – 92 and 57 units – and the first episode begins within half a bar of secondary GS on the way to the second episode (GS of 57 is 21·8:35·2). The two episodes therefore define an expanding GS sequence the same as was seen with the first movement of *La mer* (Fig. 7.8 on page 85) and very similar to that of *L'isle joyeuse* (Fig. 5.1 on page 50).

If the alternative measurement from page 19 is followed, and the cadenza considered as equivalent to just two of the surrounding 6/8 bars (four units), the proportions remain accurate to within a crotchet beat throughout: the total length becomes 148 units and the coda begins after 91 (shown in brackets in Fig. 10.2), still accurate GS to nearest whole numbers. As it is, model precision is less important in such a free piece as this than in a taut structure like *L'isle joyeuse*, and this corresponds with the cadenza's ambiguity here, whereas the notation of the 'quasi-cadenza' in *L'isle joyeuse* allows no such ambiguity of measurement.

Knowing that Debussy intended *D'un cahier d'esquisses* to sound like an improvisation, one would not expect proportional structure to be too intricate, and this is generally so. The cadenza, though, is prepared by the piece's three

Fig. 10.2: *D'un cahier d'esquisses*

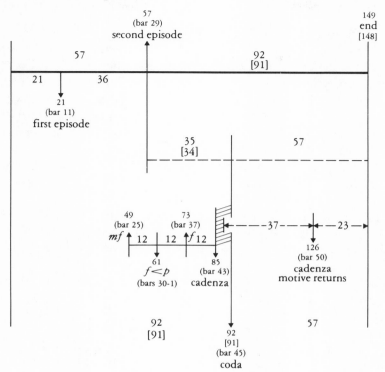

points of dynamic focus at bars 25, 30 and 37, which lead to it via a sequence of 12:12:12 units. This reduced proportional importance of dynamics matches their less important formal role here than in more vigorous pieces like 'Reflets' or *L'isle joyeuse*.

It might be thought inconsistent that the points of tonal return in Fig. 10.2 subtend GS rather than symmetrical divisions. But in this context it is logical, since here they are also points of formal departure; to form a symmetrical sequence with them would certainly have an instinctively square or sedentary effect on the piece's progress.

The piece's date of composition, its D♭ key, its *divisi*-cello-like opening, and other thematic resemblances, all leave us in little doubt about which *cahier d'esquisses* the title refers to – making the proportional similarity to the first movement of *La mer*, already mentioned, particularly striking. Like *L'isle joyeuse* it suggests structural experiments in preparation for *La mer*.

139

'Mouvement' (*Images* of 1905)

'Mouvement' is one of the clearest of Debussy's ternary forms, with an added coda which recalls the central section. Its tonal structure generally emphasizes the form, the diatonic outer sections (apart from the coda) firmly in C major, round a chromatic central section dominated by F♯ (with a strong B minor implication given only the briefest of realizations in bar 96), and a whole-tone coda. It was mentioned in Chapter 1 above that the main climax at bars 109–10, just before the recapitulation, is placed over the piece's GS (the total of bars is 177, GS of which is 109). Also, the beginning of the central section after 66 bars lies within a bar of GS on the way to the arrival of the main climax (GS of 108 is 66·7). These two proportional correspondences form part of a more complex network.

Bar 115 marks the piece's recapitulation tonally; but this recapitulation arrives with the first four bars from the opening section excised, their place having been taken by the four bars of recession, on F♯, from the climax (bars 111–14). This substitution is symmetrically matched by the four bars over an F♯ bass with which the piece's opening section ends. Fig. 10.3 shows how larger-scale symmetrical patterns result, with the halfway point marked by the arrival of the F♯ pedal after 88 bars – made absolutely exact if one counts up to the last actual note of the piece, a staccato crotchet.

In the outer sections the bass C in bars 34 and 144 forms symmetrical divisions within the sections, and the central 8+8-bar repeated phrase surrounding it marks these sections' internal points of GS (25:16:25), so that the outlines of the outer sections imitate in diminution the larger-scale proportional outline of the entire piece. GS of 66 is 41; of the opening section's total of 66 bars, 41 reappear in the recapitulation (bars 115–55) before the coda intervenes at bar 156. The overall reflected symmetry again brings to mind the title *Images*.

A rather exceptional event is the sudden explosion of the first climax in bar 53, correspondingly given no exact proportional preparation. This decisively tonic event, added lower in Fig. 10.3, then participates in other proportional schemes based on the work's tonal structure, shown in the diagram. This also shows the importance of the piece's final note, rather than just the final double-bar, as a tonal point of measurement here. The coda completes the design by whirling off, as it were into infinity, with an expanding GS sequence of 4+7+11 bars.

'Hommage à Rameau' (*Images* of 1905)

Like 'Mouvement', 'Hommage à Rameau' is in ternary form with a coda recalling the central section; and, as with 'Mouvement', its recapitulation is subtly masked, arriving thematically in bar 57 but not resolving tonally until bar 61. This overlap at the recapitulation is matched by the tonic pedal which

Fig. 10.3: 'Mouvement'

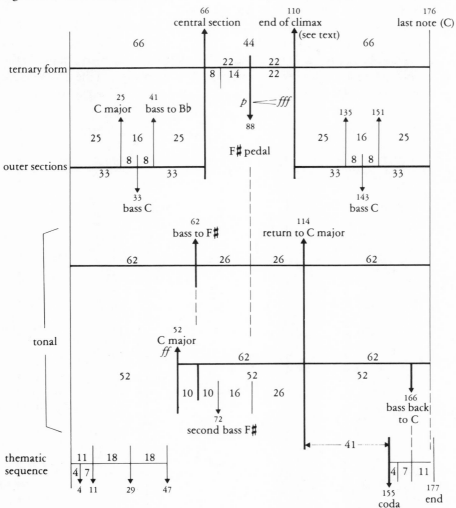

continues for the first seven bars of the central section, before the bass moves away in bar 38 (as in *L'isle joyeuse*, a large-scale phase-lag).

Again like 'Mouvement', the first and central sections of 'Hommage' both reach a dynamic culmination, the second being much the more powerful. It is also extensive: beginning *fortissimo* in bar 51, it continues the crescendo until bar 54, where the bass shifts from G to D (the tritone from the G♯ tonic) – now continuing *fortissimo*, unlike the bass G two bars earlier which was marked down to *mezzo-forte*. Debussy, incidentally, later emphasized this delayed centre of the climax, advising Marguerite Long to postpone the subsequent printed diminuendo by two bars until bar 56 (Long, 1972, 26).

141

Other evidence

Fig. 10.4 shows the proportions of the piece, measured by minim beats since the metre varies (as discussed in Chapter 2 above). Both climaxes are given 68 units of preparation, as well as forming a symmetrical arch between the piece's beginning and end, of 68:89:69 units. This all divides itself into a network of Fibonacci numbers, giving symmetrical balances (as 'Mouvement' does) to the polarity between the tonic key and its tritone. Although some of the divisions are one minim removed from ideal theoretical accuracy, to alleviate this would

Fig. 10.4: 'Hommage à Rameau'

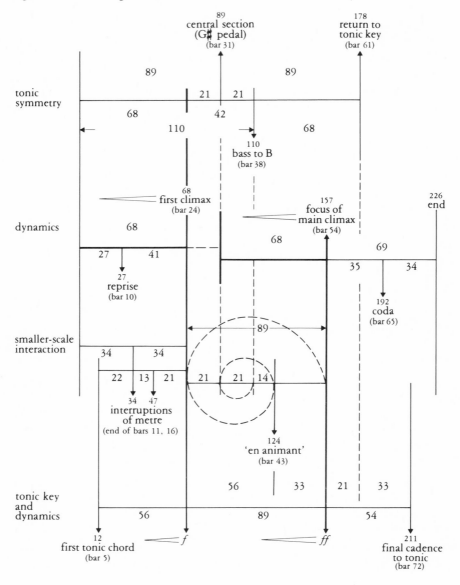

142

require more alterations of metre at musically disruptive places. As it is, the three existing metrical changes, in bars 11, 16 and 42, all help proportional accuracy, and in addition all three mark important proportional nodal points, as shown in the lower left part of Fig. 10.4. (Again, the changes of metre are audible as such only at the *end* of the bar concerned.) The postponement of the piece's first tonic chord until bar 5, matched by the final cadence five bars before the end, has a special proportional purpose, shown at the bottom of the diagram. In addition, the two climaxes form the outer divisions of a spiral sequence, matching the sense of enormous strength that slowly unwinds itself in the piece's central section.

There is another connection between 'Hommage' and 'Mouvement'. 'Mouvement' follows 'Hommage' in the *Images*, and the nearest tempo relationship between them is, perhaps surprisingly, approximately minim to minim, even allowing for a slight increase of minim speed for 'Mouvement'. (Try bars 88–110 of 'Mouvement' before setting an opening tempo!) Since the minim is already the unit of measurement in both Figs. 10.3 and 10.4, the proportions of the pieces in these diagrams can now be put directly together, as shown in Fig. 10.5. ('Hommage' is shown in bold lines, and 'Mouvement' in broken lines.)

Fig. 10.5: 'Hommage à Rameau' and 'Mouvement' in sequence

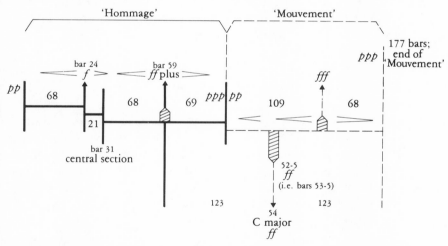

The transition between the two pieces can now be seen as placed within a minim beat of the GS between the main climax of 'Hommage' and that of 'Mouvement' (69:109 units, measuring to the centre of the climax in the latter – as accurate GS as possible without disrupting the proportions already seen within each piece). As the main climax of 'Mouvement' is placed at its GS, this completes a GS–symmetrical sequence (as accurate as possible in the context) of 68:69:109:68 units, leading from the beginning of the central section in 'Hommage', via the two pieces' main climaxes, to the end of 'Mouvement', and thus of the first series of *Images*. The earlier tonic C major climax of 'Mouvement'

also lies over the halfway point between the main climax of 'Hommage' and the end of 'Mouvement', taking the point of measurement as within bar 54 of 'Mouvement' – well within the two bars of *fortissimo*.

Therefore the dynamic shape of 'Mouvement' grows logically out of the momentum built up by 'Hommage', in a way similar to the relationship linking the last two movements of *La mer*, completed in the same year. The difference here is that, aptly, the two pieces can be separated and still retain their individual proportional coherence.

If we now complete this set of *Images* by including 'Reflets dans l'eau' at the beginning, connections continue. The nearest relationship of pulse between 'Reflets' and 'Hommage', which follows it, is a crotchet of 'Reflets' (half a bar) to a minim in 'Hommage' (the unit of measurement used in Figs. 10.4 and 10.5). In 'Reflets' the first tonic return arrives after 68 of these units (34 bars); precisely the same happens in 'Hommage', at bar 24. In 'Hommage' each of the two climaxes has 68 units of preparation, and this is related by GS (bijugate Fibonacci numbers) to the arrival of the main climax in 'Reflets' after 110 units (55 bars). Therefore the shape of 'Hommage' grows logically from that of 'Reflets', their first tonic returns related by transposed symmetry, and their dynamic shapes by GS. Those relationships among the three pieces give special weight to a letter from Debussy to Jacques Durand in 1905 (Debussy, 1980, 140), specifically requesting that the three pieces be issued in a single volume, rather than separately (as Durand had presumably intended).

'Cloches à travers les feuilles' (*Images* of 1907)

As already mentioned on page 4, 'Cloches à travers les feuilles' is another clear example of a GS dynamic arch, with its single climax, at bars 31–2, placed at its GS point. (Taking the minim beat of the outer sections as the unit of measurement, this is continued by the dotted minims of the central section – a continuity made explicit by the semiquaver sextuplets across bars 23–4 and 39–40. The resulting total is 95 units, GS of which is 58·7, leading to the second half of bar 31, with the piece's only moment of *fortissimo*.)

By Debussy's strict standards of not repeating himself, it might appear risky for him to have begun his second series of *Images* (whether deliberately or not) just as he began the first series two years earlier, with a GS dynamic arch form. But in the case of 'Cloches' the large-scale tonal procedures of 'Reflets' are reversed. 'Reflets' begins and ends diatonically, its central portion dominated by chromaticism, whereas 'Cloches' has predominantly chromatic outer sections, surrounding a strongly tonal (mostly lydian and pentatonic) central section (bars 24–39). This tonal system again pivots on a symmetrical arrangement of minor thirds, with the opening and recapitulation based on (rather than in) G and C♯

respectively, and the central section oscillating from E to B♭ and back, before finishing on C♯.

As shown in Fig. 10.6, the climactic two bars, in B♭ major, are symmetrically placed within the diatonic central section. The preceding proportions all lead by GS to (and over) the climax, and the recapitulation, restoring whole-tone modality at bar 40, subtends the GS (32:20) between the beginning of the central section and the end of the piece. The first main section (bars 1–23) also forms a smaller ternary sequence within the piece's overall one (again, a wave within a wave); this follows a GS sequence of 22:13:8 units leading to the emergence of tonal definition at bar 24. The subtle touch of then withholding the bass E until bar 26 (where the lydian A♯ disappears) means that its arrival, marking the diatonic centre of the entire piece, divides it, as exactly as possible in terms of half bars, at its halfway point (47:48 units).

The comparison – and contrast – between this piece and 'Reflets dans l'eau', as the respective opening pieces of the 1907 and 1905 *Images*, are the more remarkable because the two pieces are almost precisely the same length – 95 and

Fig. 10.6: 'Cloches à travers les feuilles'

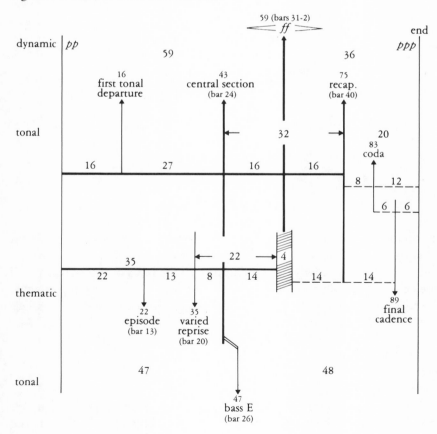

94 units respectively, measured in both cases by minim units at a very similar tempo – with their climaxes placed identically, at 58–9 units.

There are more detailed correspondences, shown in Fig. 10.7. (The necessity of the additional unit in 'Cloches' can be seen from Fig. 10.6.) Of these, the most notable is the parallel siting of the main tonal turning point (after 42 bars and 43 units respectively), which forms in each piece the primary GS between the first tonal departure and the climactic centre (26:16 bars in 'Reflets', 27:16 units in 'Cloches'). But is this parallel not illogical, given that the tonal procedure in 'Cloches' at that point is the reverse (chromaticism to diatonicism) of that in 'Reflets'? The answer seems to be that in 'Cloches' the dramatic relationship of the tonal polarities also is inverted: the opening chromaticism is languid, like the opening diatonicism of 'Reflets'; and the new tonal clarity at bar 24 comes as an increase in dynamism, like the corresponding transition to chromaticism in 'Reflets'. In the light of that, the proportional procedure in 'Cloches' makes sense.

Fig. 10.7

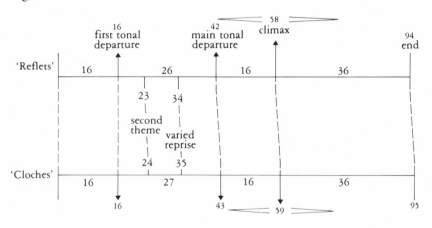

These peculiar hidden correspondences between two ostensibly very different forms invite the question of whether Debussy was deliberately setting himself a challenge – seeing how closely he could approach the basis of the earlier model structure of 'Reflets', but now from the absolutely opposite direction tonally, and consequently with a completely original effect. (Also compare the parallels in Fig. 10.7 with those involving 'Reflets dans l'eau' in Fig. 4.8 on page 44.)

'Poissons d'or' (*Images* of 1907)

To a rather less clear degree than 'Mouvement' or 'Hommage à Rameau', 'Poissons d'or' can be described in ternary-plus-coda terms. Bars 1–29 form the opening section, with bars 22–9 forming a varied reprise and transition. Bars 30–85 form a central development section, all derived thematically from the opening section, leading from bar 30 to the piece's *sforzandissimo* climax in bars 84–5. This central portion is subdivided thematically into three parts at bars 46 and 55. A very condensed recapitulation ensues, now over varied chromatic harmony, leading into the tonic resolution of the cadenza and coda from bar 94 to the end.

These outlines are carefully blurred: the transition to the central section is not only prepared tonally in bar 26 but also dovetailed in between bars 28 and 33, and the recapitulation is anticipated strongly from bar 80 onwards. Nonetheless, bar 30 is clearly recognizable as an unprecedented turning point texturally and thematically, and Debussy's dynamics (ignored by all too many pianists) indicate bars 84–5 as the proper culmination of the preceding dynamic accumulation. Bar 86, despite its chromatic harmony, takes up the recapitulation melodically from bar 3 of the opening section, so that the two climactic bars, 84–5, really take the place that bars 1–2 occupied in the opening section. Bars 84–5 therefore can be taken as forming a structural overlap, belonging both to the central section and the recapitulation.

Dynamically 'Poissons d'or' bears some similarity to 'Jeux de vagues', indulging in a number of sudden, irregularly spaced dynamic eruptions before beginning a sustained approach by four-bar phrases, from bar 64, to the main climax – placed much nearer the end of the piece than those of the other *Images* already studied.

Measurement of its proportions was discussed on page 19; the cadenza, 37 quaver beats long (beginning slightly below tempo, but definitely continuing the pulse), counts as the equivalent of 6⅙ bars of 3/4, bringing the piece's total dimensions to 102⅙ units of 3/4. (The extra ⅙, present for musical reasons, has a negligible effect on the overall calculations and can safely be disregarded here.)

Fig. 10.8 shows its proportional sequences, taking the centre of the main climax as the point of measurement, in view of the climax's double structural role. The piece's opening and final sections are related by GS (29:18); the beginning of the long crescendo and ostinato to the main climax divides the central section in GS of 34:21, and consequently the entire piece likewise (63:39, or thrice 21:13). The final tonic resolution at bar 94, beginning the cadenza, is symmetrically placed (9:9) within the final section, and the cadenza's dynamic peak, confirming the tonic key, takes up a similar position within these latter 9 units.

The earlier dynamic peaks then form GS–symmetrical sequences, as does the thematic grouping in the central section, giving proportional emphasis to the beginning of the long crescendo (bar 64) and the main climax. Unlike 'Jeux de vagues', 'Poissons d'or' is the last movement of its suite; accordingly the proportional sequences leading to the main climax then resolve themselves by GS within the movement, or at its end.

Fig. 10.8: 'Poissons d'or'

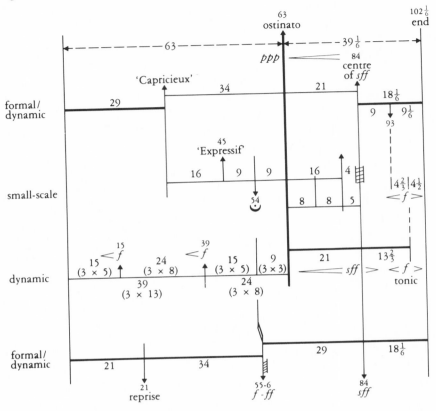

As the finale of the 1907 *Images*, the large-scale proportional outline of 'Poissons d'or' can be compared with that of 'Mouvement', the finale of the 1905 *Images*. This is shown in Fig. 10.9. The symmetrical divisions from 'Mouvement' now become GS ones, with the general outline of 'Mouvement' ellipticized in the later piece. For two pieces so different in many respects, this hidden relationship is remarkable; it can then also be linked to the proportional outline of 'Dialogue du vent et de la mer', the other finale composed in the same period of Debussy's career. This is shown lower in Fig. 10.9.

Both 'Cloches à travers les feuilles' and 'Poissons d'or', from the 1907 *Images*, can therefore be seen as logical and adventurous variants of the proportional models used for their equivalents in the earlier 1905 *Images*. Since the 1905 *Images* are such a sophisticated, virtually model, embodiment of the proportional principles Debussy had developed up to then, it would have been futile for him merely to repeat their structural sophistication in later works. Instead, the *Images* of 1907 advance a stage, experimenting with the earlier ideas to find how much they can be ellipticized, inverted, or subverted without losing their musical relevance and coherence. ('Et la lune descend sur le temple qui fut', the central

Fig. 10.9: Comparisons (not to scale)

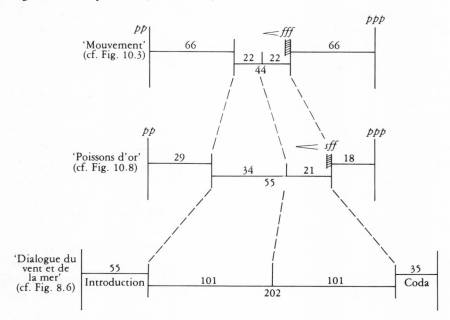

piece of the 1907 *Images*, has no such direct connections with the first series of *Images*. It goes a stage further again by avoiding any large dynamic surges.)

Prélude à l'après-midi d'un faune

Different writers have viewed this analytically elusive masterpiece in various ways; summing them up in his own perceptive discussion, William Austin (1970, 74) observes that 'perhaps the disagreement is more about the meaning of the labels than about the way the music coheres'. The most logical labels appear to be the ones used by Jean Barraqué (1972, 86), recognizing the sections from figure *3* to bar 54 and from *8* to *10* as developments of the opening part up to *3*, with a closer approximation to recapitulation, albeit much varied, not arriving until *10*, and the central section lasting from bar 55 to figure *8*. (The importance of *3* as the work's main pivot of departure is underlined by the presence there of the work's only anacrusis, subtly brought to the surface from the earlier lead-in to *2*.) This gives the work, for all its fluidity, a distinct arch form, with its main climax in the central portion; and the sections can conveniently be labelled A *A'* B *A"* A_r. (The italicization of the two transitional *A* sections refers to their freer relationship to the opening section, by comparison with the final recapitulative A_r section.)

Strangely, none of the existing analyses considers the piece's important undulating dynamic accumulation as crucial to the architecture. There is only one *fortissimo*, in bar 70; after this has subsided, the music never rises above *piano* (collectively, or *mezzo-forte* in individual voices) and is mostly *pianissimo*. But the main climax is prepared by an earlier undulating dynamic sequence – the clearest example of this in Debussy's music up to that time – which largely defines the paragraph articulation up to bar 54, with main divisions at *1*, *2*, *3* and bar 55, and subsidiary articulation at *4*, *5* and *6*.

In measuring the proportions of this piece the metrical modulations between *3* and *4* have a curious effect. Debussy indicated that the quaver remains constant throughout the passage, which means that at *10* a crotchet beat is still worth two of the quaver units with which the piece opened. Between *10* and *11*, triplets are gradually re-introduced into the 4/4 metre, until at *11* the notation changes to dotted crotchets, continuing the pulse of the preceding crotchets with their triplet subdivision. The new dotted crotchet, therefore, is still worth 2 units in terms of pulse continuity, instead of the 3 units of a dotted crotchet at the opening of the piece – despite the fact that from *10* it is quoting virtually the same music. Of the many effects of transformation that this work's arch form undergoes in its recapitulative stages, this is one of the oddest; and even if one has no interest in measuring proportions, to the sensitive listener the memory of the metrical gear-change between *3* and *4* – perpetrated twice to emphasize the point – is likely to leave an instinctive inkling that the recapitulation is somehow working on a differentiated rhythmic level from the opening.

The arithmetical effect on proportions is that from *11* to the end, the 9/8 and 12/8 bars have to be regarded as modified 3/4 and 4/4 bars, consisting respectively of 6 and 8 units, a unit being the constant quaver pulse of the piece as measured up to *10*. (This is no suggestion that the last nine bars would be felt as groups of six or eight beats; the reasoning of pages 17–18 applies again.) This gives a total of 817 units for the entire piece.

Fig. 10.10 shows the resulting large-scale proportions. The first paragraph lasts 72 units, and this exactly defines the positioning of the climax in the second paragraph, 72 units after its beginning at *1*. The third paragraph beginning at *2* similarly reaches its peak after 72 units, and the fourth one (the *A'* section) expands this by GS, its culmination being centred 113 units after its beginning ($72 \times 1{\cdot}618 = 116$, GS to within three units, or half a bar). The lead-in to the main climax in the central section begins again 72 units after the beginning of that section, leaving another 72 to the end of the section.

The resulting series of dynamic peaks, taken by itself, follows a Fibonacci sequence up to the third peak, with only one inaccuracy of one quaver beat (234 instead of 233), too insignificant to matter. Only the main climax does not continue this Fibonacci sequence; this is because from the third peak (bar 47) onwards a larger sequence takes over, as will be described shortly.

The paragraph at *2* then begins a GS sequence linking *2*, the anacrusis to *3*, the central section at bar 55 and the recapitulation at *10* – all accurate to within two quavers ($689 \times 0{\cdot}618 = 425{\cdot}8$; $425 \times 0{\cdot}618 = 262{\cdot}7$; $264 \times 0{\cdot}618 =$

Fig. 10.10: *Prélude à l'après-midi d'un faune*

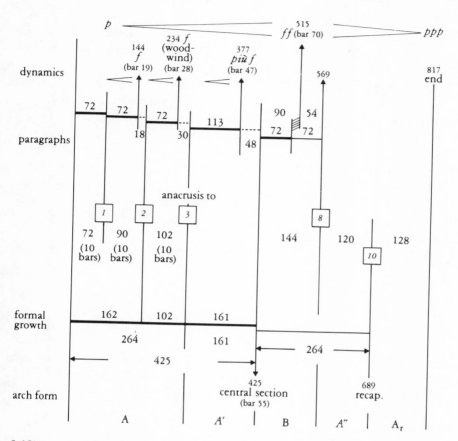

163)—remarkable accuracy in view of the larger metrical structure involved.

Incidentally, a notable relationship with bar structure here is that the gradual expanding sequence of the first three paragraphs comprising the opening A section—72:90:102 units—is contained by a 10+10+10-bar sequence—the growth being achieved by gradual metrical expansion between *1* and *3*.

The one main division not covered by this formal GS sequence is the beginning of the *A"* section at *8*. This is because the central section's length instead imitates the opening Fibonacci dynamic sequence, comprising 144 units. The central section's *fortissimo* climax divides this into 90:54 units—as near as possible to GS in terms of crotchet beats. GS of 817, the work's total of units, is 505—ten units, or 1⅔ bars, from this main climax after 515 units. This is the largest inaccuracy yet; though only 1·2% of the entire length involved, its presence allows the climax maximum GS accuracy inside the central section.

There exists a variant reading of the dynamics at that point. In Debussy's own two-piano arrangement, which probably antedates the full score, the climax is

151

spread over bars 68–70, with twin *forte* peaks (no *fortissimo*) indicated in bars 68 and 70.[1] In this state the climax lies exactly over the overall GS point (inside bar 68), but loses its GS accuracy within the central section. In percentage terms the inaccuracy is more evenly spread by the full score's modification to *fortissimo* in bar 70 only – apart from the broader surge produced by this single *fortissimo* with its three bars of powerful crescendo.

The other discontinuity in Fig. 10.10 is that the climax at bar 70 does not continue the Fibonacci sequence of the earlier peaks, as already mentioned. This is because from *4* onwards four-bar groups of 3/4 metre (24-unit groups) gradually assume preponderance, running continuously from the peak in bar 47, via all the intermediate points of formal articulation, to the end of the central section at *8*, where the metre changes to 4/4. (The only exception is at *5*, where the line is still kept smooth, and proportional continuity is maintained instead by GS of 24:38:24.) Figure *4*, beginning this new symmetrical sequence after 315 units, lies within three units (half a bar) of the entire piece's secondary GS, after 312 units.

Finally, Fig. 10.11 shows how all the final points of resolution in the piece

Fig. 10.11

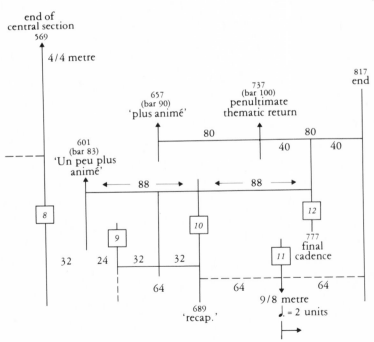

1. Debussy's manuscript of the two-piano version (collection of Mme Jobert-Georges, Paris; photographic copies in the Centre de Documentation Claude Debussy) corresponds to the printed two-piano score in this matter, just as his manuscript full score (Music department of the Bibliothèque Nationale, Paris: Ms. 17685) corresponds to the printed full score.

produce a comprehensive series of interlocking symmetrical divisions, drawing the piece to its serene close. They include figure *11*, where the notation reverts to dotted crotchets, the dotted crotchet now being worth only two units, as described on page 150 above. This symmetry might appear banal or inevitable in view of the larger metrical groupings, were it not that the frequent changes of metre in the final parts of the piece make such symmetries, even without the intricate overlapping, most unlikely to have arisen fortuitously. (The reader who doubts this is invited to find a way of changing the proportions without destroying most of the symmetries.)[2]

Of all Debussy's works up to 1894 studied here, *L'après-midi* evidently contains the most sophisticated proportional organization. Apart from this, Arthur Wenk (1976, 152) has pointed out one other numerical correspondence – that the piece comprises the same number of bars (110) as Mallarmé's poem comprises lines. Fortuitous, perhaps, but the coincidence is made more remarkable by the simultaneous presence of the other numerical systems just described – particularly since the above analysis has pointed out another numerical counterpoint between bar measurements and quaver measurements in the opening part of the piece.

Other works

From about 1894 onwards, up to the pieces studied so far in this book, virtually all Debussy's works show proportional organization, although to varying degrees of structural importance. For example, in the *Nocturnes*, whose forms are still more conventionally definable in ternary and rondo terms, proportional structure is present but less dominating than in *La mer*. Or in the *Children's corner* proportional structure, although present, plays a less vital role than in the piano *Images*.

Two movements from the year 1901 appear to have no such thorough proportional frameworks: the 'Toccata' of *Pour le piano* and the two-piano piece *Lindaraja*. With the 'Toccata', a more conventional piece in many ways, this is not too surprising. With *Lindaraja* it is of more interest because of its affinities (shown in Ex. 27) with both the 'Prélude' of *Pour le piano* and the slightly later 'Soirée dans Grenade' from *Estampes*, two pieces thoroughly organized into proportional sequences. *Lindaraja*, involving no discernible ones, gives, for all its dramatic moments, less impression of these being coherently paced and

2. Debussy himself tried one of the only possibilities. In his pre-orchestral draft of *L'après-midi* (published in facsimile in Debussy, 1963), bar 101 was omitted. This omission, of 8 units (remembering the metrical idiosyncrasy described on page 150 above), allowed a large-scale balance of 120:120 units across the recapitulation at figure *10* (instead of 120:128 as in Figs. 10.10 & 10.11), but at the cost of destroying nearly all the symmetries in Fig. 10.11. (Debussy later added the missing bar to the manuscript by pencilling 'bis' above bar 100 – again, a case of proportions being made exact by repeating a bar.)

Ex. 27
(a) *Lindaraja*, bars 35–8

(b) *Pour le piano*, 'Prélude', bars 43–5

(c) *Lindaraja*, bars 129–32

(d) 'La soirée dans Grenade', bars 23–8

aligned than the other two related pieces do. This judgment is admittedly subjective, but it is shared by many commentators, and finds implicit corroboration in Debussy's decision to keep *Lindaraja* unpublished (it was not printed until 1926).

Later orchestral scores and *Pelléas*

Other developments of the proportional techniques already seen in the *Images* of 1907 continue in the orchestral *Images* and in *Jeux*. The dramatic frameworks of 'Gigues' and 'Rondes de printemps' (from the *Images*) and of *Jeux* all show a particular relationship to 'Jeux de vagues'—an avoidance of sustained dramatic accumulation in the earlier part of each work, making way decisively for two sustained build-ups to large climaxes in the later part of the score. Fig. 10.12 shows the parallel. (The ballet *Khamma* also tends towards this dramatic shape, but less exactly.)

Fig. 10.12: Comparisons (not to scale)

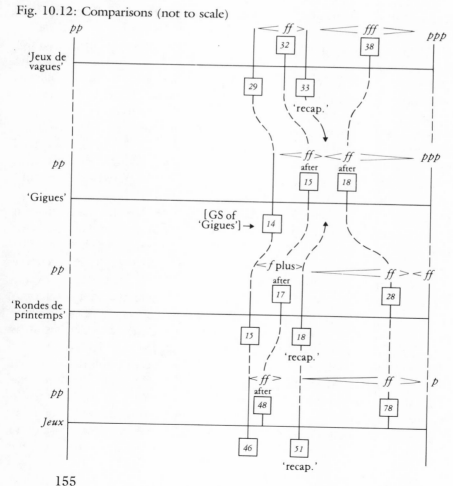

Other evidence

All these scores, however, have quite different general proportions: although they all have GS and symmetrical organization, their differences of musical substance logically lead to different solutions of proportional balance. Unlike 'Jeux de vagues', they are all complete musical entities, and accordingly their proportional sequences all complete themselves by the end of the piece. It can very quickly be guessed that this archetypal dramatic shape, particularly important to Debussy, first found form in his *oeuvre* in *Pelléas et Mélisande*. In this case the shape was, of course, implicit in Maeterlinck's drama. But similar basic forms are fundamental to much drama of all epochs; our analysis leads us back to Debussy's acute sensibility to literature and drama.

To study *Pelléas* properly from this aspect would require another book; but one proportional occurrence can quickly be mentioned. The climax of the opera, Act 4 Scene 4 (the first scene Debussy set), accumulates its tension in a clear sequence of events; its role in the opera's form is obviously parallel to that of the passage leading to *78* in *Jeux*, or the passage leading to *38* in 'Jeux de vagues'. Its main dramatic pivot, after Pelléas's and Mélisande's declaration of love, is the point of literally no return, as Pelléas and Mélisande, in the garden, hear the castle doors lock for the night (top line of page 255 in the Durand vocal score, at the double-bar). This divides the scene's total of 1316 crotchet beats in exact GS of 813:503 (taking the scene's musical beginning as the 6/4 on page 232 of the Durand vocal score) – as accurate as anything yet traced in this book. Pelléas's and Mélisande's declaration of love (page 244 in the Durand vocal score) is placed over the exact halfway point of these first 813 beats.

Similarly, there is not space here to analyse the other orchestral scores – in any case it is healthier to leave some challenges for the reader. But there is a special interest in showing some aspects of *Jeux*, provided it is remembered that this, without thorough musical analysis, can only tell us a very limited amount about this complex and magnificent score.

Measurement should be explained here, as the score does not always make it clear what should be done. (As mentioned before, Debussy notated his scores for the performer's convenience, not the analyst's.) The basic unit of pulse adopted is the opening crotchet, which becomes, slightly accelerated, the dotted crotchet of the 3/8 bars. This relationship also applies between *78* and the end. In between, all printed tempo relationships are followed – for example, the 2/4 bar (at $\quarternote = \eighthnote$) being treated as $\frac{2}{3}$ of a unit, the 3/4 bar at *27*, *29* and *43* (where $\eighthnote = \eighthnote$) as two units, and so forth. But at *49* the musical relationship is different: this time the preceding rhythm has completely collapsed, and the crotchet of the new 3/4 metre (no tempo relationship specified this time) is taken as re-establishing the basic unit of pulse. Similarly at *78*, again with no relationship specified, the crotchet beat musically takes over from the preceding 3/8 bar, rather than $\eighthnote = \eighthnote$, because the cross-rhythms leading into *78* prevent any audible quaver continuity across the transition. (To take a basis of $\eighthnote = \eighthnote$ in these last two cases would also make the 3/4 uncomfortably fast, unlike the examples at *27, 29* and *43* where ♪ = ♪ was specified.) Even though some of those relationships are not specified in the score, they are all musically logical, and they result in a proportional system that accords perfectly with the logic of all the others already seen in this book.[3]

Fig. 10.13: Proportions in *Jeux*

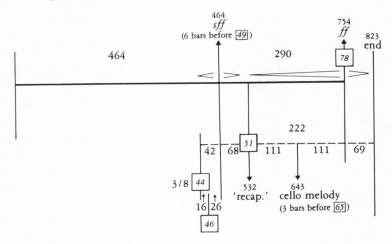

Fig. 10.13 shows the resulting large-scale proportions. The focus of the penultimate climax, at bar 429 (six bars before *49*), is at the primary GS on the way to the final climax at *78* (GS accurate to within two bars, or 0.3% of the distance measured). A GS–symmetrical sequence then links those two climaxes with first the recapitulation (to use the term freely) at *51*, then the entry of the sustained string melody–which Debussy had stealthily withheld all through the piece until then – in bar 566 (five bars after *64*), and lastly the end of the work–all the divisions here being accurate to within a bar.

It is not only those musical ways of defining tension and structure (*sensation et forme*) that are familiar from 'Jeux de vagues'; we also saw the same numbers in

3. At *35* the first printing of the score had ♪ = ♪ , which Debussy then changed to ♩ = ♪ for subsequent printings. Yet ♪ = ♪ seems more musically logical (for example, the violin pizzi-cato figure). Debussy obviously had difficulty in deciding: in the manuscript full score (Music department of the Bibliothèque Nationale, Paris: Ms. 966) he gives ♪ = ♪ (visibly changed thus from ♩ = ♪); but the ♪ = ♩ two bars earlier was originally ♪ = ♪ . In his annotated copy of the first printing of the full score (Bibliothèque François Lang, Royaumont, France), he left the printed ♪ = ♪ unchanged at *35* but reverted to ♪ = ♪ two

bars earlier. Does the confusion suggest that Debussy had to extricate himself from a mistake in counting?–an understandable one, given the metrical complexity. The question arises not only because of his obvious difficulty in decid-ing, but also because the solution he finally adopted was the best one proportionally rather than the most logical one musically.

Debussy's piano reduction of *Jeux*, antedat-ing the full score, is one bar shorter, the bass entering one bar, instead of two, after *38*. The effect on overall proportions is fairly negligible, though.

use there – particularly 222, divided 111:111 (Fig 9.9 on page 124). At the same time this correspondence shows the distance Debussy had travelled in the intervening seven years. 'Jeux de vagues' traverses 222 units from its beginning to its main climax; *Jeux* traverses 222 quite similar units merely from its recapitulation to its final climax – a *tour de force* of controlling tension, achieved here by extraordinary harmonic skill, moulded into a new mixture of large- and small-scale construction. In 'Jeux de vagues' small-scale 'foreground' dynamic sequences had given way at a well-defined point (figure *29*) to larger 'background' ones; in *Jeux* Debussy mixes the two types, incorporating an unpredictable sequence of small-scale dynamic undulations *within* the overall accumulation between *51* and *78*, these subsidiary surges contributing to, but never obscuring, the main large-scale surge.

A complication in *Jeux* is that Debussy is known to have remodelled the final section at a late stage, extending the passage before *78* and also the final page.[4] This was done at Diaghilev's request; but Debussy's unusual compliance (he refused to change a note of *Khamma* for Maud Allan) suggests he also favoured the idea. Again it proves he was not working from an unalterable plan. What the earlier version may have involved proportionally is uncertain without more thorough analysis; but one possibility is that Debussy might have thought in terms of different tempo relationships at various points – possibly accounting for the problem discussed in note 3 on page 157.[5]

Préludes

The *Préludes* are somewhat exceptional; in most of them (but not all) some proportional structure can be found, but usually less consistently or intricately than in the piano *Images*. One possible explanation is simply that many of the *Préludes* are sufficiently short to remove the need for more complex hidden unifying devices. Another reason comes from the title *Prélude*, suggesting that a sense of incompleteness at the end of such pieces is apt. An example is 'Brouillards', which fades out in mid-phrase, harmonically on a question mark; this is matched by the piece's proportional sequences, similarly left unresolved at its close.

Some of the *Préludes* somewhat exceed their brief, amounting to larger, complete musical edifices more akin to the *Images*. 'Ce qu'a vu le vent d'ouest'

4. The manuscript piano reduction score (Music department of the Bibliothèque Nationale, Paris: Ms. 1008) contains the original versions of these passages, scored out but still legible.

5. The manuscript of *En blanc et noir* (Music department of the Bibliothèque Nationale, Paris: Ms. 989) shows one instance where, in extending a passage at proof stage, Debussy also changed its tempo relationship to the surrounding sections. (This is the same passage referred to in note 11 on page 9 above.)

and 'La cathédrale engloutie' (Book 1), and 'La terrasse des audiences' and 'Feux d'artifice' (Book 2), are the clearest examples, and all four form proportional systems. That of 'La cathédrale', of special interest, is examined now.

'La cathédrale engloutie'

With one exception, this piece follows an arch form, ABCBA, with the main divisions at bars 28, 47, 72 and 84, and the two outer portions forming introduction and coda. Although the sections are all thematically related, they are still clearly distinguished in other ways. The 27-bar introduction contains the one departure from a pure arch form—an anticipation in bars 7–13 of the central C section, so that this long introduction itself forms a ternary sequence—again, a wave within a wave.

Fig. 10.14: 'La cathédrale engloutie' as printed

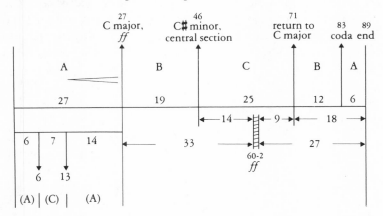

Fig. 10.14 shows the piece's dimensions as printed. Despite the allure of the 89-bar total, no consistent proportional tendency whatever is visible. But this piece poses a much more practical problem. For performers, it is impossible to set a suitably 'profondément calme' tempo at the beginning that does not have funereal consequences from bar 22 onwards (and in bars 7–13). The only way to offset this, by speeding up in bars 18–21, involves the embarrassment of contradicting Debussy's instruction 'sans presser' at bar 20.

The solution comes from the fortunate fact that Debussy recorded the piece on piano roll in 1913 (Welte-Mignon roll no. 2738, available until recently on a Telefunken LP record, GMA 65, issued in 1962). He simply plays bars 7–12 and 22–83 at exactly double the speed of the remainder – logically, since it results in continuity of triple metre at all the tempo transitions. This is surprisingly little known, though it was first documented by Charles Burkhart in 1968. Burkhart also considers bars 86–9 to be at the faster speed, but this is less clear: Debussy makes a considerable rallentando in bars 84–5, and bar 86 could be considered as a return to the ordinary slower tempo from the rallentando. It is therefore not considered here as a doubling of speed.

The problem of why this is all unmarked in the score is discussed below. The other problem about this evidence is that a piano roll cannot guarantee exact reproduction of the original tempo since, unlike a record or tape, its pitch is unaffected by playback speed; also, piano rolls can be edited. (At least, though, this one is known to be by Debussy, unlike some Duo-art rolls issued under Ravel's name but actually played by Ravel's friend Robert Casadesus.)[6] But this way of playing the piece, apart from being musically logical, was also known to some of Debussy's acquaintances, including Alfred Cortot (Burkhart, *ibid.*, lists them all), who recorded the piece on disc with the same tempo changes. Debussy's stepdaughter, Mme de Tinan (then Dolly Bardac), who was resident in the Debussy household when the *Préludes* were composed, has confirmed in conversation that Debussy played those two sections at double speed.

Taking a bar of the slow tempo as a unit, each of the fast bars is now equivalent to half a unit. Fig. 10.15 shows the result. The 89 bars produce a total of 55 such units, 34 of them at the faster tempo (bars 7–12 and 22–83) and the remaining 21 at the slower tempo. The climactic section arrives after 21 units, the GS; and

Fig. 10.15: 'La cathédrale engloutie' with Debussy's recorded modifications

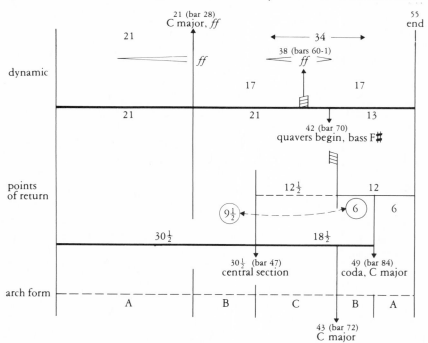

6. Information kindly supplied by Gregor Benko (formerly of the International Piano Archives now housed at the University of Maryland). These piano rolls are discussed further in Appendix 2 below.

the arrival of the central (C) section forms a GS of 30½:18½ units on the way to the coda.

The lengths of the two B sections are related by GS of 9½:6 (=19:12); the tonic return at bar 72 (second B section) subtends a near-symmetrical division of 12½:12; and the coda's arrival divides these latter 12 units 6:6. (The very slight inaccuracies in the ratios of 30½:18½ and 12½:12 are mutually explanatory: to correct one would exacerbate the other.) Just anticipating the recapitulation at bar 72, the quaver movement begins at bar 70, after 42 units, over a tritonal bass F♯, completing a 21:21 division around the climactic first tonic arrival in bar 28. The piece's remaining climax, in bars 61–2, lies over the halfway point (17:17 units) between the first climax and the end.

Why the tempo changes are not indicated remains mysterious; they are equally absent in the only known autograph.[7] But the necessary indication ♩ = ♪ , at bar 43 of 'Ce qu'a vu le vent d'ouest' (present in the printed score), is also missing from the same manuscript, providing at least one other instance of a tempo instruction so obvious to Debussy's musical instinct that he appears to have taken it as read (like the g♮"s in *L'isle joyeuse*, mentioned earlier on page 49 note 1).

The manuscript of 'La cathédrale' does contain one piece of circumstantial evidence: in bars 70–3 the quavers are notated as semiquavers, with the bar-line between bars 70 and 71 omitted; and the minims in bars 72–3 are obviously changed from what were initially crotchets. This is shown in Ex. 28. Rather than

Ex. 28: Autograph manuscript of 'La cathédrale engloutie', bars 67–73 (reproduced by courtesy of The Robert Owen Lehman Foundation and of The Pierpont Morgan New York)

soil what is an unusually beautiful manuscript, Debussy refrained from scoring out the semiquaver bars, and instead noted neatly in the margin that 'ces doubles croches sont des croches' (these semiquavers are quavers). But this manuscript, in view of its exceptional immaculateness — even for Debussy — must have been recopied from an earlier draft (as is known to have been Debussy's normal practice). His mistake in bars 70–3 suggests that the draft from which he was copying may have had a different metrical notation, which he was now altering in the course of recopying. The concentration necessary could easily have been sufficient to distract him from remembering to supply instructions for changing

7. The autograph of the complete first book of *Préludes* forms part of The Robert Owen Leh- man foundation, on deposit in The Pierpont Morgan Library, New York.

the tempo. (Also, the two doublings of speed come, like so many manuscript problems, at the beginnings of new lines.)

The alternative argument, that he simply could not count well enough to cope with these metrical complications, is hardly borne out by the metrical intricacies successfully negotiated in, for example, the first movement of his Sonata for Flute, Viola and Harp. Whatever the answer, it cannot change the proportions documented in the music itself, as Debussy intended it to be heard.

The last works

Some of the last works of 1915 onwards appear to carry the process of subverting proportional systems to its full conclusion, by ultimately defying their logic and largely avoiding the types of proportional system found in earlier works. *En blanc et noir* eschews obvious GS sequences almost completely, and the forms of the Sonatas and *Etudes* are less dependent on them than earlier works have been seen to be. This does not disprove the relevance of GS to earlier works; it merely reflects that some of the late works explore a very different idiom – particularly with the elliptical density of some of the *Etudes* or *En blanc et noir*. When GS–symmetrical sequences are clearly present, as in 'Pour les huit doigts' (bijugate Fibonacci numbers, counting by crotchet beats), they are not always resolved at the ends of the pieces. Sometimes other clear numerical sequences are involved, such as the 34 bars of the central section of 'Pour les octaves' (bars 49 – 82), divided $10 + 9 + 8 + 7$. Some simple GS constructions remain: the last of all Debussy's piano pieces, the *Elégie* of December 1915 (now republished by Jobert, Paris 1978), begins and ends quietly, reaching its climactic point after 13 of its total of 21 bars.

To investigate those aspects of Debussy's late style properly would require another book. But the tendency can be summed up briefly by saying that Debussy, continuing his constant evolution away from the musically obvious, sometimes moved clear even of any instinctive expectations and rewards that might be involved in following GS and symmetrical sequences – avoiding the subconsciously expected proportional move, just as his earlier works develop by forestalling the expected melodic or harmonic follow-through. When proportional systems are partly present, as in some of the *Préludes* or *Etudes*, they could simply initiate musical relationships that can then be continued and developed in different ways.

It can be added that if Debussy was unaware of his proportional systems, the subconscious judgment responsible first of all for organizing them with such precise logic would later have had to avoid completely – and still subconsciously – the possibility of such occurrences in a selected number of the late works.

'The golden mean, as Aristotle says, keeps you from bein' a golden ass.'

— Lord Peter Wimsey

Chapter 11

External evidence

It may have seemed churlish in the preceding chapters not to accept quietly that Debussy's *divin nombre* letter about 'Jardins sous la pluie' establishes that he planned his proportional systems consciously. But the remark is arguably not explicit enough to be absolutely conclusive; on the more positive side, to pursue the question further can lead to other worthwhile discoveries. If the proportional structures were really subconciously formed, then the subject awaits psychological research well beyond the scope of this book, and Gustav Fechner has been vindicated to a degree he could hardly have dreamt of. If, on the other hand, they were consciously formed – or even just if they reached their final exactitude with Debussy's conscious assistance – then two main questions follow. First, where did he learn the idea? Second, why was he so secretive about it?

The existence of the second question of course makes the first harder to answer. In addition, Debussy's childhood education was so irregular that we can trace little of what he was formally taught then.[1] Nor can we examine his library, now dispersed; in any case much of what he read in his formative years was probably borrowed or read in his favourite bookshops, discussed more below.

But when we speak of his formative years, it is well to remember how long his musical formation took, as already seen in Chapter 4 above. One of the most decisive periods in Debussy's life came at the end of his student days when, freed from his institutional studies, he was caught up by the Symbolist movement, spending more time among writers and painters than with fellow-musicians. These circles form one focus for this chapter's investigation.

Another important event was his first childhood encounter, at about the age of nine, with the artistic avant-garde, brought about through the eccentric figure of Charles de Sivry, brother-in-law of Paul Verlaine and, according to Emile Goudeau (1888, 109), 'musician too, but more particularly a cabbalist passionately embroiled in occult science'. De Sivry encountered the young Debussy through knowing Debussy's father during the 1871 Paris Commune, after which de Sivry's mother, by then Mme Mauté de Fleurville, took charge of the

---

1. According to Julia d'Almendra (1965, 110), who interviewed Debussy's sister Adèle in 1948, Debussy spent a good part of his infant years not with his parents but with his aunt in Cannes. There he was even trained in the music- al liturgy of the cathedral, and d'Almendra suggests this as the origin of his love of the old modes and of Palestrina and his contemporaries.

young Debussy's musical education. What Debussy heard and learned in this radical milieu must have contributed largely to his subsequent disrespect for the academic establishment when he went on to study at the Conservatoire in 1882. (His Conservatoire studies appear to have included no incitements to compose by proportional systems.)

It is easier to trace what Debussy would have heard among the Symbolists. Proportional balance has always been regarded as basic to composition in the visual arts, as documented notably in Paul Sérusier's *ABC de la peinture*, a substantial part of whose thirty-five constituent pages is devoted to proportions – and of this, almost four pages (pages 16–17 and 19–20) to the Golden Section. Although the book did not reach print until 1921, it was intended as a handbook of traditional teaching, with ideas Sérusier had gathered since early in his career, when one of his closest associates was the painter Maurice Denis – who in turn was a friend and artistic collaborator of Debussy's in the late 1880s (he designed the cover illustration for *La damoiselle élue*). Denis's own interest in numbers and proportion is discussed later in this chapter.

Numerical structure has an equally long pedigree in literature, going back at least to Virgil, incorporated either as proportions or by more esoteric systems of number symbolism – or, in some cases, by both simultaneously. G. E. Duckworth (1962), Alastair Fowler (1964; 1970) and Gunnar Qvarnström (1966) demonstrate some of the most striking examples of number systems lurking below innocent façades in famous literature.

The Symbolists were specially interested in this subject for two reasons – the possible cabbalistic and other hidden connotations of the numbers themselves on the one hand, and, on the other, the more practical use of numbers in shaping and balancing forms. Evidence of the former will be discussed further on. Apropos of the latter, the Symbolists' (and Debussy's) famous preoccupation with *plaisir* – in its proper meaning and in its artistic role – was a thoroughly scientific pursuit for them, not just a dilettantish hedonism as is still often supposed. One of the most precise expressions of this scientific quest can be found in the writings of the mathematician Charles Henry.

A shy figure, whose reputation suffered almost complete eclipse after his death in 1926 until a recent resurgence of interest, Henry was a crucial background presence to the Symbolist movement in the 1880s and 1890s, particularly as a recognized mentor to the 'Hydropathes', a large, loosely knit association of avant-garde artists in the 1880s. Through the 'Hydropathes' and his literary friend Gustave Kahn, Henry became one of the closest friends of Jules Laforgue, whose art criticisms, well known to Debussy, are very obviously influenced by Henry's scientific approach. Through Laforgue, Henry also became acquainted with the musical Ysaÿe brothers, with whom Debussy became friendly some years later. Most notably, Henry was a co-founder of the influential Symbolist journal *La Vogue*, and his writings figured widely in other Symbolist journals – including *La Revue Blanche*, in whose pages Debussy's 'Monsieur Croche' later made his début. (Félix Fénéon, the editor of *La Revue Blanche*, was one of Henry's most enthusiastic supporters.) According to David Arkell (1979, 42), Henry was also the model, or one of them, for Paul Valéry's *Monsieur Teste*, from which Debussy later rather shamelessly pillaged – to Valéry's irritation – for his own 'Monsieur Croche'.[2]

Henry was particularly concerned to demonstrate numerical relationships that can be linked with such sensations as 'harmonious' and 'inharmonious' combinations of colour, or with concordant and discordant shapes and angles in the composition of drawings. In Henry's view these qualities could be analysed in terms of the same mathematical equations as could the curves and angles of a musical melodic line. In short, Henry sought to give simple and workable definition to the relationships between mathematics and art in ways that could also link all the arts – an extension of the quest that had motivated the work of others like Gustav Fechner, whom Henry frequently mentions. It was predominantly from Henry's theories that Georges Seurat's and Paul Signac's Neoimpressionism was derived (thoroughly documented by William Homer, 1964); Camille Pissarro also followed this school for a time before breaking away, finding that the applications of the theories were becoming too stereotyped – again, too much like a *formule*.

In relating his theories to music Henry took a special interest in the theoretical writings of Rameau, and there his prime concern, as with the ancient Greeks, was the numerical relationships inherent in melody, harmony and rhythm. It is in his more general aesthetic writings that discussion of larger-scale proportion appears, and prominent in this is discussion of the Golden Section.

Henry's first publication on aesthetics, the *Introduction à une esthétique scientifique* of 1885, quickly shows his breadth of reference: by pages 5–6 he has illustrated the artistic criteria he is dealing with by touching on the most marked stylistic traits of artists as varied as Leonardo da Vinci, Rameau and Edgar Allan Poe. Should that have failed to raise the young Debussy's eyebrows, Henry immediately groups Leonardo and Rameau together as the two artists who, he considers, 'pursued farthest the science of aesthetics' (*ibid.*, 5). His next sentence takes as an example Leonardo's illustrations for his friend Luca Pacioli's GS treatise *De divina proportione* of 1509. By page 6 Henry's discussion has included

2. José Argüelles (1972) gives a complete bibliography of Henry's writings, together with a thorough study of his work and influence on the Symbolist movement. Henry's acquaintance with the Ysaÿe brothers is documented in his correspondence with Laforgue, edited many years later by Debussy's close friend Georges Jean-Aubry (Laforgue, 1922, vols. 4–5). Laforgue himself met the Ysaÿe brothers through the journalist Théo Lindenlaub, a known acquaintance of both Henry and Debussy. Whether Debussy knew Laforgue personally is not known; Laforgue died shortly after Debussy's return from Rome.

Henry's friendships with Laforgue and other writers are traced further by David Arkell (1979, especially 41–3). Remarkably, Debussy was one of the earliest admirers of Laforgue in the 1880s, when Laforgue was still virtually unknown except to his friends. Some fascinating evidence of this has been gathered by Margaret G. Cobb (1982).

both Gustav Fechner and Adolf Zeising, the latter also owing his fame to GS treatises of 1854 and 1884. Page 15 takes up proportions specifically, singling out 'harmonic proportion' and Golden Section because they alone combine the properties of geometric series with addititive or subtractive functions. The latter he gives in its two names of *section d'or* and 'la *divine proportion* de Pacioli'.

Page 20 takes up music more specifically, but less in terms of large proportions than in terms of the shape of melodies considered as curves, or as a line turning through a different angle with each new note. Making the analogy with sculpture, Henry quotes at length from Eduard Hanslick on the subject of 'arabesque' and its aesthetic importance – a recurrent subject some years later in Debussy's writings. By page 30, after more precise numerical analysis of musical intervals and of the significance of temperament in tuning, Henry's discussion has again become more general, and among other ideas raised in the closing paragraphs is the presence of spirals in nature. For a pamphlet of thirty-one pages, the amount of attention given to some of Debussy's favourite topics, quite apart from GS and spirals – Rameau, Edgar Allan Poe, arabesque, and precise links between the arts – is very remarkable.

Most of Henry's aesthetic publications are similarly short; only 'L'esthétique des formes' (first published in instalments in *La Revue Blanche* in 1894–5) is considerably longer, summing up the basis of various of his earlier works, and again discussing the Golden Section. Since Henry's other writings include articles such as 'Loi d'évolution de la sensation musicale' (1886), *Wronski et l'esthétique musicale* (1887a), and *La théorie de Rameau sur la musique* (1887b), it is hard to imagine that the young Debussy would not quickly have fastened on them. When the *Introduction à une esthétique scientifique* appeared in 1885, Debussy was in Rome; but we have some idea, from Debussy's correspondence with friends such as the Parisian bookseller Emile Baron (quoted in Ambrière, 1934), of how carefully, even in Rome, he followed Parisian avant-garde literary and other artistic developments. As we saw in Chapter 4, it was shortly after 1885 that GS and symmetrical organization began to appear in a thoroughly organized way in Debussy's music – particularly in 'Spleen'.

When Henry's subsequent aesthetic papers appeared, Debussy was back in Paris and mixing in circles that included various friends of Henry – notably the eccentric poet and inventor Charles Cros, known for his interest in ancient secret traditions of art (Goncourt, 1891, 70). This part of Debussy's life is strangely shadowy, different acquaintances tending to give different accounts of his interests and circles of friends, suggesting that he moved somewhat silently among many of them. Since Debussy was still largely unknown at the time, few bothered to document his movements – not that Debussy would have encouraged any such attempts. There is no record of whether Debussy ever met Charles Henry, though if he ever attended the occasionally 300-strong gatherings of the 'Hydropathes' he must have been aware of Henry's influence there. In any case, we have so much documented discussion of Henry's work, in books that Debussy must have known (such as Charles Morice's 1889 literary manifesto *La littérature de tout-à-l'heure*), in numerous reviews of Henry's writings in Symbolist and other journals, perhaps implicitly in the connection between Messieurs Croche and Teste, and in later recollections by people who were friends of Debussy's at the time – notably in Maurice Denis's *Théories* – that it is inconceivable that Debussy, with his insatiable curiosity and literary appetite, could have remained unaware of the exact nature of Henry's work.

A more curious aspect of Debussy's interests, little mentioned by most of his friends, was his preoccupation with the occult. While this had become something of a fad in *fin-de-siècle* Paris (see, for example, Lionel Carley's amusing anecdotes (1975, 50) which include Delius infuriating Strindberg at a Parisian séance by making the table spell out *m-e-r-d-e*), Debussy's interest appears as something much more serious, in common with that of many Symbolist artists – reflecting the underlying Symbolist belief at the time that science was on the verge of breakthroughs that would establish new links, or re-establish ancient ones, with both art and religion.

Debussy's occult involvements were first documented by Léon Guichard (in Lockspeiser, 1965, 272–7), who tracked down Debussy's association with Joséphin Péladan's rather tub-thumping neo-Rosicrucian movement in the early 1890s, and his abortive musical collaboration with the occultist playwright Jules Bois in 1892. It appears that Debussy was occupied with *ésotérisme* even during his stay in Rome from 1885–7, his letters to Emile Baron (Ambrière, 1934) requesting supplies of not only Symbolist journals but also such titles as *Rose + croix* by Albert Jounet (known then as an occultist and cabbalist), and Charles Morice's *Le chemin de la croix*. Neither of the titles has been traced, unfortunately. One may well wonder whether such interests had been inculcated at an early age (together with ideas about number?) by Charles de Sivry.

By the time of Debussy's return from Rome in 1887, a central Parisian rallying-point for both esoteric and Symbolist devotees was establishing itself in the shape of the bookshop and publishing house L'Art Indépendant of Edmond Bailly, another *ésotériste* of widely remarked erudition. Alain Mercier (1969, 126) considers Bailly's influence primarily responsible for the new spread of interest in esotericism around that time, and the poet and *ésotériste* Victor-Emile Michelet, who was actually on the scene, describes the shop in more detail (1937, 66–80), as does Debussy's poet friend Henri de Régnier (1926). According to Michelet Debussy was one of the most regular callers (it was Bailly who first published Debussy's *Cinq poèmes de Baudelaire* and *La damoiselle élue*). In Michelet's words (1937, 75):

Able to express himself freely there, Debussy let himself be thoroughly impregnated with Hermetic philosophy [involving reputedly ancient Egyptian theories of magic and alchemy]. Besides his reading on that subject and conversations with Edmond Bailly, who was a student of the esoteric side of both Occidental and Oriental music, he became acquainted with the sacred music of the Hindus [*sic*] through frequenting the Sufi Inayat Khan and his two brothers.

167

Among the shop's other frequent visitors were Mallarmé; Gustave Moreau, at that time Debussy's favourite painter (Lockspeiser, 1962, 230); Villiers de l'Isle-Adam, whose Rosicrucian play *Axël* became one of Debussy's unfinished operatic projects; Odilon Redon; Huysmans; the engraver and sculptor Félicien Rops; Degas; Toulouse-Lautrec; and Régnier. Régnier himself (1926, 89) mentions Verlaine and Laforgue as having been visitors in earlier years before Bailly took the shop over from Edouard Dujardin, the editor of *La Revue Indépendante* and founder of *La Revue Wagnérienne*. Some of those that Debussy met there he may already have known from the Chat Noir before his stay in Rome. One wonders what books and journals filled Bailly's bookshelves (Charles Henry's writings must surely have been there), or what conversation passed between the shop's visitors. Michelet documents some of the ideas in the air by quoting a letter he received in 1890 from Mallarmé (Michelet, 1937, 67):

Mon cher confrère,
Thank you for sending me your study *De l'ésotérisme dans l'art*. It interests me quite personally. For I'd find it difficult to conceive anything or to follow it up without covering my paper with geometry that reflects something of the mechanism of my thinking. Occultism is the commentary on the pure signs obeyed by all literature, the immediate projection of the spirit.

Votre très persuadé,
Stéphane Mallarmé.

If this is a rather unusual view of Mallarmé, Alain Mercier (1969, 123 seq.) tends to corroborate it, giving other evidence of Mallarmé's interest in geometry, equations and cabbala. Unfortunately no detailed record seems to be available of exactly what was discussed at Mallarmé's *mardi* gatherings. According to Walzer (1963, 186), Debussy was quite an early *habitué* of the *mardis*, even before his close friend Pierre Louÿs.[3]

---

3. Some fascinating glimpses of the Parisian literary world from the 1880s to the 1920s come from the large collection of correspondence (now in the Carlton Lake Collection at the Humanities Research Center, University of Texas at Austin) between Victor-Emile Michelet and various literary and artistic friends, much of it concerning his work as editor of the periodical *La Jeune France*. The letters amply document both the professional esteem and the affectionate regard in which Michelet was held by as wide a range of artists as Villiers de L'Isle-Adam, Edmond Bailly, Théophile Gautier, Eugène Carrière, Jules Massenet, the singer Emma Calvé, Debussy's early friend Maurice Bouchor (whose letters to Michelet include questions about cabbala), Georgette Leblanc, Charles Morice, and Debussy's friends and artistic collaborators Gabriel Mourey and Ricardo Viñes. Debussy's acquaintance with Michelet would have continued through the involvement of both of them in the literary Société Baudelaire in the 1890s and 1900s; it was from the Société's archives that Debussy's correspondence with Michelet recently emerged (via a dustbin), on the subject of proposed music (never completed) by Debussy to accompany a performance in 1903 of Michelet's esoteric play 'Le pèlerin d'amour'. This episode is fully documented by Robert Orledge (1982, pp. 266–8 and p. 368 note 29), and also by R.-E. Knowles (1954, 230–1), whose sympathetic study of Michelet's career provides further fascinating glimpses of Parisian literary life of that period.

It is also tantalizing that no record exists of Debussy's conversations with Inayat Khan and his brothers; apart from any more arcane knowledge, they may have been a main source for Debussy's later use of Eastern modes, as already seen in *L'isle joyeuse* and *La mer*. More precise knowledge of Debussy's interests can be gleaned, however, from Villiers de l'Isle-Adam's *Axël* – though sadly Debussy's musical sketches for it have disappeared. Like Goethe's *Faust*, which Debussy also knew,[4] *Axël* makes prominent reference to the magic significance of the pentagram (Mariel edition, 1960, 195) – a figure at the centre of most esoteric symbolism, and the most basic geometric manifestation of the Golden Section, as its lines divide one another uniquely by GS. Pierre Mariel, in his introduction to *Axël* (*ibid.*, 25–7), shows that much of *Axël*'s symbolism, including the preoccupation with the pentagram, is derived from Eliphas Lévi's *Dogme et rituel de la haute magie*, where the pentagram (*pentacle*, which Lévi spells *pantacle*, as Villiers then also does) figures prominently. Lévi includes the following description of what geometrically can only be the Golden Section (Lévi, 1896 [English edition], 87):

By the Pentagram also is measured the exact proportions of the great and unique Athanor necessary to the confection of the Philosophical Stone and the accomplishment of the Great Work.

If Lévi's passage sounds fatuous to our ears, this does nothing to lessen the influence the book had on the circles Debussy was frequenting in the 1880s and 1890s. Mercier (1969) documents this influence in some detail, listing many admirers of the book who knew Debussy (such as Catulle Mendès) as adepts of cabbalistic systems of number virtuosity that go well beyond the range of just the measurement of spiral lengths discussed in Chapter 8 above. Mariel (1960, 23) more specifically mentions Debussy as being influenced by the *Dogme et rituel*, although this might be hard to prove.

To be fair to Lévi, the sentence quoted above, like most occult alchemical writing, is meant allegorically in terms of the human soul, not just the making of solid gold. (This alchemical context also makes explicit the traditional association of GS with alchemy, already implicit in the name *section d'or*.) One could interpret Lévi as saying that in occult belief the proportion measured by the pentagram – that is, the Golden Section – purifies the soul and elevates the spirit. Whatever one thinks of this, the passage documents how GS was considered then among those with esoteric leanings, in addition to its purely aesthetic treatment by Charles Henry. This belief in the magic or health-giving properties of GS and the pentagram, incidentally, is well documented through the ages, traceable as far back as the Pythagorean school (see for example the *Encyclopaedia Britannica* article on Pythagoras). One implicit relic of this philosophy in music

4. Robert Godet (1926, 63–5), recounting Debussy's knowledge of *Faust*, and even of such authors as Schopenhauer, sums up: 'Debussy avait un cerveau égal à tous les tâches, à toutes celles du moins qui se passent du concours de la sottise ou de la pédanterie.'

is the fact that the standard 5-line musical staff is still known in Italian as the 'pentagramma' ('pentagrama' in Spanish).

Debussy's break with Péladan's movement in the early 1890s was not surprising, since Péladan's flamboyant ways contrasted as sharply with Debussy's natural secretiveness as with traditional Rosicrucian secretiveness. Whether Debussy continued esoteric activities after this is harder to ascertain; but a rather extraordinary dossier of esoteric political intrigues (Schidlof, 1967, 23) lists Debussy as Grand Master until his death (possibly a figurehead role) of the then highly secret Rosicrucian *Prieuré de Sion*, a movement that came to recent public prominence in connection with the mysterious history at the turn of the century of Rennes-le-Château.[5] The musician Numa Libin also recounts in conversation that Maggie Teyte, whom he knew well, related to him that when she knew Debussy (from 1907 onwards) he was still involved in esoteric activities, including esoteric Egyptology.

However all this may be, and however much Debussy may have differed with Péladan, there is much he may have learned from Péladan's very wide knowledge; it is a pity that their letters to each other are untraced since vanishing in Emma Debussy's disastrous auction of 1933. According to Paul Arnold (1955, 268), Péladan's musical theories were derived from Pythagoras and Plotinus, both known as avid disciples of number and numerology, and this recalls Debussy's reference to Plato in his letter about *divin nombre* and 'Jardins sous la pluie'. Plato's surviving writings do not in fact explicitly discuss GS, though it is implicit in the pentagonal faces of one of the five Platonic solids, the dodecahedron. But more relevant to Debussy's context, Plato is traditionally linked with GS – for example, by Matila Ghyka (1949, 224) and Ernő Lendvai (1971, 115).[6]

One other correspondence with Péladan, though it proves little, is so odd as to be worth relating. In 1892 Péladan published his allegorical Rosicrucian novel *Le panthée*, whose central figure is an impoverished composer, Bihn, no doubt partly drawn from Péladan's acquaintance with Debussy and Satie. Working constantly on his *Symphonie de l'or*, Bihn dreams of escaping with his mistress

5. This is now documented by Baigent *et al.* (1982), developed from the material presented by Henry Lincoln in two television programmes (Lincoln, 1979). Part of Lincoln's evidence concerned a precise connection with Nicolas Poussin's painting *Les bergers d'Arcadie*, shown to be designed around the pentagram; and this gives a special slant to an otherwise enigmatic dictum in Péladan's rules for the 1892 *Salon des Rose + Croix* – that among the types of painting to be rejected were 'all landscapes except those composed in the manner of Poussin' (Péladan, 1892, 292). In an earlier book on the subject of Rennes-le-Château, Gérard de Sède (1977,

28n) claims that the central character in the affair, Béranger Saunière, was entertained *chez* Debussy in 1891.

6. Lendvai's reference, though, results from his having taken Plato's description of geometric series in general (from the *Timaeus*) for one of GS. François Lasserre (1964, 89) explains more precisely that Plato's contemporary Eudoxus was said in Classical times – by Eudemus – to have learnt his geometrical proofs about the Golden Section from Plato, and that this tradition has lived on.

from the wretchedness of city life to an idyllic existence on the island of Jersey. One wonders what Péladan's thoughts were when Debussy, twelve years later, himself eloped to Jersey with Emma Bardac, while he was at work on *La mer*, his own *symphonie de l'or* in the special sense we saw in Chapters 7–9 above.

Various passages in Debussy's published articles suggest he sympathized with Charles Henry's or Péladan's numerological views. Defending the music of Rameau, Debussy takes up Rameau's scientific approach to music, recalling

the old Pythagorean theory that music should be reduced to a combination of numbers: it is the 'arithmetic of sound' just as optics is the 'geometry of light'. (Debussy, 1977, 255.)

An ardent reader of Baudelaire, Debussy might have felt this beyond mere abstract theory. Baudelaire's essay *Du vin et du hachish* describes a particularly vivid experience of music as numbers (1961, 338) – from which it is not a long step to the vortexes and spirals of *La mer* (pages 77 and 97 above), with their exact numerical manifestations.

In her study *The Rosicrucian enlightenment*, Frances Yates makes frequent mention of the traditional Rosicrucian view of music as a scientific art, or an esoteric science, quoting examples like Vitruvius (much discussed by Debussy's contemporaries), who listed 'the arts and sciences based on number and proportion' as 'music, perspective, painting, mechanics and the like' (*ibid.*, 38). Yates also frequently emphasizes the Rosicrucian movement's prime interest in reform and renewal of the arts, seen as an image of the cosmos. Debussy's general affinity with this credo hardly needs further elaboration here, and it perhaps echoes particularly in another Debussy comment that 'Music is a mysterious mathematical process whose elements are a part of Infinity' (Debussy, 1977, 199).[7]

Other documentation exists of the ideas with which Debussy came into contact in the 1880s and 1890s. Maurice Denis published his accumulated theoretical ideas in 1912. Besides almost immediate mention of Charles Henry's work (1912, 3), he frequently expounds the importance of number:

True, it is easier to grasp the law of proportions, the mystery of the *sacred measures* [*saintes mesures*], the methods of synthesis in hieratic Egypt or ancient Greece ... (*ibid.*, 179)

From this subordination of nature to human sensibility and reason emerge all the rules: good proportions, the measure whereby one can ... find the numerical rapports as well with the Japanese as with the Egyptians – proportions that coincide in fact with our instinctive need for symmetry, equilibrium and geometry ... (*ibid.*, 267–8)

Denis, like his friend Sérusier an enthusiastic student of numbers, is doubtless referring to more varied and complex number systems than just GS; but it again

7. The oft-quoted passage, from an interview in April 1904, in which Debussy is credited with saying 'Il faut débarrasser la musique de tout appareil scientifique' is completely unreliable. In a letter to Louis Laloy the day after the 'interview' appeared in print, Debussy ridiculed its inaccuracy: 'C'est extraordinaire comme ce soi-disant musicien entend mal ...' (Debussy, 1971, 273 and 319; also in Lesure, 1962, 9 and 46).

illustrates to what extent Debussy was surrounded by such thinking at the very time numerical structures began to appear clearly in his music.

Early in the 1890s, through Pierre Louÿs, Debussy became friendly with the young Paul Valéry. Many years later, in his lecture *Histoire d'Amphion*, Valéry reminisced:

> I told Debussy I envisaged an extravagant operatic system based on an analysis of means and on strict principles ... Thus the orchestra and singers had profoundly different tasks; the dramatic action, mime and dance were all rigorously separated and produced each at its own rate, for well-determined durations. The same applied to the overall duration, divided and even timed by the clock. (Valéry, 1960, 1281)

This, the only recorded conversation between the two artists, probably dating from the mid-1890s (Lesure, 1977, 153), centres on the two principles of strict temporal proportion and structural counterpoint. Such a bureaucratic execution of the principles might hardly have appealed to Debussy, but once again we find him involved in such discussion. Valéry's other well-known passion at the time was Classical architecture; his interest in number was more precisely documented quite a few years later in 1931, when he wrote a preface to Matila Ghyka's GS treatise *Le nombre d'or* (whence the epigraph on page 23 above).

Even if Valéry's plan was not to Debussy's liking, a letter Debussy wrote to Georges Hartmann in 1897 tells us that Debussy's method was similarly to prepare a groundplan of a work before writing in the music: 'The musical plan of the *Chevalier d'or* is ready, and I just need about two and a half months to finish it' (Cobb, 1977, 46).[8]

We know, too, that Debussy shared his friends' critical alertness to architecture. Another letter to Georges Hartmann in 1898 (Roy, 1964, 118) finds Debussy railing for a good few paragraphs at what he considers the appalling architecture of the Opéra-Comique. Carried away in a vein of lyricism, he finishes:

> These people seem to know nothing about light, and consequently about the whole theory of luminous undulations [*la théorie des ondulations lumineuses*], the mysterious harmony that links up the different parts of an edifice ...

If this, tantalizingly, is not more technically specific, it still shows Debussy's strength of feeling on the subject; it also provides an excellent analogy to Debussy's own procedure six years later in *L'isle joyeuse* – one of his most luminous pieces – in terms of the dynamic undulations that serve to link up the piece's formal framework, as we saw in Chapter 5 above.[9] Such an alertness to architecture is hardly surprising, in any case, from one who had been brought up in the redesigned Paris of Baron Haussmann, characterized by its geometric groundplan of intricate but long alignments, converging on *étoiles* and other

8. No trace has ever been found of this work, with its rather Rosicrucian-sounding title.

9. Architects I have asked about this have various views. It seems most likely that Debussy

points of focus (rather as Debussy's structural counterpoints do) – and with its twenty constituent *arrondissements* arranged in an expanding spiral round the centre (which is why Paris can still be heard referred to colloquially as 'l'escargot').

A more explicit connection between architecture and his music appears in a letter from Debussy to Georges Jean-Aubry in 1908 (Cobb, 1977, 46), where Debussy expresses disquiet about Ricardo Viñes's way of playing his new second series of *Images*:

... he needs to put in some hard work on them. He still doesn't feel their architecture clearly, and, despite his incontestable virtuosity, he distorts their expression.

Again architecture and expression – *forme et sensation* – are connected; and, as we saw in Chapter 10 above, the architecture in these pieces is very unconventional.

His articles as a critic confirm a sharp awareness of musical architecture; a good reason for documenting all this will soon be seen. One of the clearest instances is his review in 1901 (Debussy, 1977, 22–3) of Paul Dukas's Piano Sonata:

... If you look at the third part of this sonata, you'll find, underneath the apparently picturesque exterior, a powerful force that controls, almost imperceptibly, the rhythmic tension as if by a steel spring [*un mécanisme d'acier*] ... You could even say that the emotions themselves are a structural force, for the piece evokes a beauty comparable to the most perfect lines found in architecture ...

Not only does this again link expression directly with form, but also the possible analogy of a spring (the passage is hard to render exactly in English, but this interpretation is reasonable) recalls the spiral in his own 'Hommage à Rameau', seen in Fig. 10.4 on page 142 above – a piece composed not long afterwards. Whatever the case concerning this detail, Debussy's last sentence anticipates the character of 'Hommage à Rameau' most precisely.

A more technical issue suggests that Debussy was using GS consciously. This is that the numerical sequences found in the analyses above nearly always reduce themselves at some stage to the Fibonacci series, the most convenient way of carrying out otherwise unwieldy GS calculations. This applies throughout 'Spleen' (the first comprehensive GS structure in his *oeuvre* – page 35 above); in 'L'âme évaporée' (page 37); in the incomplete dynamic sequences of Figs. 4.4–4.5 (page 40); in the opening dynamic sequence of *L'après-midi* (page 151); in 'La cathédrale engloutie' (page 160); in the most dynamic sections of

was referring to techniques used since ancient times to prevent monotony on the outside of a building all made of the same material. This is done by managing the relief of the walls and outlines so as to vary the amount and angle of light and shadow striking various parts of the walls, and, in the process, to emphasize the overall proportions. In musical terms this would be equivalent to the juxtapositions of modes and changes of texture and dynamics that help define the waves and formal outlines in *L'isle joyeuse*. Whatever the case, it tends to confirm that the issues Debussy was referring to were sophisticated architectural ones. I am grateful to Kenneth Buffery for enlightening conversation on this subject.

L'isle joyeuse (pages 54–5), 'Reflets dans l'eau' (pages 25–7), 'Hommage à Rameau' (page 142) and 'Poissons d'or' (page 148); in the Introduction to 'Dialogue du vent et de la mer' (page 97) and the earlier version of the Introduction to 'De l'aube à midi sur la mer' (page 89); and finally in the 1915 *Elégie* (page 162). Fibonacci numbers are also important in pieces not analysed here, including *Masques*, 'Pagodes' from *Estampes*, the 'Prélude' from *Pour le piano*, the *Prélude* 'Ce qu'a vu le vent d'ouest', and the introductory part of 'Rondes de Printemps'.

In addition to this we have the oddity that the plan of 'L'âme évaporée' (as seen in Fig. 4.2 and pages 37–8) appears artifically contrived, since some of its numerical intricacies, through they make up a Fibonacci network, could not have been intuited by a subsconscious sensitivity to GS–symmetrical division. Or if the incomplete Fibonacci systems seen in the *Ballade, Nocturne,* and the 'Menuet' from the *Suite bergamasque* (Figs. 4.4–4.5, page 40) were subconsciously intuited, this subconscious sensitivity would have had to work exactly for part of each piece and then suddenly switch itself off, which is hard to accept logically. Was Debussy experimenting in those pieces – with the discipline of writing to a set scheme, or by juxtaposing proportioned sections or whole pieces (as in the *Suite bergamasque*) with unproportioned ones?

If he was, this might have resulted from his observation that he had already intuitively approximated to GS in songs like *Beau soir* (page 33 above); we know *Beau soir* still in his mind over this period, since he had it published in 1891, about eight years after its composition. To link intuition with conscious technique in this way would have been specially in keeping with Jules Laforgue's views on the matter, which Debussy must have been reading at about that time (quoted in this book's Preface).

If all or some of the above supposition is correct, why was Debussy so secretive about it? One answer is simply that secretiveness was basic to his personality – 'Il était très secret' is usually one of the first comments one hears in conversation with those who knew him – possibly connected, too, with the habitual secrecy of esoteric circles. But Debussy generally avoided any technical description of his own music – for example, nowhere in his letters or writings do we find even the whole-tone scale named – and this reflects the fact that, in the most exact sense, he was the absolute professional, or *anti-dilettante*, whose professional pride lay in letting the music speak for itself. After all, virtually no composers before Schoenberg explained their precise techniques either, and though Schoenberg did, his aesthetic and temperament were far removed from Debussy's. Nor would Debussy have wanted to divulge any more techniques to the imitators of his style in the 1900s, who, he insisted, were in danger of making him loathe his own music.

Debussy also had to be on guard against misunderstanding from critics, some of it misguided, some of it wanton. More than a few critics considered his style too esoteric and contrived, and for Debussy to have let information leak about geometric construction would have been folly, virtually telling critics where to pounce. We know this was Debussy's point of view because he used the argument himself when writing in defence of Rameau (Debussy, 1977, 255):

[Rameau] was perhaps wrong to write down all these theories before composing his operas, for it gave his contemporaries the chance to conclude that there was a complete absence of anything emotional in the music.

Another article finds him putting this more aggressively (*ibid.*, 127): 'Moreover, I think it is dangerous to initiate the layman into the secrets of musical chemistry' – the main implication of this being a full awareness of techniques he was not prepared to divulge.

Did Debussy divulge anything more specific to friends? If he did, it would doubtless have been in confidence, and if so, it seems that confidence was respected. Nonetheless, some remarks from his friends are worth noting for what they may imply. Robert Godet, one of Debussy's most trusted friends, wrote to him in 1917 to compliment him on how the Sonata for Flute, Viola and Harp seemed in quite a new way to suspend itself in the air without visible support. Godet continues (Lesure, 1962, 82):

Of course, you have never abused the function of scaffolding, and you have always excelled – if anyone did – at flattening it with one kick once the edifice was complete.

Georges Jean-Aubry, with whom Debussy shared a love of Jules Laforgue's works, had a similar view. Writing in 1920 of Debussy's essential *goût de la liberté*, Jean-Aubry defines this as 'non pas le goût du désordre ... mais une secrète discipline à soi-même imposée' (1920, 193–4). Whatever they meant precisely, it is evident that those two intimates of Debussy's mature years accepted not only strict discipline in Debussy's music but also its complete compatibility with his musical freedom.

One particularly wonders what Jean-Aubry meant, because it was to him that Debussy first enthused in 1908 about André Caplet, who was soon Debussy's most trusted musical collaborator: 'This Caplet is an artist. He knows how to create sonorities and, with a pleasing sensitivity, he understands proportions [*il a le sens des proportions*] ...' (Debussy, 1957, 23). In 1909 Caplet was arranging *La mer* for two pianos, and in connection with the arrangement we find Debussy writing to him in a genial mood (*ibid.*, 40): 'You're the guardian angel of corrections ... and you're jolly good at counting! [*vous savez joliment bien compter!*]' What had Caplet been counting in *La mer*? Their correspondence gives no more clues; but numerical preoccupations would have been well in character with Caplet's known penchant for mysticism.

If, after all this, we have still not nailed Debussy down with proof more conclusive than his *divin nombre* letter, we can only congratulate him on having covered his tracks so efficiently, if indeed he did all this consciously – though his general secretiveness gives more weight to an odd slip like the *divin nombre*.

175

Might that letter be an example of the well-known subconscious urge to leave a clue somewhere when one has perpetrated the perfect crime? Whatever the case, it helps establish the perspective of this discussion if we also view it from the other side, considering what necessarily follows from the belief that Debussy's use of GS was completely unconscious.

One would have to accept immediately that he was also unaware of the exact nature of many of his most sophisticated forms, like 'Jeux de vagues', whose construction is inexplicable unless proportions are taken into account. This would require Debussy to have had a most unmeticulous lack of interest in exact architectural aspects; but we have just seen a profusion of his views telling us otherwise, in addition to his remarks on proportions quoted in Chapter 1 (page 9, note 11).

In the case of 'Jardins sous la pluie', if GS was not his conscious preoccupation, what was he referring to in his letter? As mentioned in Chapter 10, no other system is visible in the plan shown on page 137 above (Fig. 10.1); if one were, it would inevitably not have allowed the simultaneous GS precision of Fig. 10.1 – brought to maximum accuracy by the bar he added to the proofs. And if he counted bars in 'Jardins sous la pluie', did he avoid doing this in other pieces, despite the interest in number many of his associates had?

In 1889 Maurice Emmanuel records Debussy saying he 'could do with less four-bar phrases' in César Franck's symphony (Lockspeiser, 1962, 208). What about *L'isle joyeuse* and 'Jeux de vagues'? If he was not aware of the structural purpose of their four-bar sequences, it would suggest that his critical faculties had regressed since 1889; and his music otherwise hardly supports this idea. All this would have to apply to a composer who extolled 'the need to understand – so rare among artists' (Debussy, 1977, 254).

If there are some difficulties in accepting the idea that Debussy used GS consciously (mainly the lack of any trace of arithmetic on his surviving sketches), there seem to be considerably more indigestible contradictions involved if we take the other point of view. But the answer must be one or the other, and the more plausible option seems clear for the moment, though it is well not to adopt too fixed a position, since more evidence could appear that might either complicate or simplify the question. Whatever the exact answer, it does not change what the musical scores contain, and only affects two or three sentences of our provisional conclusions.

Roger Nichols (1977, 157) calls GS 'a structural and proportional device which does not draw attention to itself' – a description that could hardly ask for better corroboration than the way Debussy's use of GS managed to evade detection for almost a century. If deliberate, Debussy's strategy was well-nigh perfect, to the extent even of convincing many commentators that such strict procedures would be incompatible with his music. There is another important aspect, though, to this relationship between strictness of execution and freedom of expression. All the dimensional changes and variants traced in the chapters above were achieved simply by Debussy's extending or compressing the same musical material – by repeating a bar or a pair of bars, or conversely by eliminating some such repetition, or by stretching one bar to two or compressing two into one. Such an inherent flexibility of line, with all the advantages it brings, must also lead dangerously near at times to the stifling chasm of infinite possibilities. Ravel is an obvious example, among many, of a composer whose inner resources found their fullest stimulation when his outer ones were most strictly limited, and it is equally arguable that strict proportioning actually made composition easier in many respects for Debussy, anchoring the music down where apt, and providing the necessary way of balancing and controlling the new formal freedom his music had won in other respects. This again is in keeping with the general views on freedom and discipline expressed by Debussy's friends Godet and Jean-Aubry, quoted on page 175 above.

Edgar Allan Poe was one of the most dominating of all the literary influences on Debussy, and his essay 'The philosophy of composition' – virtually a catech-ism to many of the Symbolists – puts this relationship between expressive freedom and formal strictness neatly in focus. Poe's aim in this essay is to scotch completely the idea of artists forming their works in an inspired haze, without any idea of the precise mechanisms that shape them. Selecting 'The Raven' as one of the best-known and dramatically most effective of his poems, he explains:

It is my design to render it manifest that no one point in its composition is referrible either to accident or intuition – that the work proceeded step by step, to its completion, with the precision and rigid consequence of a mathematical problem.

Poe then lists in relentlessly logical detail a chain of coldly calculated decisions covering all aspects of the poem's composition, from its optimum overall length to the choice of the word 'Nevermore' as a refrain largely because of its asso-nance. Every possible technique is used to exploit and manipulate the reader's instinctive responses and expectations, building the tension all the while towards the poem's climax. Opinions vary as to whether Poe's tongue is in his cheek at times, so clinical seems his claimed manipulation of the reader's emotions; but the beauty of his position is that if indeed his tongue is in his cheek, then he is merely applying the same techniques one storey higher: all his technical explana-tions, and the surprises he springs with them, are similarly playing cat and mouse with the reader's expectations and responses.

On an immediate level, Poe's strategy could easily be adapted to define the logical course of detailed construction in a piece like Debussy's 'Reflets dans l'eau'. The analogy also extends more generally to the way Debussy's equally exact systems help the music to reach, unfiltered, to more powerful levels of emotional response in the listener, by avoiding the standard forms that drive more conventional music into the net of the listener's intellectually conditioned judgment. This is exemplified by the structural nature of *La mer*, where Debussy evidently wanted to keep the work's peculiar but very fundamental use of sonata form from being superficially audible. More important here, the smaller formal units and associated geometric structures make up the motives, subjects and developments in the underlying process of transformation and renewal, so that the larger sonata scheme effectively works one storey above (or below) the apparent level of argument – further extending the possible analogy with Poe's techniques.

Edward Lockspeiser had a constant preoccupation with this aspect of Debussy as an explorer and communicator of the remoter corners of dream consciousness, where emotions tell their truths unstifled by intellectual prejudice or inhibition. In his lecture 'Debussy's concept of the dream', Lockspeiser explored this idea along the line of Debussy's idolization of Poe and Turner, and it led him to an intriguing intuitive coincidence. Discussing parallels of dream images between Debussy and Turner, he played recorded extracts from *La mer*, and followed by quoting from an article by (the then) Sir Kenneth Clark:

This dream-like condition reveals itself by the repeated appearance of certain motifs which are known to be part of the furniture of the unconscious ... One of these is the vortex or whirlpool, which became more and more the underlying rhythm of [Turner's] designs ...

Turner's are not the only spirals that can be associated with *La mer*. The first edition of *La mer* appeared with a reproduction on the cover, at Debussy's request, from Katsushika Hokusai's print 'The hollow of the wave off Kanaga-wa', a copy of which also hung on Debussy's study wall (Pl. 1). The dominating motive of the print is the wave, whose lower outline curves in a logarithmic spiral, admittedly broader than Debussy's variety. In addition, the GS divisions indicated around Pl. 1 show how close the composition comes to overall GS – marking especially the upper extremity of the wave, the side of its lower curve, and the top of Mount Fuji.

Another of the most popular of Japanese prints at the time, which Debussy is likely to have known (and of which Monet had a copy), was Andō Hiroshige's 'The whirlpools at Awa' (Pl. 2), whose main motive speaks for itself, and which also approximates closely to overall GS composition (vertically, the division between water and land; horizontally, the centre of the vortex). Debussy's love of Japanese art is well known; whether or not he knew this print, it well illustrates the preoccupation with such shapes and compositions in Japanese art.

It is even possible that the spiral shapes hidden in Dubussy's music might have some intended significance relative to the spiral configuration of the human inner ear. This might sound too far-fetched were it not that a precise parallel can be drawn once again with Laforgue's essay on Impressionism, which stresses the relationship between the techniques of Impressionist painting and the workings of the human eye.

Pl. 1: 'The hollow of the wave off Kanagawa' from Katsushika Hokusai's *Thirty-six views of Mount Fuji, c.* 1820–9 (reproduced by courtesy of the Trustees of the British Museum)

Time will tell what further conclusions may result from the present study, once its findings have been put together with material from other fields, or material that may emerge in the future. As far as performing the music is concerned, it is worth remembering that the above analyses have all been made from what Debussy wrote in his scores; to try to emphasize the forms and shapes any further would be like trying to enhance a Renoir *baigneuse* by sketching in her skeleton. In this respect Robert Godet's comment, already quoted on page 175, about 'flattening the scaffolding with one kick once the edifice is complete' can equally aptly be applied to the music's performance. At the same time, the analyses above prove how precisely judged Debussy's indications are, and how crucial to the forms: there is even less excuse now than there ever was for the rhythmically and dynamically perverse performances of his music that tend to claim stylistic authenticity, often in the name of 'what imbeciles call Impressionism'.

The reader wishing some respite from Golden Sections is recommended to Anton Ehrenzweig's book *The hidden order of art*. Despite what the title might suggest, Ehrenzweig hardly touches on aspects like proportional techniques, but rather pursues in detail, and with much sympathetic understanding, the complexity of relationships in the various arts between subconscious inspiration and conscious techniques. This not only develops Laforgue's thoughts on the matter, but can give useful perspective to the present book's findings.

179

Other evidence

Ehrenzweig's thesis is that art has always evolved by breaking up surface continuities in order to exploit more hidden levels of cohesion; and that when the more hidden relationships, through development, become the obvious surface techniques, their fecundity dies (or to use Debussy's term, they become *formules*). As an example he mentions the practice among Romantic symphonists of helping unity by quoting from earlier movements in later ones, and points out the irony that the model this technique was derived from – the finale of Beethoven's Ninth Symphony – used the device for the absolutely opposite purpose of wrenching the finale away from the worlds of the earlier movements

Pl. 2: 'The whirlpools at Awa' from Andō Hiroshige's *Famous places in the sixty-odd provinces*, 1855 (reproduced by courtesy of the Victoria and Albert Museum)

180

(1967, 219–20). The argument has obvious affinities with the relationship between the surface argument in Debussy's music, the sort of surface interruptions that we saw in pieces like 'Jeux de vagues', and the hidden cohesion at deeper levels that those interruptions established.

Another main part of Ehrenzweig's thesis is that in general a crucial part of artistic creation is an oscillation between very precise critical phases and ones of more intuitive receptiveness to new inspiration. He suggests that on a smaller scale, too, more rapid alternations of these states are a normal part of healthy waking consciousness (*ibid.*, 203), and that their rhythm may be instrumental in defining our sense of time. Although he does not pursue this further with music, it invites more study. Not only basic rhythm and metre, but also the subtler large-scale rhythms and alternations of types of structures that we have seen in Debussy's music: for the sensitive listener these all might affect aspects of this psychological rhythm, and thus be instrumental in defining our sense of musical time and proportion – as well as in explaining music's ability to warp our sense of time away from clock time. This also makes obvious why good musical proportions cannot just be defined theoretically, but have to be matched to the music's content by the most critical intuition.

These are merely fragments of ideas that invite exploration. In short, the present book is likely to, and should, raise more questions than it answers. The hope is that its findings have helped define some of those questions more clearly, and may suggest some ways of investigating them. If more findings result that topple some of the opinions expressed in the preceding pages, I shall be entirely content.

Appendix 1

Measuring the arc length of a logarithmic spiral

(cf. page 105)

This can in fact be done without any recourse to mathematics: one simply lays a piece of thread or string along the arc of Fig 8.1 on page 97, marks off the length involved and then measures it by the same units as in the diagram. Obviously this rather crude method is not conducive to maximum accuracy; hence the calculation below.[1]

Even the calculation cannot give complete accuracy, for the reason that the musical plan represented in Fig. 8.1 follows Fibonacci numbers, which represent GS only to the nearest whole numbers. Therefore the points of intersection of a true logarithmic spiral, based on exact GS, will not correspond absolutely to the bar divisions in each case. The error, however, will always be very small – in this case a maximum of c. 0.3% of the diameter of the measured portion of the arc.

To define the spiral, two exact radii are required, together with the angle traversed by the arc between one and the other, which in the case of Fig. 8.1 is 900 degrees, or 5π radians. If we follow the Fibonacci proportions of Fig. 8.1 and take the spiral's point of focus (which of course it never reaches) as 34 units from the left edge of Fig. 8.1, the arc begins at $r = 3$ and ends at $r = 34$.

The logarithmic spiral (see Fig. A.1) is defined by

$\log r = K\theta$ (where K is a constant).

Fig. A.1

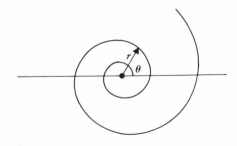

1. I am grateful to Drs David Jeffrey and Anand Sivaramakrishnan for showing me how to make the calculation, and to Andrew Uttley for confirming the result by alternative computer calculations.

Appendix 1

If natural logarithms are used, we obtain

$\ln r = k\theta$, where $\ln r$ denotes natural logarithm of r,

or $r = e^{k\theta} = \exp(k\theta)$, where exp is calculated by using natural log tables backwards. (Small k is a new constant.)

If the spiral begins at $\theta = \alpha$ and goes to $\theta = \beta$,

$$\theta = \alpha \Rightarrow r_1 = 3 = e^{k\alpha}$$

$$\theta = \beta \Rightarrow r_2 = 34 = e^{k\beta}$$

In this case also $\beta - \alpha = 5\pi$

To find k: $\quad \frac{r_2}{r_1} = \frac{34}{3} = \frac{e^{k\beta}}{e^{k\alpha}} = e^{k(\beta - \alpha)} = e^{5k\pi}$

$$\frac{34}{3} = e^{5k\pi} \Rightarrow k = \frac{1}{5\pi} \ln \frac{34}{3} = 0.1545553...$$

The reason for using natural logarithms is that the following equation then applies to find arc length:

$$\text{Arc length} = \sqrt{1 + k^{-2}} \, (e^{k\beta} - e^{k\alpha})$$

(This equation, derived from simple calculus, has been known for some centuries.)

Substituting for k, $e^{k\alpha}$ and $e^{k\beta}$

$$\text{Arc length} = \sqrt{1 + 0.1545553^{-2}} \, (34 - 3)$$

$$= 202.957 \text{ (accurate to 3 decimal places).}$$

In Fig. 8.6 (page 102) the central total of bars between Introduction and Coda must be an even number, to permit the symmetrical division at the end of the Exposition; 202 (101 + 101) is the nearest even number to the result above.

Alternatively one can calculate by taking two other fixed points (for example, $r_1 = 8, r_2 = 21$), making these the exact points of spiral intersection rather than the two points in the above calculation. One could then find k (which would be very marginally different) and calculate arc length with appropriate modifications to the above formula for arc length to cover the extension of the arc beyond the limits of the new r_1 and r_2. A further alternative is to begin with only one fixed radius (or diameter) and define k by means of exact GS:

$$\frac{r_1}{r_2} = GS = \frac{\sqrt{5} - 1}{2} \text{ whenever } r_1 \text{ and } r_2 \text{ are } \pi \text{ radians apart.}$$

Because the Fibonacci series only approximates to exact GS, resulting arc lengths can vary between 199 and 206, depending on the fixed points chosen; again 202 is the nearest even number to the mean of those results.

If indeed Debussy was more adept with numbers than is generally known, it could account for another hidden relationship linking the two spirals in the outer movements of *La mer*. That of Fig. 8.1 is based on the Fibonacci series, and that of Fig. 7.2 (page 77) is based on the summation series 7, 9, 16, 25, 41, 66...,on which the whole first movement is built. These two series, both defining circular figures, are related by π, the number that defines the measurement of circular arcs. That is, if one multiplies 3, 5, 8, 13, 21..., by π, one obtains, to nearest whole numbers, 9, 16, 25, 41, 66 and so on.

Appendix 2

Proportional intrigue in other composers' music

Various types of proportional correspondence, including GS, can be found in music by composers of many styles, schools and eras – though it is important to add that they are untraceable in equally large quantities of excellent music by many of the same composers. In many cases where GS is present, the musical evidence suggests that it is unlikely to have been applied consciously; also it often tells us little about the music that is not already obvious in orthodox terms. For example, E. J. P. Camp's investigation into the positioning of double-bars in Mozart sonata movements (1968) needs to be supplemented by more detail of what happens inside the sections – especially any unorthodox procedures – before one can guess why the double-bar is at the GS in some movements but not in others. In this respect John Rutter's more detailed proportional study (1975) of Beethoven's Fifth Symphony has more to tell us, suggesting how departures from the sonata norm are used to build up proportional and dynamic strength in terms of large-scale rhythms. Some of the proportions Rutter goes on to trace in Haydn and Mozart (*ibid.*) were almost certainly deliberately planned, since they involve other ratios besides GS. Haydn, Mozart and Beethoven are linked, too, by their connections with Freemasonry – even though only Mozart's involvement in it is known to have been very thorough.

Some cases of numerical structure in music are well known to have been deliberate. Brian Trowell's analyses (1979) of highly sophisticated numerology in music by Dunstable have proved themselves specially practical by helping to solve paleographic problems in manuscript sources. Newman Powell (1979) maps this field further, showing Fibonacci numbers in other medieval music, and giving an unusually lucid description of the special properties of GS. In recent music, some deliberate Fibonacci constructions by Křenek, Nono and Stockhausen are described by Jonathan Kramer (1973). Berg's preoccupation with numbers, particularly the number 23 (but apparently not the Golden Section), has long been known, on his own admission. Only recently, though, did the discovery by Douglass Green and George Perle of annotated sketches, and then of an annotated full score, of Berg's *Lyric suite* permit an appreciation of how intricately Berg practised numerical construction (Perle, 1977).

On the other side, Camp (1968, 33) mentions that Schoenberg, questioned about the Golden Section, disclaimed use of it (perhaps because the Fibonacci series contains the number 13?). Schoenberg's use of the term Golden Section to describe the relationship between dominant, tonic and subdominant keys (1978, 132) is a different matter, obviously intended metaphorically rather than mathematically. Roger Nichols also reports in conversation that Messiaen, asked in 1978 about GS, similarly disclaimed use of it – perhaps more surprisingly in view of his mysticism. It might make an interesting project – not attempted here – to investigate whether Messiaen's music nonetheless reveals any intuited GS patterns.

Ernő Lendvai's detailed study (1971) of Bartók's music is still controversial, mainly because some wayward arithmetic undermines the accuracy of many of his claims of GS construction. Lendvai also dodges the question of whether Bartók used GS consciously (if we accept that some of Lendvai's proportional conclusions are valid). This is discussed in more detail in Chapters 2 and 7 of Howat (1979) and in Howat (1983). The case cannot be proved one way or another since Bartók, perhaps wisely, left no explicitly incriminating evidence in letters or surviving sketches. On the other hand, any argument that Bartók – a voracious reader and an avid student of natural history – was unaware of GS has to contend with such immediately obvious details as the xylophone solo that opens the third movement of his *Music for strings, percussion and celeste*: the repeated f'''s follow a sequence of 1, 2, 3, 5, 8, 5, 3, 2, 1 per crochet beat between the beginnings of bars 2 and 4.

To investigate these other composers in detail is beyond the scope of this book; but three examples of GS construction are remarkable enough to be worth describing below. None of them has accompanying evidence, either in the manuscripts or in the composers' letters, to prove whether the use of GS was conscious or not. But the constructions are clear and logical, and also account for idiosyncrasies in the music's construction.

Schubert: Piano Sonata in A, D.959, first movement exposition

The first 81 bars of this movement, from Schubert's penultimate sonata, are a model of normal sonata exposition – tonic first group to dominant second group, linked by a modulating transition passage in bars 28–54. In performance it is easy to imagine the imminence of the double-bar in bars 78–81. Instead, at bar 82 the music plunges into a turbulent and chromatic development of the earlier transition material, before the main second subject returns in bar 117, leading to the double-bar and repetition. In normal terms this is unaccountable, yet it sounds convincing; what is its logic?

Fig. A.2 shows the layout of this passage, 132 bars long the first time, and 130 when repeated (counting over the cadence to C major the second time, as is logical). In every way the main turning point is the division after bar 81, separating the orthodox, diatonic part of the exposition from its irregular, tonally unstable adjunct. GS of 132 is 81·58, and of 130 is 80·34, so this main

187

division is within two-thirds of a bar of the exposition's primary GS for both the first and second times.

Fig.A.2: Schubert Sonata in A, D.959, first movement exposition

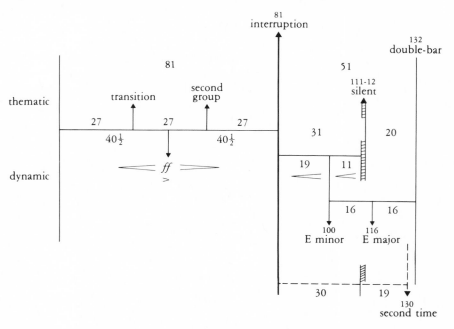

These first 81 bars – the stable portion – are divided 27:27:27 by the three thematic groups (first group, transition and second group) and also 40½:40½ by the section's dynamic apex, the *fortissimo* accented chord halfway through bar 41. Conversely, the irregular portion from bar 82 onwards is dominated by GS, the main division being at the silent bar 112 that marks this portion's climax (31:20 bars the first time, 30:19 the second). The sudden cadence to E minor and *subito piano* in bar 101 similarly mark the GS on the way to the silent bar (19:11 bars). From there to the double-bar (first time) the 32 bars are divided 16:16 by the return to tonal stability with the second subject in bar 117.

For all the music's difference from Debussy's idiom, the structural principle is the same one as we saw in *L'isle joyeuse* (Fig. 5.6 on page 55 above) and in *La mer* (Fig. 7.2 on page 77) – symmetry up to the GS point followed by GS after it. The principle of exposition, too, appears to be working in counterpoint on two levels, the 'surface' exposition up to bar 81 itself forming the first group of a more elemental exposition of stability against instability, symmetry against asymmetry. Again it is a disruption of surface coherence (after bar 81) that allows the more potent structure to develop under the surface. (And another disruption of surface coherence – the silent bar 112 – allows it to return to symmetry and tonal stability.) It should be added that in the movement's recapitulation the proportions are altered – but then it is no longer an exposition.

Schubert scholarship of the last decades has found enough evidence to quash the old notion of Schubert dashing off his masterpieces without careful preparation (see, for example, Reed, 1972); and this example must add to the intrigue of how he worked. (Some surviving sketches for the movement show that he did not originally sketch it to the above dimensions.) Whatever the answer, it might involve Jacques Chailley's study (1975) of *Winterreise*, in which Chailley unexpectedly found himself concluding that Schubert must have been involved in Freemasonry – a subject on which Chailley already had expertise from an earlier investigation of Mozart's *Zauberflöte* (1972). (Chailley also pointed out that Schubert would have been wise to keep any Masonic activity secret in the political climate of the time.) The structure analysed above also gives off a specific whiff of Freemasonry, in that the first 81 bars, divided 27:27:27, form 3 blocks of 3 to the power 3. (The movement's coda – another strange adjunct to the structure – again is 27 bars long.) Together with many other curious types of structural contrivance – tonal and other – in Schubert's music, this invites more study.

Ravel: 'Oiseaux tristes' from *Miroirs* (1904–5)

Of the five pieces comprising *Miroirs*, 'Oiseaux tristes' presents the simplest formal outlines. Its ternary form is clear as ABAA', the A' consisting of a cadenza and coda following a condensed recapitulation (bars 21–4). Leaving out for the moment the cadenza and coda, the main ABA portion of the piece – bars 1–24 – forms a dynamic arch beginning and ending *pianissimo*, and reaching a *forte* climax in bar 15. Counted by crotchet beats (since bar lengths vary), this section comprises 89 units, and the height of the dynamic arch is reached after 55 of these, making the dynamic arch clearly proportioned by Fibonacci numbers. The top part of Fig. A.3 shows this. The portions of the arch before and after the peak are also divided no more than one crotchet beat away from the intermediate points of GS, with the key change after 33 crotchets (bar 10), the onset of the central section with the agitated bird-calls after 47, and the recapitulation after 75 crotchets. The tonality at the climactic point is also the most remote key (E) reached from the piece's tonic E♭ minor, as well as the tritone from the B♭ which forms the first and last note of the dynamic arch.

Thus far there is no ambiguity whatever in the measurement of dimensions. The cadenza complicates this; as with the cadenza of Debussy's *D'un cahier d'esquisses* the normal rhythm is suspended, and it has to be related to what surrounds it in a musically realistic rather than literal way.[1] In 'Oiseaux tristes'

1. Vlado Perlemuter (1970, 24) confirms this, relating that Ravel warned him against playing the cadenza 'too literally. The *Lent* applies only to the chord and its prolongation before moving quite rapidly into the cadenza.'

Fig. A.3: Ravel: 'Oiseaux tristes' from *Miroirs*

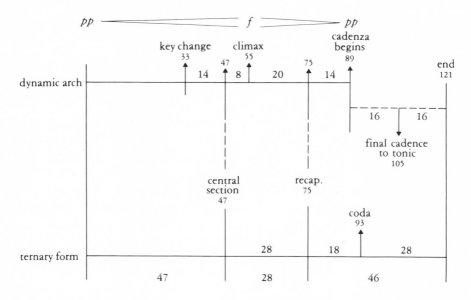

the predominating metre is 4/4; bar 26, following the cadenza, is in 4/4, and although bar 24, preceding it, is marked 2/4, both the harmonic motion and the dynamic gradation there give effectively a bar of 4/4 beginning halfway through the notated bar 23. The cadenza could then provisionally be counted as a group equivalent to a 4/4 bar, thus taking literally the semibreve in the bass.

If this is done, the length of the entire piece comes to 121 units. GS of 121 is 75:46, defining exactly the point of recapitulation (bar 21) and, to within a crotchet, the beginning of the central section after 47 units, as shown in the lower sequence of Fig. A.3. The coda similarly coincides with the GS between the recapitulation and the end, completing a GS arch sequence of 28:18:28 (accurate to the nearest crotchet) within the larger one of 47:28:46. All this shares the logic already seen in the Debussy examples: in the more static formal outlines the Golden Sections are balanced to form symmetrical arches, whereas the more dramatic element of the piece, the dynamic arch, avoids symmetry.

From Fig. A.3 it can be seen how harmoniously the two sequences are linked, the outlines of the ternary form growing logically out of the momentum of the dynamic arch. As a concluding link between the two sequences, the 32 units of cadenza plus coda are divided 16:16 by the final cadence to the tonic chord at the beginning of bar 29.

Even the small inaccuracies in Fig. A.3 can be logically accounted for. Were the recapitulation to enter at its theoretically ideal point in the dynamic arch – after 76 units – the piece would have to finish after 123 units. The resulting 34-unit length (instead of 32) from the end of the dynamic arch to the end of the piece would either disrupt the 16:16 ratio around the final cadence at bar 29, or necessitate its expansion to 17:17 – which would then cause metrical complications at a musically inappropriate point.

It is, incidentally, remarkable that this analysis should hinge on the same complication of measurement – the cadenza – as Debussy's *D'un cahier d'esquisses*, for Ravel is known to have written 'Oiseaux tristes' under the conscious influence of the structural ideas Debussy had just incorporated in *D'un cahier d'esquisses*.[2]

Like Debussy (and apparently unlike Schubert), Ravel makes frequent use of GS, notably throughout the *Miroirs*. The most sophisticated example is 'Alborada del gracioso', a virtual compendium of proportional devices, including a large-scale GS sequence derived thematically from a small-scale one related to it by the ratio $\sqrt{5}$ (from which is derived the exact value of GS, as shown on page 2 note 1 above).[3] As a subtle structural encore, Ravel orchestrated 'Alborada' in 1918, extending some passages to allow more time for orchestral colour and crescendo accumulation. This new version, inevitably breaking up some of the old proportional correspondences, erects new ones in their place.

Other works by Ravel showing GS construction include three dynamic arch forms – the songs *Si morne!* and *Les grands vents venus d'outre-mer*, and the piano piece *A la manière de Borodine*. More intricate GS construction, using Fibonacci numbers, is apparent in the Sonata for Violin and Cello and the late Sonata for Violin and Piano, as well as in parts of *Le tombeau de Couperin* (for example, in the 'Fugue' the first inverted entry occurs after 21 bars and the first stretto after 34). The third of the *Miroirs*, 'Une barque sur l'océan', goes further by mixing GS with another number system developed from powers of 3, contained inside clearly defined musical blocks, and then ingeniously developed in conjunction with the GS tendencies.

In general Ravel was known to be fascinated by hidden challenges, well

2. A Duo-art piano roll of 'Oiseaux tristes' (Duo-art no. 082), supposedly performed by Ravel himself, is among those mentioned on page 160 above as possibly having been made by Robert Casadesus. The carelessly articulated rhythm audible on this particular roll (obscuring the difference between duplet and triplet quavers, and thus the underlying crotchet pulse, at transitions such as bars 3–4) is therefore not definitely attributable to Ravel; nor is the aleatory treatment of bars 10–11 in the 'Ravel' Duo-art roll of 'La Vallée des cloches', also from *Miroirs*. The confusion over the authorship of these rolls is compounded by the fact that a recent issue of them on disc (Everest X-912) – no doubt done in all innocence – reproduces the 'Toccata' from *Le tombeau de Couperin* at a grindingly slow pace – just about the speed at which Ravel, a notoriously uneven pianist, might have

been able to play it! M. Jean Touzelet kindly clarified the matter by playing me his own copy of the 'Toccata' roll (Duo-art no. 086) on a properly adjusted Duo-art Steinway set to the speed indicated on the roll, producing a much more credible performance.

3. The $\sqrt{5}$ relationship is achieved in whole-number terms by a combination of GS and symmetry. 5 is thus related to 11 by 5+3+3, 13 to 29 by 13+8+8, 21 to 47 by 21+13+13, etc. Those are the numbers concerned in 'Alborada', counting in 6/8 units from the beginning, giving a fascinating pattern of thematic derivation. The logic of this arithmetic can be followed from the formula for GS in Chapter 1 above: if ϕ (the value of GS) is taken as the smaller value, 0·618034, then $\phi = \frac{\sqrt{5}-1}{2} \Rightarrow \sqrt{5} = 1 + 2\phi$, or $1 + \phi + \phi$.

exemplified by a highly ingenious piece of (non-GS) virtuoso construction quietly concealed in the 'Pantoum' of the Piano Trio, detected recently by Brian Newbould (1975). All this musical evidence gives a precise focus to Ravel's enigmatic remark to Maurice Delage: 'My *Trio* is finished. I only need the themes for it' (Stuckenschmidt, 1969, 149). One must suspect that Ravel knew well what he was doing; learning his craft in the Paris of the early 1890s he would have been aware of the same currents of thought as was Debussy, with whom he was then still on good terms.

Fauré: 'Reflets dans l'eau' from *Mirages* (1919)

Fauré's choice of poem (from the Baronne de Brimont's set of *Mirages*) might suggest homage to Debussy, who had died the year before. At the same time the superficial parallel shows how different their idioms were – notably in this song's avoidance of any strong dynamic surge. But there is a more concealed correspondence.

The poem's seven stanzas, all the same length, are spread to different lengths in the music – respectively 13, 11, 9, 11, 12, 17 and 38 minim units, indicating special treatment for the last stanza, with its quietly sinister climax to the poem ('Si je glisse ...'). In a through-composed setting, Fauré runs his main musical transitions in counterpoint with the verse, preventing the musical transitions from coinciding with beginnings of stanzas until the crux – the beginning of the final stanza at bar 33. Thus the opening 2/2 metre expands in bar 18 to 3/2, aptly at the word 'caresses' in the first line of the third stanza – the word-painting underlined by an inversion of the hitherto constant texture, and a slightly feverish glimpse of the tonic key through the chromaticism. In response, the 2/2 metre returns in bar 25, just before the end of the fifth stanza, and lasts until the end of the song. The first of those metrical changes arrives after 34 minim beats, and the other one after 55, leaving 56 units to the end.

Fig. A.4 shows, in addition to this simple Fibonacci sequence, how the final 56 beats are arranged to accommodate the poem's climax in the last stanza. The quaver movement, constant since the song's beginning, is interrupted halfway through bar 33, after 72 units, to make way for the menacing 'Si je glisse, les eaux feront un ronde fluide ...' The accompaniment to this ripples in three phrases of triplet then duplet quavers, until the original accompanying texture returns in the second half of bar 44, the ripples having subsided. From the interruption in bar 33 to the end of the ripples in bar 43 there are 21 units (counting the rest in bar 44 apart); the surrounding sections, each of 17 units (to the nearest whole number), make up a total of 34, balancing the song's climactic section by GS and setting it symmetrically in the centre of the last 56 units. (The extra unit – 56 instead of 55 – is present because to produce exact Fibonacci numbers again in the second half of the song would involve another interruption of the 2/2 metre.

Fig. A.4: Fauré: 'Reflets dans l'eau' from *Mirages*

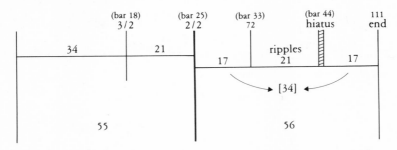

Presumably Fauré, no slave to *rigueur*, decided that musical exigencies took priority – especially in this case the dramatic effect of the structural hiatus in the bar 44.)

GS is completely absent from the other three *Mirages* and, as far as can be seen, from most of Fauré's output. If this example of Fibonacci construction was unconsciously intuited, what happened to the intuition in all his other music? Might Fauré have been paying homage to Debussy on more than one level, quietly incorporating what he perhaps knew was a technique special to Debussy (as well as to Fauré's former pupil Ravel)?

Whatever the answers in the above three analyses, there is a distinct possibility that such techniques have been in the conscious equipment of many composers, who, finding them in earlier music, have quietly borrowed or developed them. This certainly applies to some twentieth-century composers: Peter Maxwell Davies is one who has confirmed it in conversation, mentioning Dallapiccola as one of various composers with whom he has discussed proportional and other hidden techniques in music of the past. The point is also implicit from all the analyses in this book that, with many composers, the more a piece flouts formal norms the more one might suspect other types of discipline in its formal organization.

Appendix 3

'Reflets dans l'eau' (*Images* of 1905)

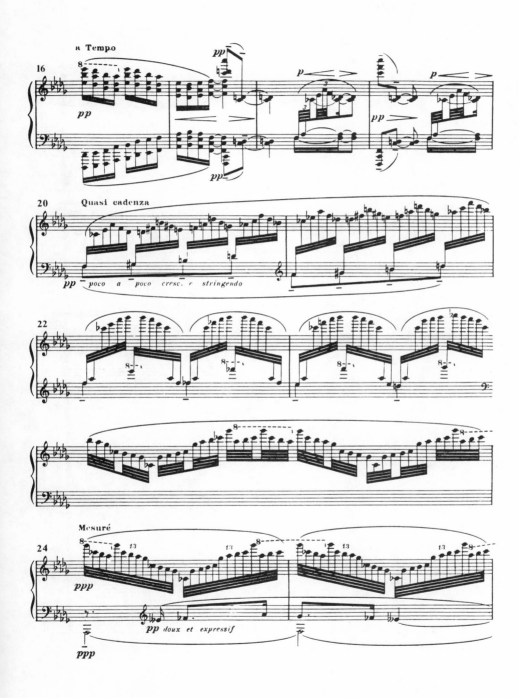

195

'Spleen' (*Ariettes oubliées*)

'Clair de lune' (*Suite bergamasque*)

L'isle joyeuse

213

215

Textual commentary

Three sources have been available for each piece reproduced above. In each case source 3 is a second edition corrected or revised from the first edition, and this source 3 has been taken as the basis for the text above. In the cases of 'Reflets dans l'eau' and *L'isle joyeuse* the firm of Durand no longer has records of the exact dates of issue of those second editions (the works were reprinted about every two years) but can confirm that the corrections were supplied by Debussy. In the case of 'Clair de lune' the corrected edition was probably issued shortly after Debussy's death when the firm of Fromont was taken over by Jean Jobert (in 1923); in case the corrections were not from Debussy's pen, they are listed at the end of the commentary to 'Clair de lune' below. For the other three pieces, though, differences between source 3 and the earlier ones are listed only if the source 3 reading is not an obvious correction or retouching of the earlier versions, or if the variant is of special importance to the above analyses. Not listed are editorial slurs, printed ⁓⁓⁓, and other additions printed in square brackets. All bar numbers and unit totals in the musical texts are editorial. The abbreviations 'u.s.' and 'l.s.' stand for upper staff and lower staff.

'Reflets dans l'eau' (no. 1 of *Images, première série*)

Sources: (1) autograph: Music department of the Bibliothèque Nationale, Paris: Ms. 998

(2) first edition, prepared from (1) above, by A. Durand et fils, Paris, October 1905, imprint no. D.&F. 6615 (1)

(3) corrected edition from the same plates, Durand *c.* 1910–15.

No proofs or other copies corrected by Debussy have been traced.

Bars 15, 33 – 4, 79–80: – – – – – after 'Rit.' and 'Molto rit.' in (1) only.
Bar 18, u.s.: tie c♭'–c♭' present in (1) only.
Bar 22, u.s.: second note, g♭''' in all sources, presumably should be e♭''' as in more recent Durand reprints.
Bar 23: no diminuendo has been added; although absolute *subito ppp* in bar 24

seems unlikely, opinions must vary if and where to begin any diminuendo.

Bars 24–8, u.s.: by normal convention this passage should be in demisemiquavers, not hemidemisemiquavers as in all sources. Perhaps just carelessness; but other manuscripts of Debussy's (discounting a few obvious slips) also suggest that he tended to work on the basis that a group of 13, 14 or 15 (as in this passage) is nearer to 16 (normal hemidemis) than to 8 (normal demis). His notation has therefore been retained, not only because the context prevents any confusion, but also – possibly Debussy's reason for notating as he did – because it avoids what would otherwise look misleadingly like changes of speed leading into bars 24 and 29.

Bar 29, u.s.: Debussy's arithmetic is correct (10+4+2 hemidemisemiquavers in the first half of the bar); but, despite the concurrence of all sources, perhaps the figuration should include a c''' before the b♭''.

Bar 36, u.s.: last group demisemiquavers in all sources.

Bar 50, u.s.: double dot in all sources after ♪; an alternative solution to removing a dot (as here) would be to follow with a demisemiquaver upbeat. Cf. bar 65, but also bar 54.

Bar 54, u.s.: all sources erroneously have ♪.. before the octave F♯, and a crotchet tail on the last quaver c♮'''d♮'''.

Bars 59–60, l.s.: all sources have crotchet bass notes instead of minims as in the surrounding bars. Perhaps an oversight; perhaps an implication of increased turbulence in these two central climactic bars (cf. the analysis in Chapter 3 above).

Bar 93: how to play the first chord, combining the *tenuto* marks with the arpeggiation, is not clear. (1) lacks the arpeggiation sign, suggesting that Debussy too had doubts. Vlado Perlemuter reports that in later years (*c.* 1915) Debussy instructed Marcel Ciampi to play it thus:

'Spleen' (no. 6 of *Ariettes oubliées*)

Sources: (1) autograph: Bibliothèque François Lang, Abbaye de Royaumont, France

(2) first edition, prepared from (1), by E. Girod, Paris 1888, imprint no. E.G. 6122

Textual Commentary

(3) second edition from new plates by E. Fromont, Paris 1903, imprint no. E.1422 F.(6).

No proofs or other copies corrected by Debussy have been traced.

The text follows that of (3) without alteration except to omit the English translation. Debussy revised the song for the 1903 edition, retouching some harmonies and textures, and moving some vocal entries back or forward by up to a crotchet; exceptionally, the final 'hélas' is 1⅓ bars earlier in (1) and (2), on two f♭'s (♪♩), but with the piano part underneath as in (3). None of the variants in any way affect the analysis in Chapter 4 above.

'Clair de lune' (no. 3 of *Suite bergamasque*)

Sources: (1) first proofs with Debussy's corrections: Music department of the Bibliothèque Nationale, Paris: Rés. Vma. 286
(2) first edition by E. Fromont, Paris 1905, imprint no. E.1404 F.
(3) second edition from new plates but using the same imprint no., J. Jobert, Paris *c.* 1923

No autograph or other copies corrected by Debussy have been traced.

Bar 7, u.s.: tie from final e♭' lacking in (3); present in (1) and (2).
Bar 17, l.s.: (3) has *m.g.*; (1) and (2) correctly have *m.d.*
Bar 21, u.s.: all sources have a superfluous dot after crotchet g♭".
Bar 33: *4* lacking in (3); present in u.s. of (1) and (2).
Bar 52, l.s.: final ♩ ↱ lacking in all sources.
Bars 58, 65, l.s.: *2* lacking in all sources.
Bars 59–65, l.s.: the inconsistency of the bass note values has been left untampered with, since the only consistent solution (a dotted minim tied to a dotted crotchet in each bar) would clutter the score. The inconsistency implies that such exactitude is not desired: that the bass notes are to be sustained but without their subsequent point of release being made obvious.

Alterations made for source (3): bars 7, 17, 33: cf. commentary above / bar 6, u.s.: dot to minim e♭' / bars 18–19: *2, 6* to u.s. / bar 21: *6* to both staves / bar 23: *6* to u.s. / bars 35–6, l.s.: slur only on first beat of 35 in (1) and (2) / bar 36, u.s.: ♮ to b'' / bar 61, l.s.: ♭ moved from d' to c' / bar 69, u.s.: dot to d♭ '''.

224

L'isle joyeuse

Sources: (1) autograph: Music department of the Bibliothèque Nationale, Paris:
Ms. 977

(2) first edition, prepared from (1), by A. Durand et fils, Paris 1904, imprint no.
D.&F. 6446

(3) corrected edition from the same plates, Durand *c.* 1910–15.

No proofs or other copies corrected by Debussy have been traced.

Bars 9, 15, 16, 66, u.s.: ♮ to g″ in (3) only; see page 49 note 1 above.

Bars 13, 113–14, 240: all *tenuto* marks editorial; cf. respectively bars 12, 103–4
and 109–10, 236.

Bar 18, beat 3: perhaps Debussy meant the *mf* that appears in all sources, but a
lapse of concentration when recopying seems a more probable explanation in view of the similar echo effects in bars 17 and 19–20.

Bar 63: no diminuendo in any sources; cf. commentary above to bar 23 of
'Reflets dans l'eau'.

Bars 117–44: see page 62 above regarding an early sketch variant.

Bars 139–40, u.s.: *tenuto* marks on the first note of each beat lacking in (2) and
(3) are implied in (1), where bars 138–40 u.s. each appear as ⁒ .

Bars 148–51, 166–77, u.s.; 204–7, 212–15, u.s & l.s.: the dotted crotchets
should possibly be tied in pairs or fours (if so, it is not the only repeated
detail Debussy overlooked, as has already been seen). The solution is not
clear enough, though, to justify changing the text.

Bars 156–7: (1) gives these bars as in Ex. 11 on page 62 above.

Bar 161, l.s.: the staccato dot in all sources is probably a carelessly written
intended *tenuto* mark; cf. bar 164.

Bar 242: ∧ (l.s.) and > (u.s.) editorial; cf. bar 238./ All sources have a staccato
dot as well as a *tenuto* mark above beat 1, u.s.; but in (1) the dot appears
above the *tenuto* sign and was probably an accident; cf. bar 238. / The
other inconsistency with bar 238 – the notation of the second and third
beats, u.s., common to all sources – has been left unchanged.

Bar 254, l.s.: change to bass clef lacking in all sources.

Bibliography

Abravanel, Claude (1974): *Claude Debussy: a bibliography* (Detroit Studies in Music Bibliography no. 29), Detroit.

d'Almendra, Julia (1965): 'Debussy et le mouvement modal dans la musique du XXᵉ siècle', in *Debussy et l'évolution de la musique au XXᵉ siècle*, ed. Edith Weber, Paris 1965, pp. 109–26.

Ambrière, Francis (1934): 'La vie romaine de Claude Debussy', *La Revue Musicale*, no. 142 (January 1934), pp. 20–6.

Argüelles, José A. (1972): *Charles Henry and the formation of a psychophysical aesthetic*, London.

Arkell, David (1979): *Looking for Laforgue*, London.

Arnold, Paul (1955): *Histoire des Rose+Croix*, Paris.

Aronowsky, S. (1959): *Performing times of orchestral works*, London.

Austin, William (1970): *Debussy: Prelude to 'The afternoon of a faun': an authoritative score*, London.

Baigent, Michael; Leigh, Richard; and Lincoln, Henry (1982): *The Holy Blood and the Holy Grail*, London.

Barraqué, Jean (1965): 'Debussy: ou l'approche d'une organisation autogène de la composition', in *Debussy et l'évolution de la musique au XXᵉ siècle*, ed. Edith Weber, Paris 1965, pp. 83–96.

—— (1972): *Debussy*, Paris.

—— (posth.): 'Debussy: ou l'approche d'une organisation autogène de la composition', unpublished analytical notes on *La mer* (developed from 1965 version), left incomplete at Barraqué's death in 1973.

Baudelaire, Charles (1961): *Oeuvres complètes*, ed. Y.-G. le Dantec and Claude Pinchois, Paris (Bibliothèque de la Pléiade).

Bergson, Henri (1910): *Time and free will*, translated by F. L. Pogson, London.

Berman, Laurence (1974): 'Debussy, "Jeux de vagues"': response (unpublished) to paper by Douglass M. Green (1974), read to the annual meeting of the American Musicological Society, Washington, D.C., 3 November 1974.

Burkhart, Charles (1968): 'Debussy plays "La cathédrale engloutie" and solves metrical mystery', *Piano Quarterly*, 65 (Fall 1968), pp. 14–26.

Camp, E. J. P. (1968): 'Temporal proportion: a study of sonata form in the

226

piano sonatas of Mozart', Ph.D. dissertation, Florida State University.

Carley, Lionel (1975): *Delius: the Paris years*, London.

Carter, Elliott (1977): *The writings of Elliott Carter*, compiled, edited and annotated by Else Stone and Kurt Stone, Bloomington, Indiana.

—— see also Edwards.

Chailley, Jacques (1972): *The magic flute, Masonic opera*, translated by H. Weinstock, London.

—— (1975): *Le voyage d'hiver de Schubert*, Paris.

Church, A. H. (1904): *On the relation of phyllotaxis to mechanical laws*, London.

Clark, Sir Kenneth (1959): 'Turner's look at nature', *The Sunday Times*, 25 October 1959.

Coan, C. A.: see Colman (1912; 1920).

Cobb, Margaret G. (1977): 'Debussy in Texas', *Cahiers Debussy*, n.s., *1* (1977), pp. 45–6.

—— (1982): *The poetic Debussy: the song texts and associated letters*, collected and annotated by Margaret G. Cobb, Boston.

Colman, Samuel (1912): *Nature's harmonic unity: a treatise on its relation to proportional form*, edited by C. A. Coan, New York.

—— (1920): *Proportional form: further studies in the science of beauty* (with C. A. Coan), New York.

Cook, Theodore A. (1903): *Spirals in nature and art*, London.

—— (1914): *The curves of life*, London.

—— (1922): 'A new disease in architecture', *The Nineteenth Century*, *91* (1922), p. 521.

Crevel, Marcus van (1959; 1964): *Jacobus Obrecht: opera omnia*, vols. 6 and 7 (Missae *Sub Tuum Presidium* and *Maria Zart*), edited with commentary and analysis by Marcus van Crevel, Amsterdam 1959 (vol. 6), 1964 (vol. 7).

Debussy, Claude (1927): *Lettres de Claude Debussy à son éditeur* [Jacques Durand], Paris.

– —— (1938): *La jeunesse de Pelléas: lettres de Claude Debussy à André Messager*, collected and edited by J.-André Messager, Paris.

—— (1957): *Claude Debussy: lettres inédites à André Caplet (1908–1914)*, collected and edited by Edward Lockspeiser, foreword by André Schaeffner, Monaco.

—— (1963): *Prélude à l'après-midi d'un faune*, facsimile reproduction of Debussy's draft in short score, with foreword by Roland-Manuel, Washington (The Robert Owen Lehman Foundation).

—— (1971): *Monsieur Croche et autres écrits*, Debussy's critical writings and interviews compiled and edited by François Lesure, Paris.

—— (1977): *Debussy on music*: collected critical writings and interviews, compiled and edited by François Lesure, translated and annotated by Richard Langham Smith, London.

Bibliography

—— (1980): *Claude Debussy: lettres 1884–1918*, compiled and edited by François Lesure, Paris.

—— see also Austin; Cobb (1982); Pommer.

Denis, Maurice (1912): *Théories*, Paris.

Duckworth, G.E. (1962): *Structural patterns and proportions in Vergil's Aeneid*, Ann Arbor, Mich.

Durand, Jacques: see Debussy (1927).

Edwards, Allen (1971): *Flawed words and stubborn sounds: a conversation with Elliott Carter*, New York.

Ehrenzweig, Anton (1967): *The hidden order of art*, London.

Eimert, Herbert (1961): 'Debussy's "Jeux"', *Die Reihe*, 5 (English edition), Bryn Mawr, Pa., pp. 3–20.

Emmanuel, Maurice: '[Debussy's] conversations with Ernest Guiraud', in Lockspeiser (1962), pp. 204–8.

Erickson, Robert (1967): 'Time relations', *Journal of Music Theory*, 7 (1967), pp. 174–92.

Fechner, Gustav (1876): *Vorschule der Aesthetik*, 2 vols., Leipzig (Breitkopf & Härtel).

Fowler, Alastair (1964): *Spenser and the numbers of time*, London.

—— (ed.) (1970): *Silent poetry: essays in numerological analysis*, London.

Franz, Marie-Louise von (1974): *Numbers and time*, London.

Gervais, Françoise (1971): *Etude comparée des langues harmoniques de Fauré et de Debussy*, 2 vols., special numbers, 272–3, of *La Revue Musicale* (1971).

Ghyka, Matila (1927): *Esthétique des proportions dans la nature et dans les arts*, Paris.

—— (1931): *Le nombre d'or*, 2 vols., Paris.

—— (1946): *The geometry of art and life*, New York.

—— (1952): *Philosophie et mystique du nombre*, Paris.

Godet, Robert (1926): 'En marge de la marge', in *La jeunesse de Claude Debussy*, special number of *La Revue Musicale*, vol. 7 no. 7 (1 May 1926), pp. 51–86.

Goncourt, [Edmond](1891): *Journal des Goncourts*, ser. 2, vol. 2, Paris.

Goudeau, Emile (1888): *Dix ans de Bohème*, Paris.

Green, Douglass M. (1974): 'Debussy's "Jeux de vagues" and the orchestral sketch in the Sibley Music Library', unpublished paper read to the annual meeting of the American Musicological Society, Washington, D.C., 3 November 1974.

Guichard, Léon: 'Debussy and the occultists', in Lockspeiser (1965), pp. 272–7.

Hambidge, Jay (1920): *Dynamic symmetry: The Greek vase*, New Haven.

—— (1924): *The Parthenon and other Greek temples: their dynamic symmetry*, London.

228

—— (1948): *The elements of dynamic symmetry*, New Haven.

Henry, Charles (1885): *Introduction à une esthétique scientifique*, Paris (also in *La Revue Contemporaine*, 2 (August 1885), pp. 441–69).

—— (1886): 'Loi d'évolution de la sensation musicale', *La Revue Philosophique*, 25 (1886), pp. 81–7.

—— (1887a): *Wronski et l'esthétique musicale*, Paris (Editions de la vogue).

—— (1887b): *La théorie de Rameau sur la musique*, Paris (Editions de la vogue).

—— (1888a): *Rapporteur esthétique et sensation de forme*, Paris (also in *La Revue Indépendante*, April 1888, pp. 73–90).

—— (1888b): *Cercle chromatique ...*, Paris (also in *La Revue Indépendante*, May 1888, pp. 238–89).

—— (1889): 'Le contraste, le rythme et la mesure', *La Revue Philosophique*, 28 (October 1889), pp. 356–81.

—— (1891): *Harmonie de formes et de couleurs*, Paris.

—— (1895): *Quelques aperçus sur l'esthéthique des formes*, Paris (originally a series of articles, 'L'esthétique des formes, in *La Revue Blanche*, 1894–5).

—— see also Argüelles.

Homer, William (1964): *Seurat and the science of painting*, Cambridge, Mass.

Howat, Roy (1977): 'Debussy, Ravel and Bartók: towards some new concepts of form', *Music & Letters*, 58 (July 1977), pp. 285–93.

—— (1979): 'Proportional structure in the music of Claude Debussy', Ph.D. dissertation, Cambridge University.

—— (1983): 'Bartók, Lendvai and the principles of proportional analysis', *Music Analysis*, 2/1 (March 1983), pp. 69–95.

Jankélévitch, Vladimir (1949): *Debussy et le mystère*, Neuchâtel.

—— (1968): *La vie et la mort dans la musique de Debussy*, Neuchâtel.

—— (1976): *Debussy et le mystère de l'instant*, Paris.

Jean-Aubry, Georges (1920): 'L'oeuvre critique de Debussy', *La Revue Musicale*, vol. 1 no. 2 (1 December 1920), special Debussy number, pp. 191–202.

—— see also Laforgue.

Jonas, Oswald: see Schenker.

Jounet, Albert: *Rose+Croix*, place and date of publication untraced (probably Paris, *c.* 1885).

Jourdan-Morhange, Hélène: see Perlemuter.

Knowles, Richard-E. (1954): *Victor-Emile Michelet: poète ésotérique*, preface by Gaston Bachelard, Paris.

Kramer, Jonathan (1973): 'The Fibonacci series in 20th-century music', *Journal of Music Theory*, 17 (Spring 1973), pp. 110–48.

Laforgue, Jules (1922): *Oeuvres complètes*, 6 vols., ed. G. Jean-Aubry, Paris.

Langham Smith, Richard: see Debussy (1977).

Lasserre, François (1964): *The birth of mathematics in the age of Plato*, London.

229

Bibliography

Le Corbusier [pseud. of Jeanneret, Charles Edouard] (1954): *The modulor: a harmonious measure to the human scale universally applicable to architecture and mechanics,* translated (from the first French edition of 1948) by P. de Francia and A. Bostock, London.

Leigh, Richard: see Baigent *et al.*

Lendvai, Ernő (1971): *Béla Bartók: an analysis of his music,* London.

Lesure, François (1962): *Claude Debussy: textes et documents inédits,* special number of *La Revue de Musicologie,* vol. *48,* no. 125 (July–December 1962).

—— (1977): *Catalogue de l'oeuvre de Claude Debussy,* Geneva.

—— see also Debussy (1971; 1977; 1980).

Lévi, Eliphas [pseud. of Constant, Alphonse-Louis] (1856): *Dogme et rituel de la haute magie,* Paris.

—— (1896): *Transcendental magic: its doctrine and ritual,* translated from the above by A. E. Waite, London.

Lincoln, Henry (1979): 'The priest, the painter and the Devil' and 'The shadow of the Templars', two television programmes in BBC2 *Chronicle* series, 20 and 27 November 1979.

—— see also Baigent *et al.*

Lockspeiser, Edward (1962): *Debussy: his life and mind,* vol. 1, London, reprinted Cambridge 1978.

—— (1963): 'Debussy's concept of the dream', *Proceedings of the Royal Musical Association,* 89 (1962–3), pp. 49–61.

—— (1965): *Debussy: his life and mind,* vol. 2, London, reprinted Cambridge 1978.

—— (1973): *Music and painting,* London.

—— see also Debussy (1957).

Long, Marguerite (1972): *At the piano with Debussy,* London.

Mariel, Pierre: see Villiers de l'Isle-Adam.

McKay, James (1977): 'The Bréval manuscript: new interpretations', *Cahiers Debussy,* n.s., *1* (1977), pp. 5–15.

McManus, I. C. (1980): 'The aesthetics of simple figures', *British Journal of Psychology,* vol. *71* part 4 (November 1980), pp. 505–24.

Mercier, Alain (1969): *Les sources ésotériques et occultes de la poésie symboliste,* vol. 1, Paris.

Messager, Jean-André: see Debussy (1938).

Michelet, Victor-Emile (1890): *De l'ésotérisme dans l'art,* by Emile Michelet, Paris.

—— (1903): 'Le pèlerin d'amour', one-act lyric verse fantasy, in *La porte d'or,* collection of poems by Michelet, Paris (Paul Ollendorff), pp. 197–227.

—— (1937): *Les compagnons de la hiérophanie: souvenirs du mouvement hermétiste à la fin du XIXe siècle,* Paris.

Moevs, Robert (1969): 'Intervallic procedures in Debussy: Serenade from the

Sonata for Cello and Piano, 1915', *Perspectives of New Music*, vol. *8* (Fall–Winter 1969), pp. 82–111.

Morice, Charles: *Le chemin de la croix*, place and date of publication untraced (probably Paris, *c.* 1885).

—— (1889): *La littérature de tout-à-l'heure*, Paris.

Nattiez, Jean-Jacques (1975): *Fondements d'une sémiologie de la musique*, Paris.

Newbould, Brian (1975): 'Ravel's Pantoum', *The Musical Times*, *116* (March 1975), pp. 228–31.

Nichols, Roger (1967): 'Debussy's two settings of "Clair de lune"', *Music & Letters*, *48* (July 1967), pp. 229–35.

—— (1972): *Debussy*, London.

—— (1977): *Ravel*, London.

—— (1980): 'Images of Debussy', series of ten programmes on BBC Radio 3, 1 July–2 September 1980.

Orledge, Robert (1982): *Debussy and the theatre*, Cambridge.

Pacioli, Luca (1509): *De divina proportione*, Venice (modern editions: Milan 1956 with English translation; German translation by C. Winterberg, Vienna 1889).

Pascoe, Clive (1973): 'Golden proportion in musical design', D.M.E. dissertation, University of Cincinnati.

Péladan, Joséphin (1892): *Le panthée (+ Acta Rosae Crucis Templi)*, Paris.

Perle, George (1977): 'The secret programme of the Lyric Suite', *The Musical Times*, *118* (August–October 1977), pp. 629–31, 709–13, 809–13.

Perlemuter, Vlado (1970): *Ravel d'après Ravel* (with Hélène Jourdan-Morhange), Lausanne.

Poe, Edgar Allan: 'The philosophy of composition', in *The complete works of Edgar Allan Poe*, ed. James A. Harrison, New York 1902 (reprinted 1965), vol. 14, pp. 193–208.

Pommer, Max (1972): Preface to Peters edition of *La mer* (pp. xvii–xxii), Leipzig.

Powell, Newman W. (1979): 'Fibonacci and the Golden Mean; rabbits, rumbas and rondeaux', *Journal of Music Theory*, vol. *23* no. 2 (Fall 1979), pp. 227–73.

Purce, Jill (1975): *The mystic spiral*, London.

Qvarnström, Gunnar (1966): *Poetry and numbers*, Lund.

Reed, John (1972): *Schubert: the final years*, London.

Régnier, Henri de (1926): 'Souvenirs sur Debussy', in *La jeunesse de Claude Debussy*, special number of *La Revue Musicale*, vol. *7* no. 7 (1 May 1926), pp. 89–91.

Rogers, Michael R. (1977): 'The Golden Section in musical time: speculations on temporal proportion', Ph.D. dissertation, University of Iowa.

Rolf, Marie (1976): 'Debussy's *La mer*: a critical analysis in the light of early sketches and editions', Ph.D. dissertation, University of Rochester, Eastman School of Music.

231

Bibliography

Rothwell, James A. (1977): 'The phi factor: mathematical proportions in musical forms', Ph.D. dissertation, University of Missouri at Kansas City.

Roy, Jean (1964): 'Trois lettres inédites de Claude Debussy réunies par Jean Roy', in *Claude Debussy 1862–1962 [sic]: livre d'or*, special number, 258, of *La Revue Musicale* (1964), pp. 118–20.

Rutter, John (1975): 'The sonata principle', Open University Course A 241 (*Elements of music*), Milton Keynes.

Ruwet, Nicolas (1962): 'Note sur les duplications dans l'oeuvre de Claude Debussy', *Revue Belge de Musicologie*, *16* (1962), pp. 57–70 (also in Ruwet, *Langage, musique, poésie*, Paris 1972).

Salzer, Felix (1952): *Structural hearing: tonal coherence in music*, 2 vols., New York.

Samson, Jim (1977): *Music in transition*, London.

Schenker, Heinrich (1954): *Harmony*, edited and annotated by Oswald Jonas, translated by Elizabeth Mann Borgese, Chicago.

Schidlof, Léo R. (1967): *Dossiers secrets de Henri Lobineau*, Paris (Philippe Toscan du Plantier).

Schoenberg, Arnold (1978): *Theory of harmony*, translated by Roy E. Carter, London.

Scholfield. P. H. (1958): *Theory of Proportion of Architecture*, Cambridge.

Scott, Cyril (1924): *My years of indiscretion*, London.

Sède, Gérard de (1977): *Signé: Rose+Croix: l'énigme de Rennes-le-Château*, Paris.

Sérusier, Paul (1921): *ABC de la peinture*, Paris.

Siegele, Ulrich (1978): *Bachs theologischer Formbegriff und das Duett F-dur*, Neuhausen–Stuttgart.

Souvtchinsky, Pierre (1939): 'La notion du temps et la musique', *La Revue Musicale*, no. 191 (May–June 1939), pp. 70–80.

Stockhausen, Karlheinz (1959): '... How time passes ...', *Die Reihe*, *3* (English edition), Bryn Mawr, Pa., pp. 10–40.

Stravinsky, Igor (1947): *Poetics of music*, New York.

Stuckenschmidt, H.-H. (1969): *Maurice Ravel: variations on his life and work*, translated by S. R. Rosenbaum, London.

Thompson, D'Arcy Wentworth (1917): *On growth and form*, Cambridge (new editions 1942 and 1961).

Trevitt, John (1973): 'Debussy inconnu: an inquiry', *The Musical Times*, *114* (September–October 1973), pp. 881–6, 1001–5.

Trowell, Brian (1979): 'Proportion in the music of Dunstable', *Proceedings of the Royal Music Association*, *105*, (1978–9), pp. 100–41.

Valéry, Paul (1960): *Oeuvres*, ed. Jean Hytier, Paris (Bibliothèque de la Pléiade).

Villiers de l'Isle-Adam, J.-M. M. P. A., Comte de (1960): *Axël*, edited with an introduction by Pierre Mariel, Paris.

Walzer, Pierre-Olivier (1963): *Essai sur Stéphane Mallarmé*, Paris.

Webster, J. H. Douglas (1950): 'Golden-mean form in music', *Music & Letters*, *31* (July 1950), pp. 238–48.

Wenk, Arthur B. (1976): *Claude Debussy and the poets*, Berkeley.

Whittall, Arnold (1975): 'Tonality and the whole-tone scale in the music of Debussy', *The Music Review*, *36* (November 1975), pp. 261–71.

Wittkower, Rudolf (1949): *Architectural principles in the age of humanism*, London.

—— (1960): 'The changing concept of proportion', *Daedalus*, *89* (Winter 1960), pp. 199–215.

Yates, Frances (1972): *The Rosicrucian enlightenment*, London.

Zeising, Adolf (1854): *Neue Lehre von Proportionen des Menschlichen Körpers*, Leipzig.

—— (1884): *Der Goldne Schnitt*, Halle.

Index

acoustic scale, 48–9, 54, 55, 56, 60, 61, 62,
    74–6
alchemy, 169
Allan, Maud, 158
arabesque, 166
    see also Debussy, Claude, works: *Arabesques*
arch form, 33, 73–4, 76, 78–9, 81–2, 83, 85,
    89, 149, 159, 191

Bach, Johann Sebastian, 13
Bachelard, Gaston, theories of, 16n
Bailly, Edmond, 167–8
Bardac, Emma, *see* Debussy, Emma-Claude
Bardac, Hélène (Dolly), *see* Tinan Mme
    Gaston de
Baron, Emile, 166, 167
Barraqué, Jean, 64, 70, 71, 133
Bartók, Béla, 15, 48
    proportional structure in the music of, 6,
        187
    Concerto [no. 2] for Violin and Orchestra,
        15
    Music for strings, percussion and celeste, 187
Baudelaire, Charles, 46, 168, 171
    see also Debussy, Claude, *Cinq poëmes de*
        Charles Baudelaire
Beethoven, Ludwig van, 6
    Symphony no. 5, 186
    Symphony no. 9, 180
Berg, Alban, 186
    Lyric suite, 186
bisection
    in music, *passim*
    in nature, 22
Bois, Jules, 167
Bouchor, Maurice, 168n
Bourget, Paul, 36

cabbala, 13, 168 and n, 163, 167, 169
cadenza, 17, 18–20, 23n, 28, 60, 138, 147,
    189–91
Calvé, Emma, 168n
Capet, Lucien, *Poème* for Violin and
    Orchestra, 9n

Caplet, André, 175
Carrière, Eugène, 168n
Carter, Elliott, 14, 16n
Casadesus, Robert, 160, 191n
Centre de Documentation Claude Debussy,
    see under Debussy, Claude
Chasseigne, Anne-Marie (Liane de Pougy), 7
Chat Noir, 168
Ciampi, Marcel, 223
Coates, Albert, 15
Constant, Alphonse-Louis (Eliphas Lévi),
    169
Cortot, Alfred, 160
Cros, Charles, 166

Dallapiccola, Luigi, 193
Davies, Peter Maxwell, 193
Debussy, Adèle (sister of Claude), 163n
Debussy, (Achille-)Claude
    architecture, views on, 172–3
    autograph manuscripts, 6, 7, 8, 9n, 19,
        23n, 34n, 38n, 40n, 44, 49n, 62,
        65, 66, 82, 87–92, 96n, 105–9,
        128n, 131, 152n, 153n, 157n,
        158n, 161–2, 222–5
    Centre de Documentation C. D., x, 152
    discarded titles to published works, 44n,
        132, 157n
    errors in printed editions, x, 23n, 49n, 67,
        113n, 159–60, 222–5
    Impressionism, views on, 28–9
    letters of, 6–7, 9n, 23n, 29, 88, 128n, 136,
        137, 144, 171n, 172, 173, 175
    modes, use of, 13, *48–9, 54–6,* 59, 60, 61,
        62, *74–6,* 79, 86, 98, 144–5, 169
    'Monseur Croche, antidilettante', 164–5,
        167
    number, views on, 171
    occult associations, 167–71
    other composers, views on, 9n, 133, 173
    performance of his music, 24, 28, 83–4n,
        141, 143, 147, 159–60, 173, 179,
        223

Index

Index